THE POLITICAL MIND

ALSO BY GEORGE LAKOFF

Metaphors We Live By
with Mark Johnson

Women, Fire, and Dangerous Things:
What Categories Reveal About the Mind

More Than Cool Reason: A Field Guide to Poetic Metaphor
with Mark Turner

Philosophy in the Flesh: The Embodied Mind
and Its Challenge to Western Thought
with Mark Johnson

Where Mathematics Comes From: How the Embodied
Mind Brings Mathematics into Being
with Rafael Núñez

Moral Politics: How Liberals and Conservatives Think

Don't Think of an Elephant! Know Your Values and Frame
the Debate: The Essential Guide for Progressives

Thinking Points: Communicating Our
American Values and Vision
with the Rockridge Institute

Whose Freedom?: The Battle over America's Most Important Idea

THE POLITICAL MIND

Why You Can't Understand
21st-Century Politics with
an 18th-Century Brain

George Lakoff

VIKING

VIKING
Published by the Penguin Group
Penguin Group (USA) Inc., 375 Hudson Street,
New York, New York 10014, U.S.A.
Penguin Group (Canada), 90 Eglinton Avenue East, Suite 700,
Toronto, Ontario, Canada M4P 2Y3 (a division of Pearson Penguin Canada Inc.)
Penguin Books Ltd, 80 Strand, London WC2R 0RL, England
Penguin Ireland, 25 St. Stephen's Green, Dublin 2, Ireland
(a division of Penguin Books Ltd)
Penguin Books Australia Ltd, 250 Camberwell Road, Camberwell,
Victoria 3124, Australia (a division of Pearson Australia Group Pty Ltd)
Penguin Books India Pvt Ltd, 11 Community Centre,
Panchsheel Park, New Delhi–110 017, India
Penguin Group (NZ), 67 Apollo Drive, Rosedale, North Shore 0632,
New Zealand (a division of Pearson New Zealand Ltd)
Penguin Books (South Africa) (Pty) Ltd, 24 Sturdee Avenue,
Rosebank, Johannesburg 2196, South Africa

Penguin Books Ltd, Registered Offices: 80 Strand, London WC2R 0RL, England

First published in 2008 by Viking Penguin, a member of Penguin Group (USA) Inc.

1 3 5 7 9 10 8 6 4 2

LIBRARY OF CONGRESS CATALOGING-IN-PUBLICATION DATA
Lakoff, George.
The political mind : why you can't understand 21st-century politics with
an 18th-century brain / George Lakoff.
p. cm.
Includes bibliographical references and index.
ISBN 978-0-670-01927-4
1. Liberalism—United States.   2. Progressivism (United States politics)   3. Political
culture—United States.   4. Conservatism—United States.   5. Communication
in politics—United States.   6. Thought and thinking.   I. Title.
JC574.2.U6L35 2008
320.01—dc22   2008010990

Printed in the United States of America
Set in Minion
Designed by Francesca Belanger

To my parents,

Herman and Ida Lakoff

The immune system, the hypothalamus, the ventro-medial frontal cortices, and the Bill of Rights have the same root cause.
—ANTONIO DAMASIO, *Descartes' Error*

Contents

THE POLITICAL MIND

Brain Change and Social Change

Radical conservatives have been fighting a culture war. The main battlefield is the brain. At stake is what America is to be. Their goal is to radically change America to fit the conservative moral worldview. The threat is to democracy and all that goes with it.

Not just here, but wherever American influence extends.

American values are fundamentally progressive, centered on equality, human rights, social responsibility, and the inclusion of all. Yet progressives have, without knowing why, given conservatives an enormous advantage in the culture war. The radical conservatives seek and have already begun to introduce: an authoritarian hierarchy based on vast concentrations and control of wealth; order based on fear, intimidation, and obedience; a broken government; no balance of power; priorities shifted from the public sector to the corporate and military sectors; responsibility shifted from society to the individual; control of elections through control of who votes and how the votes are counted; control of ideas through the media; and patriarchal family values projected upon religion, politics, and the market.

The future of democracy is at stake, now.

Social change is material (who controls what wealth), institutional (who runs what powerful institutions), and political (who wins elections). But the main battlefield of the culture war is the brain, especially how the brain functions below the level of consciousness.

Progressives have accepted an old view of reason, dating back to the Enlightenment, namely, that reason is conscious, literal, logical, universal, unemotional, disembodied, and serves self-interest. As the cognitive and brain sciences have been showing, this is a false view of reason. Oddly enough, this matters. It may sound like an academic issue, but this assumption about the nature of reason has stood in the way of an effective progressive defense and advancement of democracy. Progressives have ceded the political mind to radical conservatives.

This book addresses the problem in three parts:

Part I is an introduction to the basic ideas, about the mind and the brain on the one hand, about largely unconscious modes of political thought on the other, and about how they are inextricably linked.

Part II begins an application of these ideas; it provides elements for using them.

Part III turns to technical issues, the role of experts and their effect on our politics. We look at developments in the cognitive and brain sciences, how they are changing our understanding of technical fields like economics, international relations, evolution, and linguistics, and why those changes matter for politics.

How to Use This Book

This book has two uses: first, to give the reader a deeper understanding of our political life, and second, to make progressive political advocacy more effective. Both require utilizing the new knowledge gained over the past thirty years about how the brain and the mind work, knowledge that extends beyond politics to all areas of everyday life. It includes information about yourself that you have no direct access to and don't even know is there, even though it governs how you think, talk, and act.

This book is about modes of thought and how they are carried out. Individuals are complicated, and commonly use more than one mode of thought.

Beyond progressive and conservative ways of thinking, I will be distinguishing what I call a "neoliberal" mode of thought—

one that sometimes looks conservative to progressives and social-istic to conservatives.

Please do not confuse labels with modes of thought. People who call themselves "conservatives" may use progressive modes of thought in certain issue areas. Conversely, people who call themselves "liberals" may think in a conservative mode in certain issue areas.

Similarly, do not confuse party identifications with modes of thought. I am interested in pointing out modes of thought and their consequences, not in putting people in boxes by party affiliation.

The science of mind has lit up a vast landscape of unconscious thought—the 98 percent of thinking your brain does that you're not aware of.[1] Most of it matters for politics. The mind that we cannot see plays an enormous role in how our country is governed.

However, most of us have inherited a theory of mind dating back at least to the Enlightenment, namely, that reason is conscious, literal, logical, unemotional, disembodied, universal, and functions to serve our interests. This theory of human reason has been shown to be false in every particular, but it persists. In many aspects of life this may not matter. But in politics it can have very negative effects:

- It provides a misleading view of political ideologies and of how voters think.
- It hides from the public and the press much of what contemporary conservatism is about and is trying to achieve.
- It can hide the most important of issues.
- It can keep progressives from consciously articulating their moral vision and the moral mission of government.
- It forms the basis of neoliberal thought, which too often leads progressives to surrender their ideals without even stating them.
- And it can make both progressives and neoliberals ineffective.

The results, I believe, have been disastrous, both for America and for the world. For this reason it is urgent that we come to understand how the brain and the mind really work, especially when the subject matter is politics.

Cognitive science provides a lens on the political mind that you don't get in the daily papers or on TV or from your friends and neighbors. I hope to bring out into the open invisible aspects of social and political thought, while giving you some sense of the science of mind that reveals it.

In addition to being a cognitive scientist, I am also a concerned citizen of the United States, deeply loyal to its progressive democratic ideals. Those ideals are currently being threatened. To preserve them, we need to understand our politics as well as possible. I hope this book can not only help, but serve as a guide, and not just a guide to understanding politics, but to engaging in it effectively.

Why the Mind?

We usually parse politics into economics, power, social organization—we weigh the history of all these components. As central as they are to politics, our understanding of them depends on how we think. We have to consider the mind as a factor—or actor—in politics. Now that we have at our disposal massive new knowledge about how we think, all these strands need to be rethought—and as we shall see, such a rethinking radically changes our most basic understanding of all these dimensions of politics.

But that is the academic reason for looking at the political mind. There is an immediate compelling reason. Our democracy is in danger. That danger has its roots in money, power, social structure, and history, but its ultimate source is in the brains of our citizens.

The political divide in America is not just a material divide, as in the "two Americas." Nor is it just a religious divide. Nor is it just a matter of who controls what power. The divide is located in our brains—in the ways Americans understand the world. There we find two competing modes of thought that lead to contradictory ways of governing our country, one fundamentally democratic and one fundamentally antidemocratic. But unconscious modes of thought are not visible to the naked eye, and so they have thus far gone undiscussed in public discourse, despite their central role.

And it's not simply black and white—or blue and red. Most of us have within us versions of both modes of thought, which we each use differently in various aspects of our lives. But the antidemocratic mode of thought—better funded, better organized, and more thoroughly worked out—has been winning and fundamentally changing how our lives are governed.

Unfortunately, the full nature of the threat and what we can do about it are not widely understood. Standing in the way, oddly enough, is the view of the mind that accompanied the founding of our democracy.

You Can't Understand Twenty-first-Century Politics with an Eighteenth-Century Brain

As I travel around the country giving talks, I get the same kinds of questions over and over: Why are the Democrats such wimps? What divides them? What do they believe anyway? Why are conservatives so much better at getting their ideas across? Why haven't Democrats been able to accomplish more since they took over control of Congress in 2006? Why do poor conservatives vote against their interests? Why hasn't democratic populism worked? Now that the public sees global warming as real, why isn't it given a much higher priority? Why do Democratic candidates come out with a list of detailed programs, while Republicans don't?

The intention of this book is to answer these and scores of similar questions. But not in the usual way—that is, not in terms of history, institutions, material conditions, or social factors like class, race, and gender, as much as they matter. I'm looking for a deeper explanation.

Why did progressives not build think tanks like conservatives or invest in media the same way? They have just as much money. It's been a decade since progressives became aware of the major role of the conservative think tanks, message machine, and media control. Why has so little been done to build effective progressive institutions in these areas? It is not lack of money or resources. The usual modes of explanation themselves are not merely partial, but where they work, they too require an explanation.

What is missing is least visible: the role of the human brain and the mind.

What is it about our minds that led to our recent political history, to the one-sidedness of those institutions, and to the way in which class, race, and gender have functioned? What is it about human brains that have led us to think as we do? And ultimately, how can knowledge about the brain and the mind help to enact political change? That is the task of this book.

America was formed in the eighteenth century on grand principles deriving from the Enlightenment. The central idea was universal reason, the notion that there is one and only one form of rationality and that that is what makes us human.

Here is how the link was made between universal reason and democracy:

- Since all people have the capacity for reason, we can govern ourselves, without bowing to higher authorities like kings or popes or oligarchs.
- Reason makes us equal, and so the best form of government is a democracy.
- We use reason to serve our interests, and so an optimal government would serve the interests of all.

- Since we all have the same reason, the same laws can apply to all; thus, we can be governed by general, rational laws, not individual whims.
- Our inherent rational nature accords us inherent rights and freedoms.
- Government should be dedicated to the rational interests of all citizens, and must be structured so that no authority can overwhelm them.
- Reason contrasts with blind faith, and so government should be separate from, and independent of, religion.
- Science is based on reason, and so our government should recognize, honor, and develop scientific knowledge.
- Therefore, a government committed to reason will be a democratic government.
- When democratic values are violated, it is reason that must be restored.

It is no accident that Al Gore's blistering critique of the Bush administration is called *The Assault on Reason* and that Robert Reich's criticism of radical conservatism is called *Reason*. These ideals were triumphs of the Enlightenment that made American democracy possible in the eighteenth century. We need them more than ever today.

There is a problem with the Enlightenment, though, and it lies not in its ideals, but in the eighteenth-century view of reason. Reason was assumed to be:

- Conscious—we know what we think;
- Universal—the same for everyone;
- Disembodied—free of the body, and independent of perception and action;
- Logical—consistent with the properties of classical logic;
- Unemotional—free of the passions;
- Value-neutral—the same reason applies regardless of your values;

- Interest-based—serving one's purposes and interests; and
- Literal—able to fit an objective world precisely, with the logic of the mind able to fit the logic of the world.

If this were right, politics would be universally rational. If the people are made aware of the facts and figures, they should naturally reason to the right conclusion. Voters should vote their interests; they should calculate which policies and programs are in their best interests, and vote for the candidates who advocate those policies and programs. But voters don't behave that way. They vote against their obvious self-interest; they allow bias, prejudice, and emotion to guide their decisions; they argue madly about values, priorities, and goals. Or they quietly reach conclusions independent of their interests without consciously knowing why. Enlightenment reason does not account for real political behavior because the Enlightenment view of reason is false.

Take the old dichotomy between reason and emotion. The old view saw reason and emotion as opposites, with emotion getting in the way of reason. But Antonio Damasio showed in *Descartes' Error* that this Enlightenment view is utterly mistaken. Instead, reason requires emotion. People with brain damage that makes them incapable of experiencing emotion or detecting it in others simply cannot function rationally. They cannot feel what decisions will make them—or anyone else—happy or unhappy, satisfied or anxious.

In the political arena, Drew Westen has shown in *The Political Brain* that emotion is both central and legitimate in political persuasion. Its use is not an illicit appeal to irrationality, as Enlightenment thought would have it. The proper emotions are rational. It is rational to be outraged by torture, or by corruption, or by character assassination, or by lies that lead to thousands of deaths. If your policies will make people happy, then arousing hope and joy is rational. If the earth itself is in imminent danger, fear is rational. And if the Iraq War was really about oil—if all those people have died or been maimed or orphaned for oil—then disgust is rational.

But if you stop at conscious reason and emotion, you miss the main event. Most reason is unconscious! It doesn't look anything like Enlightenment reason.

And virtually all of it matters for politics.

You think with your brain. You have no other choice. Though we may sometimes wonder what part of their anatomy certain political leaders think with, the fact is that they too think with their brains. Thought—all thought—is brain activity.

Of course, you have no direct way of inspecting how your brain works. Direct introspection—just thinking about your brain—will not tell you about synapses and axons and cell bodies and dendrites, nor will it tell you what goes on where in your brain, much less how those synapses, axons, and so on give rise to thought. We know that we do not know our own brains.

On the other hand, most of us think we know our own minds. This is because we engage in conscious thought, and it fills much of our waking life. But what most people are not aware of, and are sometimes shocked to discover, is that most of our thought—an estimated 98 percent—is not conscious. It is below the level of consciousness. It is what our brains are doing that we cannot see or hear. It is called the cognitive unconscious, and the scientific evidence for its existence and for many of its properties is overwhelming. Unconscious thought is *reflexive*—automatic, uncontrolled. Think of the knee reflex, what your leg does when the doctor taps your knee. Conscious thought is *reflective*, like looking at yourself in a mirror. If all thought were conscious and reflective, you would know your own mind and be in control of the decisions you make. But since we don't know what our brains are doing in most cases, most thought is reflexive, not reflective, and beyond conscious control. As a result, your brain makes decisions for you that you are not consciously aware of.

Your brain is not a disembodied thought machine that could just as well be functioning in a vat; it is embodied in the deepest of ways. Your brain runs your body. It extends down through the spinal cord and out, via neural connections, spreading throughout your body. The very structure of your brain has evolved over eons to run your body. It runs your automatic functions—your heart pumps without your commanding it; you train it when you learn to read, play the banjo, or play shortstop.

It should come as no surprise then that the ideas that our embodied brains come up with depend in large measure on the peculiarities of human anatomy in general and on the way we, as human beings, function on our planet and with each other. This is not surprising when discussed in vague abstractions, but it is remarkable in detail: even our ideas of morality and politics are embodied in this rich way—those ideas are created and carried out not merely by the neural anatomy and connectivity of our brains, but also by the ways we function bodily in the physical and social world. Morality and politics are embodied ideas, not abstract ones, and they mostly function in the cognitive unconscious—in what your brain is doing that you cannot see.

Why does the embodiment of mind matter for politics? There are three reasons, none of them obvious.

First, what our embodied brains are doing below the level of consciousness affects our morality and our politics—as well as just about every aspect of our social and personal lives—in ways we are all too often not aware of. Deft politicians (as well as savvy marketers) take advantage of our ignorance of our own minds to appeal to the subconscious level. Meanwhile, honest and ethical political leaders, journalists, and social activists, usually unaware of the hidden workings of the mind, fail to use what is known about the mind in the service of morality and truth.

Second, the forms of unconscious reason used in morality and politics are not arbitrary. We cannot just change our moral and political worldviews at will. There are patterns of moral and political thought that are determined by how we function with our bodies in both the physical and social worlds.

And third, the embodied aspects of mind, as we shall see, connect us to each other and to other living things and to the physical world. It is this that ultimately determines what morality and politics should be about. This is how reason really works. It is the opposite of what most of us were brought up to believe.

We have reached a point where our democracy is in mortal danger—as is the very livability of our planet. We can no longer put off an understanding of how the brain and the unconscious mind both contribute to these problems and how they may provide solutions.

If you believe in the eighteenth-century view of the mind, you will look and act wimpy. You will think that all you need to do is give people the facts and the figures and they will reach the right conclusion. You will think that all you need to do is point out where their interests lie, and they will act politically to maximize them. You will believe in polling and focus groups: you will believe that if you ask people what their interests are, they will be aware of them and will tell you, and will vote on it. You will not have any need to appeal to emotion—indeed, to do so would be wrong! You will not have to speak of values; facts and figures will suffice. You will not have to change people's brains; their reason should be enough. You will not have to frame the facts; they will speak for themselves. You just have to get the facts to them: 47 million without health care; top 1 percent receiving tax breaks; no WMDs; ice caps melting. Your opponents are not bad people; they just need to see the light. Those who won't vote your way are mostly just ignorant; they need to be told the facts. Or they're greedy, or corrupt, or being duped.

If you believe in the eighteenth-century view of the mind, you will believe something like this, and you will be dead wrong! You will be ignoring the cognitive unconscious, not stating your deepest values, suppressing legitimate emotions, accepting the other side's frames as if they were neutral, cowering with fear at what you might be called, and refusing to frame the facts so that they can be appreciated. You will be ineffective. In a word, wimpy.

Yet those Democrats who believe in Enlightenment reason don't think of themselves as wimpy at all. They see themselves as upholding the Enlightenment democratic ideal as committed to facts, truth, and logic, and to informing those ignorant of the facts. They see facts as nonpartisan and the basis for bipartisan agreement. To hold yourself back from offending those you need to educate, you will say, takes strength. To keep stating the facts and figures over and over takes endurance (and it does): it is anything but wimpy from the perspective of Enlightenment reason.

Republicans operate under no such constraints and have a better sense of how brains and minds work. That's why they are more effective. Why didn't the Democrats accomplish more right after the 2006 elections that gave them control of Congress? It wasn't just that they didn't have votes to override a presidential veto or block a filibuster. They didn't use their mandate to substantially change how the public—and the media—thought about issues. They just tried to be rational, to devise programs to fit people's interests and the polls. Because there was little understanding of the brain, there was no campaign to change brains. Indeed, the very idea of "changing brains" sounds a little sinister to progressives—a kind of Frankenstein image comes to mind. It sounds Machiavellian to liberals, like what the Republicans do. But "changing minds" in any deep way always requires changing brains. Once you understand a bit more about how brains work, you will understand that politics is very much about changing brains—and that it can be highly moral and not the least bit sinister or underhanded.

It's fashionable among progressives to wonder why so many "red state" voters don't vote in their own economic interests. This is simply another symptom of eighteenth-century rationalism, which assumes that everyone is rational and rationality means seeking self-interest. To ask why John Edwards's economic populism doesn't enlist all poor conservatives is to make the same false assumption. People are not eighteenth-century reason machines. Real reason works differently. Reason matters, and we have to understand how it really works.

A great deal of the political strife in America and elsewhere stems from the cognitive unconscious of individual citizens. Yet while politics is on the front page of our newspapers, the results of cognitive science tend to be relegated to the weekly science pages, if they are made public at all. In this book, the neuroscience and cognitive science are brought to the front page, where the politics is. You are about to glimpse the operations of the political mind.

The question to ask, as you discover the depths of your own mind, is what to do with this new knowledge. We need a new, updated Enlightenment. The twenty-first-century view of the mind allows one to see what a New Enlightenment would be like.

The Old Enlightenment values were a great advance in their day. But we know so much more now than in the eighteenth century about what it means to be human, and what challenges face humanity. Our Constitution is in large part based on the intellectual tools and ideas inherited by its framers from Enlightenment thinkers. Those tools and ideas are no longer adequate. They have brought us great political, social, and material wonders. And, miraculously, the framers seem to have anticipated such developments, because the dynamic democracy they designed leaves open the possibility of revolutionary change. We have new wonders to discover, new dreams to dream. But they require an understanding of what contemporary brain science has taught us about who we are and how we think.

We will need to embrace a deep rationality that can take account of, and advantage of, a mind that is largely unconscious, embodied, emotional, empathetic, metaphorical, and only partly universal. A New Enlightenment would not abandon reason, but rather understand that we are using real reason—embodied reason, reason shaped by our bodies and brains and interactions in the real world, reason incorporating emotion, structured by frames and metaphors and images and symbols, with conscious thought shaped by the vast and invisible realm of neural circuitry not accessible to consciousness. And as a guide to our own minds, especially in politics, we will need some help from the cognitive sciences—from neuroscience, neural computation, cognitive linguistics, cognitive and developmental psychology, and so on.

We will further need a new philosophy—a new understanding of what it means to be a human being; of what morality is and where it comes from; of economics, religion, politics, and nature itself; and even of what science, philosophy, and mathematics really are. We will have to expand our understanding of the great ideas: freedom, equality, fairness, progress, even happiness.

And subtlest of all, we in the reality-based community will have to come to a new understanding of how we understand reality. There is a reality, and we are part of it, and the way we understand reality is itself real.

The brain is not neutral; it is not a general-purpose device. It comes with a structure, and our understanding of the world is limited to what our brains can make sense of. Some of our thought is literal—framing our experience directly. But much of it is metaphoric and symbolic, structuring our experience indirectly but no less powerfully. Some of our mechanisms of understanding are the same around the world. But many are not, not even in our own country and culture.

Our brains and minds work to impose a specific understanding on reality, and coming to grips with that can be scary, that not everyone understands reality in the same way. That fear has major political consequences. Since the brain mechanisms for understanding reality are mostly unconscious, an understanding of understanding itself becomes a political necessity.

Since language is used for communicating thought, our view of language must also reflect our new understanding of the nature of thought. Language is at once a surface phenomenon and a source of power. It is a means of expressing, communicating, accessing, and even shaping thought. Words are defined relative to frames and conceptual metaphors. Language "fits reality" to the extent that it fits our body-and-brain-based understanding of that reality. Since we all have similar bodies and brains and live in the same world, it will appear in many cases that language just fits reality directly. But when our understandings of reality differ, what language means to us may differ as well, often radically. In politics that happens so often that we have to pay close attention to the use of language.

Language gets its power because it is defined relative to frames, prototypes, metaphors, narratives, images, and emotions. Part of its power comes from its unconscious aspects: we are not consciously aware of all that it evokes in us, but it is there, hidden, always at work. If we hear the same language over and over, we will think more and more in terms of the frames and metaphors activated by that language. And it doesn't matter if you are negating words or questioning them, the same frames and metaphors will be activated and hence strengthened.

Language uses symbols. Language is a tool, an instrument—but it is the surface, not the soul, of the brain. I want us to look beneath language. New curtains won't save your house if the foundation is cracking.

The Old Enlightenment view of reason is not sufficient for understanding our politics. Indeed, it gets in the way. It not only hides the real threat to our democracy, it all too often keeps many of our most dedicated political leaders, policy experts, commentators, and social activists from being effective.

The Old Enlightenment has run its course. A New Enlightenment is upon us, ready or not. The first step is understanding and embracing the twenty-first-century mind. It's the only one we've got.

PART I

HOW THE BRAIN SHAPES
THE POLITICAL MIND

Democratizing Knowledge

Our knowledge of the mind and the brain has expanded so rapidly over the past three decades that hardly anyone has been able to keep up. Most of us have very little idea of what scientists have discovered about how our own minds and brains work—especially the vast reaches below the level of consciousness. Yet it is unconscious thought that rules our everyday lives—and our politics.

Do we have free will? Well, I can freely choose to take a sip from the tea in my teacup...There, I just took one. Can I freely choose to think just any thought? Only if my brain is structured to make sense of that thought.

Can I freely choose *not* to think certain thoughts when certain words are used and when my brain is tuned to activate those thoughts? We may have no choice. *Cut and run*. Can you *not* think cowardice?

This book is devoted to the democratization of knowledge, to bringing to a wide audience those grand new discoveries about our own minds that are crucial in understanding how our politics works. What is at stake is the deepest form of freedom, the freedom to control our own minds. To do that, we must make the unconscious conscious.

Part I consists of the basics, enough about the brain and the mind to sketch simply how political thought works.

- We begin outside politics proper, with Anna Nicole Smith and the multitude of narratives she lived out, narratives that reveal a lot about how brains work.

- Chapter 2 is about modes of thought, conservative, progressive, and neo-liberal.
- By Chapter 3, we can show how those modes of thought arise via widespread commonplace metaphors, and how the metaphors themselves arise via natural brain processes.
- Chapter 4 shows how the brain contributes to and maintains political ideologies.

Get ready. Here comes Anna Nicole Smith!

CHAPTER 1

Anna Nicole on the Brain

In late February 2007, Anna Nicole Smith was everywhere. The death of this sad woman, apparently from a prescription drug overdose, captured the nation in a way political events rarely do. Her life story was endlessly recapped on every channel, from E! to CNN: the humble Texas beginning, the early struggles, the stripping, the modeling, the marriage to an aging billionaire.

I was in New York at a gathering of journalists, and we were discussing the use of brain scans that reflected political loyalties. After a lecture, David Rieff, perhaps America's most important writer on humanitarian issues, made this surprising comment: "You'll never understand how politics works if you don't understand Anna Nicole Smith." What could Anna Nicole Smith have to do with politics—or brain scans, for that matter?

Abundant clues to the answer could be found on any TV channel that night. There were viewers calling in, recounting their emotional responses to Anna Nicole's life and death. Most of them were women, mourning her, idolizing her. To others, she was a gold digger, an empty-headed celebrity, a celebrity only because she was a celebrity. Her life and death resonated so profoundly with so many people because she exemplified a remarkable variety of narratives. Those narratives exist outside the body—in our culture—and inside the body—in the very building blocks of our brains. David Rieff was completely right—understanding the importance of Anna Nicole Smith will help us understand politics.

Narratives We Live By

Complex narratives—the kind we find in anyone's life story, as well as in fairy tales, novels, and dramas—are made up of smaller narratives with very simple structures.[1] Those structures are called "frames" or "scripts."[2]

Frames are among the cognitive structures we think with. For example, when you read a murder mystery, there is a typical frame with various kinds of characters: the murderer, victim or victims, possible accomplices, suspects, a motive, a murder weapon, a detective, clues. And there is a scenario in which the murderer murders the victim and is later caught by the detective.

The neural circuitry needed to create frame structures is relatively simple,[3] and so frames tend to structure a huge amount of our thought. Each frame has roles (like a cast of characters), relations between the roles, and scenarios carried out by those playing the roles. The sociologist Erving Goffman discovered that all institutions are structured by frames.[4] A hospital, for example, has roles like doctors, nurses, patients, visitors, operating rooms, X-ray machines, and so on, with scenarios like checking in, being examined, having an operation, being visited, and so on. The frame structure would be violated, or "broken," if, say, the visitors were performing operations on the doctors at the check-in desk.

The linguist Charles Fillmore discovered that words are all defined relative to conceptual frames.[5] Groups of related words, called "semantic fields," are defined with respect to the same frame. Thus words like "cost," "sell," "goods," "price," "buy," and so on are defined with respect to a single frame. The roles are Buyer, Seller, Goods, and Money, and the scenario is simple: first the Buyer has the Money and wants the Goods, and the Seller has the Goods and wants the Money; then they exchange Goods and Money; then the Buyer has the Goods and the Seller has the Money. Such a frame is the basis of our understanding of commercial events, of our reasoning about commercial events, and of the words that can be used of commercial events.

Scientists have discovered frames by looking for generalizations over groups of related words, forms of reasoning about some subject matter, and structures that subjects recognize as wholes with parts (roles and events in scenarios). And within the brain itself, frames are natural structures that have evolved from what brains do and are put together out of simple units.

Even the most basic actions, like physically grasping an object, have a frame structure that can be observed at the neuronal level, as Vittorio Gallese and I have shown.[6] The roles are the grasper, the object grasped, and the body part used for grasping. The scenario is simple: a movement of the arm and hand to the object, touching the hand to the object, and closing the hand around the object.

Simple frames can be combined to form more complex ones. A field hospital in a war, for example, might have all the doctors, nurses, and patients being soldiers; the hospital might be a tent on a battlefield; and the injuries would be war wounds. A bake sale combines a charity event and a commercial event, where the Goods are Baked Goods, the Sellers are the Bakers, the Buyers are Charitable Contributors, and the Money is a Charitable Contribution.

Simple narratives have the form of frame-based scenarios, but with extra structure. There is a Protagonist, the person whose point of view is being taken. The events are good and bad things that happen. And there are appropriate emotions that fit certain kinds of events in the scenarios. In a simple Rags-to-Riches scenario, for example, the initial state of the Protagonist is poverty, where the appropriate emotion is sadness; then there are intermediate states of hard work with varying emotions of frustration and satisfaction; and finally a state of wealth, with the emotions of joy and pride.

Since they are special cases of frames, narratives can be about particular people, about types of people, or about people in general. Part of what makes them cultural is that they use cultural prototypes, themes, images, and icons. In Russian fairy tales, there is the Baba Jaga, a powerful and villainous old hag living in a hut that stands on chicken legs in the woods. In Indian mythology and folklore, there are Rama (the Perfect Man), Sita (the Perfect Wife), Hanuman (Rama's helper, ultra-strong, able to fly, and able to appear in the form of a talking monkey), and Arjuna (the archer). In America, there are the comic-book figures: Superman, Batman, Spider-Man, and other superheroes. Then there are the movie and TV heroes: Rambo, Rocky, Rick in *Casablanca*, the Lone Ranger, Captain Kirk in *Star Trek*, Luke Skywalker in *Star Wars*.

But once you factor out the cultural specifics, a lot of the narratives look similar. Here is a general Rescue narrative. It has a number of "semantic roles," that is, main characters, actions, and instruments. The characters are: the Hero, the Victim, the Villain, the Helpers. The Hero is inherently good; the Villain is inherently bad. The main actions form a scenario, usually in this order: the Villainy, committed by the Villain against the Victim; the Difficulties undergone by the Hero; the Battle of Hero against Villain; the Victory of Hero over Villain; the Rescue of the Victim by the Hero; the Punishment of the Villain; the Reward for the Hero. The Villainy upsets the moral balance. The Victory, Rescue, Punishment, and Reward restore the moral balance. There is also a variant in which the Hero is the Victim. This is a Self-defense narrative: the Hero rescues himself.

It doesn't matter whether the story is about Rama, Wonder Woman, or Superman, the same general rescue structure occurs. We call this general case a "deep narrative." And this is just the narrative focused on the hero. There are plenty of other cultural prototypes: the gold digger, the martyr, the playboy, and so on.

But what is it in the brain that allows simple narratives to be combined into larger, more complex ones? What brain mechanism allows two different roles—Victim and Hero—to be identified as being the same, say, in a self-defense narrative? What in the brain allows a general narrative form, say a Rags-to-Riches narrative, to be applied in a special case?

The answer to all three questions is "neural binding." It might be easier to get at this with a concrete visual example. When you see a blue square, it appears as a single object. Yet the color and shape are registered in different parts of the brain. Neural binding allows us to bring together neural activation in different parts of the brain to form single integrated wholes.

To be a bit more precise: Parts of the brain neurally closer to the muscles and sensory organs are called "downstream"; those farther away in the brain are called "upstream." Neural signals go from downstream to upstream and back. Neural pathways from downstream regions "converge" on their way upstream at what are called "convergence zones."[7] Information from downstream and upstream is "integrated" at convergence zones via neural binding. Color and shape are registered in the brain relatively downstream. Neural binding circuitry converges farther upstream, integrating color and shape, making blue and a square into a blue square.

There are theories of how binding works, but we do not know for sure. The most prominent theory is that binding is "timelocking"—neurons firing simultaneously in different parts of the brain along connecting pathways. When they do, we experience simultaneous firing as characterizing the same entity. Another current theory is based on the coordination of so-called neural signatures—small collections of individual neurons together forming distinct firing patterns. But however it occurs, and whatever theory turns out to be correct, binding is one of the most important and most commonplace of all brain mechanisms.

The main thing to remember about neural binding is that it is not accomplished by magic; it has to be carried out by neural circuitry that links "binding sites" in different parts of the brain. Each neuron has between 1,000 and 10,000 incoming connections from other neurons, and another 1,000 to 10,000 outgoing connections. There are between 10 and 100 billion neurons in the brain, which means that the number of connections is in the trillions, as is the number of circuits. A great many of them are binding circuits.

Some bindings are long-term. I used to have a red VW Bug, and when I activate that memory, the red color is still neurally bound to the VW Bug shape. But if I want to buy a new car with a given shape, I can think of it in any color offered, via the short-term binding of color to shape. We use short-term bindings all the time, for example, when we use the existing Rescue narrative to structure a new rescue, as when a father rescues his child from drowning.

Binding circuitry consists just of neurons and connections, but has a special effect: it creates new experiences. For example, the experience of a red rose is not just an experience of a rose shape, an experience of redness, and a certain scent. Binding shape, color, and scent together provides a complex experience—the red rose, quite different from the yellow rose or white rose—and is accomplished just by neurons and connections.

Neural binding is also crucial to the time structure of a narrative. Even the simplest of narratives has a structure that is activated over time. Here are the stages:

- Preconditions—the prior context required for the narrative;
- The Buildup—the events leading up to the main, or central, event;
- The Main Event—what the narrative is mainly about;
- The Purpose—what is achieved (if there is a purpose);
- The Wind-Down—the events that end the narrative;
- The Result—the final context right afterward; and
- The Later Consequences.

There are variations on this structure, but this is typical for simple narratives. This is an "event structure." In the field of computational neural modeling, the technical term is an "executing schema," or "X-schema" for short.[8]

Even the simplest of actions, like taking a drink of water or tying your shoe, has such a structure imposed by our brain, which has to make our body work. We understand events in the world in terms of what our bodies can do. As a result, every simple narrative has such an event structure. Neural binding is the mechanism that creates a linkage between such highly general event structures and particular kinds of actions or narratives.

Take, for example, an election. Here are the bindings linking the event structure to the special case of the Election: The preconditions include the existence of political parties, the nomination of candidates, and so on. The Buildup is the election campaign; the Main Event is the election; the Purpose is to fill a public office; the Result is the power arrangement after the election; the Consequences are what comes about later as a result of the election. This is our simplest understanding of an election. Such a structure may do if you are just following, or reading about, an election. But actually running for office fills this structure out with additional lived narratives in hundreds of ways.

One of the reasons that politics lets us down is that we keep comparing it to our ideal narratives, to politics on TV or in the movies, which is tidier and better fits such structures.

Dramatic event structures are carried out by brain circuitry. The same event structure circuitry can be used to live out an action or a narrative, or to understand the actions of others or the structure of a story.

In addition, neural binding can create emotional experiences. In the area of the limbic system, the oldest part of the brain in terms of evolution, there are two emotional pathways with different neurotransmitters: one for positive emotions (happiness, satisfaction)—the dopamine circuit—and one for negative emotions (fear, anxiety, and anger)—the norepinephrine circuit. There are pathways in the brain linking these emotional pathways to the forebrain, where dramatic structure circuitry seems most likely to be located.

Activations of such convergent pathways are called "somatic markers." It is they that neurally bind the emotions (downstream, near the brain stem) to event sequences in a narrative (upstream, apparently in the prefrontal cortex, at the front and top of the brain). The somatic markers allow the right emotions to go where they should in a story. They are the binding circuits responsible for the emotional content of everyday experiences. Just as color and shape can be neurally bound, yielding an integrated experience of a red rose, so emotional content can be bound to a narrative, yielding a melodrama—a narrative with heightened emotional content. You feel fear when the heroine is threatened, and satisfaction or joy when the hero rescues her. The same is true of political experience that has a narrative structure: you may feel elated when your candidate wins the election (or is leading) and depressed or angry when your candidate loses. The circuitry characterizing winning for your hero is neurally bound to dopaminergic circuitry, which produces positive feelings when activated. Narratives and frames are not just brain structures with intellectual content, but rather with integrated intellectual-emotional content. Neural binding circuitry provides this integration.

We are now in a position to make sense of the mythic nature of Anna Nicole's life and death—and to see how it bears on politics.

In the case of Anna Nicole, there are many simple cultural narratives with ready-made emotions. Put them together and you get a roller coaster of complex emotions as well as a complex plot. (As we shall see, those simple classic American narratives that concern women are largely sexist. This is not surprising, since they have been around for a long time. That they have become permanent fixtures in the brains of so many Americans should make it all the more urgent that we recognize their existence— and their persistence—and start routing them out of our brains!)

Let's start with the Rags-to-Riches, or Pull-Yourself-up-by-

Your-Bootstraps, narrative. The Hero/Heroine starts out poor and unknown (the Precondition). He or she undergoes a series of hardships: the odds are against him/her (the Buildup). Through an exercise of will and discipline, he/she does something extraordinary (the Main Event) and so achieves success (the Purpose) and recognition (the Result), and gains respect, fame, and/or wealth for the achievement (the Consequence). This same Rags-to-Riches deep narrative occurs over and over in American political life. It has been used by Barack Obama, Alberto Gonzalez, John Edwards, Clarence Thomas. The narrative itself is an American icon, defining a version of the American dream, what every American who starts out poor should—and could—be doing.

By contrast, there is no honored narrative for the reality of Americans who work hard and can't climb the ladder of success because there are no rungs on it. There is no classic American narrative for the Cheap Labor Trap, in which companies drive down the cost of labor by outsourcing and other means, thus trapping tens of millions of workers in low-wage jobs from which they cannot escape.

A common extension of Rags-to-Riches is the Reinvention of the Self. In America, reinventing oneself is celebrated and extolled, in political cases such as Richard Nixon and Al Gore. Vickie Lynn Hogan, while a topless dancer, reinvented herself. She chose a new name with a new class identity: Vicki Lynn Hogan became Anna Nicole Smith.

When Anna Nicole was chosen to appear in *Playboy*, became first a centerfold and then Playmate of the Year, was offered a Guess? Jeans modeling contract, and married her billionaire, we have more than just Rags-to-Riches. This is the realization of the American Redemption narrative. The hero first fails and looks like a loser: she dropped out of high school, became a daytime waitress, then an impoverished single mom, then a topless dancer to make a buck. Her later successes redeem her. She has more than made up for those years as a dropout, a waitress, and a topless dancer.

Anna Nicole's marriage to the billionaire J. Howard Marshall II fits into two opposing cultural narratives:

- *The Gold digger.* She is a heartless, ruthless, manipulative, and sleazy gold digger (she met him when dancing in a topless bar), marrying a man sixty years her senior for his money, running up huge credit card bills on gowns and jewels, not even visiting him when he was dying, then challenging the claims of his son to the estate, and taking the case all the way to the Supreme Court.
- *How to marry a millionaire.* Like Marilyn Monroe or Julia Roberts in their signature roles, she is a naïve sexpot with a heart of gold that the millionaire recognizes and respects, and his respect wins her heart. As she says, "Nobody has ever respected me or done things for me. So when Howard came along, it was a blessing."

These are two different Rags-to-Riches narratives. Superimposed on top of the simple Rags-to-Riches deep narrative is what I will call the "Woman's Lot" narrative. It is about a woman trying to succeed in a man's world without an education or money: her sexuality and her determination are her main resources. She has to navigate the world of bad men, try to find a better one, and make the best use of her sexuality to succeed. There are several possible roles: the Innocent Ingénue, the Victim, the Girl with Pluck and Determination, and the Calculating Bitch. Success can come in various forms: the Nice Family, the Glamorous Star, the Hard-Driving Businesswoman, the Rich Man's Mistress, and so on. Anna Nicole, as a teenager, doted on Marilyn Monroe. The Glamorous Star meant success. Marilyn in legend—and in her Hollywood roles—was an Innocent Ingénue.

One variation on Woman's Lot is the Hooters narrative: she has to have and use big breasts to get even a menial job. Anna Nicole lost out in that narrative. Because her breasts were not big enough at the time, she could not even get a job as a night wait-

ress at Jim's Krispy Fried Chicken. She waitressed on the after-
noon shift and wound up marrying the sixteen-year-old cook at
seventeen, and having a child.

At nineteen, the possibility of the Nice Family narrative had
collapsed. She was divorced, the father was gone, and she was
penniless and raising a child. Her main asset was a sexy body.
To pay the bills, she took jobs as a topless dancer in strip clubs
in Houston. She took advantage of the Reinvention of Self narrative, changing her name. There she met her billionaire, J. Howard
Marshall II, whom she wound up marrying years later. Her rise in
the world came through her development and use of her sexuality: she followed the Woman's Lot plus Rags-to-Riches plotline.

But which version, the Innocent Ingénue or the Calculating
Bitch? The narratives are mutually exclusive, but either one could
fit her. Her public personality fit the ingénue: open, innocent, lov-
ing (her dog and her son), and fun-loving. On the other hand,
her moves were calculating, from the name change to the breast
implants to learning modeling techniques to modeling for *Playboy* and Guess? to marrying a billionaire to her movie, TV, and
weight-loss promotion deals. Pick one and it will hide the other.

Other versions of Woman's Lot fit her as well. Developing and
using her sexuality was not all that easy. She lived the Troubled
Life narrative. She had a weight problem: she gained, lost, gained
again. People pinned the Gold Digger narrative on her, damag-
ing her image. As a party girl, she drank and took drugs. She
was arrested for drunk driving and for assault. She was apparently bisexual, and was sued by a woman for sexual harassment.
She had little talent as an actress and her movies were roundly
panned, as was her reality TV show (though, because of her status as a mythic figure, it gained some cult status). Her billionaire
husband wrote her out of his will. And as she finally gave birth
to a baby girl, her beloved son died in front of her in the recovery
room of an overdose of methadone and prescription drugs. She
went into despair and soon died herself, apparently of a prescription drug overdose.

Through all this, she lived another version of the Woman's Lot and Troubled Life combined: she was used and abused by men. Her first husband left her with a child to support. Another millionaire lover gave her a mansion and then sued to get it back. She had a fling with her photographer and got pregnant. It was rumored that her men had kept her on drugs to use her sexually.

She also found herself embattled in the culture wars. In 1994 *New York* magazine ran a very smutty picture of her on its cover to advertise an article on "White Trash Nation." The educated subculture saw her as living out other narrative roles: the bimbo, the hick in Hollywood, and the redneck sexpot. To the good ol' boys, however, she was a good ol' girl.

All the while, she had become a celebrity, famous, always in the tabloids, in the movies, on TV, a staple of entertainment news. She was in the Nothing-Succeeds-Like-Success narrative. She was a celebrity because she was a celebrity, not because of any talent or good works.

Three more cultural narratives arose from the sudden death of her son: Teenage Drug Abuse—the suburban nightmare. The Death of a Child—every parent's worst nightmare. The Cycle of Death and Rebirth—one child dies as another is born.

Even at her death she was fit into cultural narratives: Live Fast, Die Young. She was in the same tragic narrative as Marilyn Monroe, Jayne Mansfield, Janis Joplin, James Dean. Even in death, she was at the center of a paternity trial, resolved in the modern way with DNA evidence—another drama. But it was a twist on the usual paternity suit, in which the father is trying to avoid paternity. Here the child comes with millions of dollars. Did the would-be fathers fit the Greedy Parent narrative, trying to make a buck on this child? Or did they fit the Protective Father narrative, trying to do right by the child, raise her and protect her? The daughter is in the world, evoking the Will History Repeat Itself narrative—to be played out in the press for decades. Will she be beautiful? How much will she inherit? Will she become a model? Will she fit any of her mother's narratives?

What makes Anna Nicole Smith a mythic figure? Fitting all these commonplace American narratives and frames at once. Rob Chilton, features director of *OK!* magazine said, "She was a great pop icon, almost like a cartoon character." Cartoon characters have no independent reality. They are understood only through the frames and cultural narratives imposed on them.

Listening to the TV talk shows right after Anna Nicole's death, I was struck by how many women identified with her and mourned her. They didn't see her as a gold digger, or a bimbo, or a no-talent celebrity. They saw her as fitting into the Woman's Lot narrative, just as they saw themselves. They saw her as a poor girl with a good heart and no education using her only resources—her body and her determination—and making it to fame and fortune with mostly good humor and a sense of fun, while going through many forms of woman's hell while taking drugs trying to cope with it all. Her death saddened them, genuinely, as the *USA Today* headline said: "Sad end to a troubled life."

We live our narratives. The lived story is at the center of modern personality theory.[9] The theory of neural computation, as we shall see later, shows how our brains not only permit this, but favor it. The typical roles played in narratives include Hero, Victim, and Helper. A doctor may not just be a doctor, but a Hero-doctor, saving people's lives. A housewife may see herself as a Victim-housewife, victimized by society's sexism. A nurse may see herself as the Helper to the Hero-doctor. Or as a Victim of Sexism in medicine. A president may see himself as a Hero rescuing a Victim-nation from a Villain-dictator. Or as leading a Battle of Good Against Evil. The roles in narratives that you understand yourself as fitting give meaning to your life, including the emotional color that is inherent in narrative structures.

The very fact that we recognize these cultural narratives and frames means that they are instantiated physically in our brains. We are not born with them, but we start growing them soon, and as we acquire the deep narratives, our synapses change and

become fixed. A large number of deep narratives can be activated together. We cannot understand other people without such
cultural narratives. But more important, we cannot understand
ourselves—who we are, who we have been, and where we want
to go—without recognizing and seeing how we fit into cultural
narratives.

We understand public figures by fitting them into such narrative complexes. That goes for politicians as well as celebrities.
Indeed, we often understand the people we know that way as well.
Who is that man or woman you met at the party last week? He or
she is, for you, the complex of narratives or frames you (mostly
unconsciously, as a matter of reflex) ascribe to him or her—sort
of like a cartoon character. Those narratives are not unique to
that person. You use the same simple ones over and over in different combinations for different people.

We know from cognitive science and neuroscience that such
narratives are fixed in the neural circuits of our brains. We know
that they can be activated and function unconsciously, automatically, as a matter of reflex. And just as we—automatically, without conscious control—see Anna Nicole and Hillary Clinton and
George W. Bush in terms of such narratives, so we see ourselves
as having only the choices defined by our brain's frames and cultural narratives. And we live out narrative choices made for us by
our brains without our conscious awareness.

My goal as a scientist and a citizen is to make the cognitive
unconscious as conscious as possible, to make *reflexive* decisions
reflective. When those choices are political choices—for president, senator, congressperson—it becomes vital for all of us that
we not be blindly driven by unconscious narratives and frames. Is
Hillary going to be framed as the long-suffering wife, the model
of the competent, deserving woman, or the calculating bitch? Do
we see her possible presidency in terms of the Dynasty narrative—a dynastic return to the Clinton years? Is it possible not to
see Hillary in terms of cultural narratives?

I think not. The cultural models are there in our brains. We are going to use them—automatically, without conscious control or even recognition most of the time.

David Rieff was right. Politics is very much about cultural narratives. For candidates it is about the stories they have lived and are living, the stories they tell about themselves, the stories the opposition tries to pin on them, and the stories the press tells about them. But in a deeper sense, politics is about the narratives our culture and our circumstances make available to all of us to live. Feminism has tried to create new narratives for women to live. But the narratives available to the Gloria Steinems and Hillary Clintons of the world were not available to Vickie Lynn Hogan. If you are raised in a culture where the only available choices are those of the Woman's Lot, feminism can seem ridiculous, or at best an upper-middle-class fantasy. Cultural narratives define our possibilities, challenges, and actual lives. The women who identified with, and genuinely mourned, Anna Nicole Smith were living out many of her life narratives. In those respects, they were Anna Nicole Smith. And because of that, they do care what happens to her daughter.

George W. Bush understood the power of the Redemption narrative. He had been an alcoholic, had a DUI violation, avoided service in Vietnam, had a shadow experience in his Air National Guard unit, failed repeatedly in business. You might think that this would disqualify him for the presidency. But the power of the Redemption narrative turned all of this around for him. In giving up drinking, he redeemed himself in the eyes of all those who live or want to live by the Redemption narrative, who forgave his "youthful indiscretions." Every failing overcome was a testimony to his character. That is why just stating the facts of his alcoholism, his DUI violation, and his military record had no effect.

Al Gore is very conscious of his use of the Redemption narrative. He even calls himself self-mockingly a "recovering politician." In successfully alerting the world to the dangers of global warming, he has redeemed himself for his failure to become president in 2000. His Nobel Prize is surely confirmation of that success.

In a New Enlightenment, cultural narratives will not be gone, replaced by cold, hard reason. Cultural narratives are part of the permanent furniture of our brains. But in the New Enlightenment we will at least be self-aware. We will recognize that we are all living out narratives. It will be normal to discuss what they might be, to raise the question of what influence they have, and whether we can or should put them aside.

There is also a dark side of narrative. The people in our national security apparatus—the military, the CIA, and private contractors—know that personal identity is largely defined by the narratives we live out. Methods of torture have been devised to break down the "subject" being interrogated by destroying the narratives that define him so that he no longer has his old identity. They then use techniques such as sensory deprivation, isolation, fear, and physical shock to forge a new identity for him in which he is dependent on his torturers and is willing to help.[10] The effects of these techniques are horrifying—and very real.

We can never go back to the naiveté of the eighteenth-century philosophers. But nor can we escape from having human brains and thinking with real human minds. What we can do is become as self-aware as possible, using what the science of the mind has to teach us.

Narrative and War

In the first Gulf War, the first President Bush first tried a self-defense narrative: Saddam Hussein was threatening the United States. He was choking off our oil lifeline. Antiwar demonstrators countered with the slogan "No Blood for Oil," and it worked. A poll taken three months before the war showed that Americans would not go to war for oil. But they would go to war for a rescue. Immediately after the poll, the president's narrative changed to the Rape of Kuwait, a rescue narrative. The daughter of a Kuwaiti diplomat, who lived in the United States but was identified falsely as a victim of Saddam's army in Kuwait, testified to seeing brutal rapes. The rape testimony shored up the Rape of Kuwait narrative. Saddam was the Villain (inherently evil, beyond reason), Kuwait was the Victim (innocent, too weak to defend herself), the United States was the Hero (the rescuer), and the coalition members were the Helpers.

When you accept a particular narrative, you ignore or hide realities that contradict it. The "innocent" Kuwait was not very nice. It was a dictatorship, a major violator of human rights. During the Iran-Iraq War, Iraq claimed, Kuwait had drilled sideways under the Iraqi border to pump Iraqi oil and take it as its own. Kuwait paid Iraq to defend it against Iran, then later insisted the money was a loan to be repaid by a financially drained Iraq. Kuwait engaged in currency manipulations to devalue Iraqi currency, allowing rich Kuwaitis to go into Iraq and buy up commodities cheaply—including the sexual services of widows of Iraqi men who had died in the Iraq-Iran War, which annoyed religious Muslims in Iraq no end. Also hidden was the source of Saddam Hussein's weaponry: the United States, which saw Iraq as an ally keeping Iran in check. The person sent by the United States to confer with its ally, Saddam Hussein, during the Iran-Iraq War was none other than Donald Rumsfeld, who was photographed shaking hands with Saddam. Narratives have a powerful effect in hiding reality.

Interestingly, the same narrative shift was used by the second President Bush in the Iraq War. First there was a self-defense narrative: Saddam was threatening the United States with weapons of mass destruction. We were both Victim and Hero. The Helpers were the Coalition of the Willing. When no WMDs were found, the rationale for the war shifted to a rescue narrative. The Victims now were the people of Iraq. The Villain was Saddam Hussein. His Villainy was oppression: spying on, torturing, killing, even raping his own citizens, while taking Iraq's oil profits for himself. The United States was the Hero, bringing democracy to the people of Iraq and freeing them of torture, rape, corruption, and killing. Once Saddam was defeated, a new Villain was found: the insurgents—Iraqis who are engaging in a civil war, or who want the United States to leave.

The deep Rescue narrative remains the same. In two different wars, under two different presidents, the same narrative structures were imposed, and the same narrative shift occurred. How is it possible for the brain to apply the same narrative structure to two different real-world cases? The deep narratives are fixed in the brain; the synapses of the neural circuits characterizing them have been so strengthened that the highly general, deep narratives are permanently parts of our brains. Neural binding allows these permanent general narrative structures to be applied to ever new special cases. That's why the same narrative structures keep recurring, from war to war, from celebrity to celebrity, from one political figure to another.

We Are in the Melodrama

It is hardly news that people who watch TV are not passive observers. Reality TV is based on the idea that the viewers play roles in the show. *American Idol* is an obvious example. MoveOn.org showed that the same was true of the Internet. Their members actively play roles in politics, sending letters to officeholders, raising money for candidates, and opening up their living rooms for their neighbors to participate in national discussions.

The latest example of active participation, as I write this, was the YouTube Democratic Debate held on July 23, 2007, in which YouTube users submitted videos of themselves asking questions of the candidates, which were then culled by the CNN staff and actually run on the debate. People who sat at home playing questioners in their imagination became real questioners. I suspect this will become a standard format.

Why?

There are two further properties of the brain that explain this, and a lot more. The same part of the brain we use in seeing is also used in imagining that we are seeing, in remembering seeing, in dreaming that we are seeing, and in understanding language about seeing. The same is true of moving. The same parts of the brain used in really moving are used in imagining that we are moving, remembering moving, dreaming about moving, and in understanding language about moving. Mental "simulation" is the technical term for using brain areas for moving or perceiving, imagining, remembering, dreaming, or understanding language.[11] It is mental simulation that links imaginative stories to lived narratives.

But what links your lived narratives to those of someone else?

Our most plausible hypothesis at present is "mirror neuron circuitry, which integrates action and perception." We apparently have "mirror neuron circuits" in the premotor cortex that fire when we either perform a given action or see someone else perform the same action.

This is not magic. Mirror neuron circuits are connected via two-way pathways to other brain areas:

1. To the primary motor cortex, which connects to motor neurons in the muscles of the body and directly controls muscle movement;
2. To the parietal cortex, which integrates sensory information arising in the visual, auditory, and somatosensory regions;
3. Via the insula to the positive and negative emotional pathways;
4. To the posteromedial cortex, which must be active in the experience of empathy, say, in compassion and admiration;[12] and
5. To the so-called super-mirror neurons in the prefrontal cortex, which modulate the activation of the mirror neurons, apparently to either enhance or limit their capacity for empathy.

Mirror neuron circuits are also apparently used in so-called mind reading, when we guess from seeing part of a familiar action what the rest of the action will be.[13]

The reason that I hedge a bit is this: the hypothesis depends on the assumption that the brains of macaque monkeys have the same structure and function as analogous regions in the human brain. An example is that we can identify the premotor cortex in the macaque monkey brain with the premotor cortex of a human being. That assumption is plausible, uncontroversial, and used widely in neuroscience research—and I am accepting it here.

In short, some of the same neural structure in the brain that is used when we live out a narrative is also used when we see someone else living out that narrative, in real life or on TV, or if we imagine it as when we are reading a novel. This is what makes literature and art meaningful. It is also what makes crossovers between reality, TV, and the Internet work. It is why Second Life can flourish on the Internet, with thousands of people finding real meaning in their second life that is not in their first.

The fact that imagining and acting use much of the same neural structure has enormous political consequences. September 11, 2001, was an event that aroused fear, even if you were just watching on TV, thousands of miles away from danger. Repeated images of the twin towers falling, in Republican ad after Republican ad, have continued to arouse fear as well. Even the language of fear—"threat," "attack"—used over and over in Republican rhetoric, can continue to evoke fear once the neural circuits have been fixed in your brain. Someone is putting that fear to political use.

In the October 17, 2004, *New York Times Magazine*, Ron Suskind wrote of his encounter with an unnamed aide of George W. Bush:

> The aide said that guys like me were "in what we call the reality-based community," which he defined as people who "believe that solutions emerge from your judicious study of discernible reality." I nodded and murmured something about Enlightenment principles and empiricism. He cut me off. "That's not the way the world really works anymore,"

he continued. "We're an empire now, and when we act we create our own reality. And while you're studying that reality—judiciously, as you will—we'll act again, creating other new realities, which you can study too, and that's how things will sort out. We're history's actors... and you, all of you, will be left to study what we do."

In many ways, those words were prophetic. The Bush administration has shown an extraordinary capacity to make real what it imagines—tax cuts, elimination of social programs, privatization of government operations, deregulation, environmental destruction for the sake of private profit, and on and on—making yesterday's political imagination into today's reality, with the public hardly noticing. Naomi Klein has documented the rise of "disaster capitalism" under the Bush administration, where private contractors get huge no-bid contracts to do jobs in disasters (such as 9/11, Katrina, Iraq) that government used to do, while government agencies are made nonfunctional through budget cuts.[14] This is essentially a major transfer of wealth from taxpayers to private corporations, an overwhelming weakening of government, and a capacity-shifting from government to corporations that profit mightily from disasters at great cost to the general public. Such relatively invisible "reality creation" is below the public radar screen. Why is this possible?

The brain supplies the reasons. First, stresses like fear (of terrorist attacks), worry (say, about finances, health care, and so on), and overwork tend to activate the norepinephrine system, the system of negative emotions. The result is a reduced capacity to notice. Second, the right conceptual framework must be in place in order to recognize apparently different events as the same kind of event.

For example, as I write this, there are three front-page news stories that seem to be about different things: Blackwater mercenaries killing civilians in Iraq, the president's veto of the continuation of SCHIP (a government-run children's health care program that has been working), and the FDA no longer having the resources to monitor food and drug safety trials. But they are about the same issue: the radical conservative political and economic agenda is putting public resources and government functions into private hands, while eliminating the capacity of government to protect and empower the public. The public has no conceptual framework to see all these as the same and to comprehend what this means, and with the stress of fear and worry and overwork, the public has little capacity to notice and to create the substantial neural structures needed to comprehend what is happening in hundreds of areas of life.

The Democratic leaders are not, as they say, connecting these dots. On the contrary, their appeal to supposed Enlightenment reason—conscious, logical, unemotional, disembodied, based on perceived self-interest, and open to rational discussion as classically conceived—plays into radical conservative hands. The facts and figures are given, but they are all about different things—violence in Iraq, children's health, drug tests. The Old Enlightenment reason approach not only fails, it wastes effort, time, and money. It does so not only because the public's mind is mostly unconscious, metaphorical, and physically affected by stress, but because its brain has been neurally shaped by past conservative framing.[15]

The same neural mechanisms behind the melodramas that tied so many people to the fate of Anna Nicole Smith—mechanisms beyond Enlightenment reason—are serving a major political purpose and hiding massive political and economic change.

With such an explanation of what is hidden and why, it becomes possible to consciously create a conceptual framework, a language, an imagery, and an appropriate emotional tone in which such major under-the-radar changes not only become visible, but their moral consequences become known. It is not easy, but it can be done—if you understand the problem.

CHAPTER 2

The Political Unconscious

Politics is about moral values. Every political leader presents his or her policies on the grounds that they are "right"—that is, they are moral. Yet basic conservative and progressive modes of thought start from very different perspectives on what constitutes morality, perspectives so different that they are virtually opposites.

How do we know this? After all, there is an opposing view, that all politics is a matter of money, power, and organization. Those are obviously vital to any winning politics. But if that were all there were to it, if there were no moral issues involved, then it would not matter who wins, except for who gets the patronage.

But in America today, moral issues are central. It does matter morally who wins.

And what does cognitive science have to do with this? The answer is the cognitive unconscious—the system of concepts that structure our brains but that we can't see directly. Most of what we understand in public discourse is not in the words themselves, but in the unconscious understanding that we bring to the words. As Charles Fillmore has shown, each word is defined relative to at least one conceptual frame.[1] Those frames evoke other frames in the system. Understanding involves drawing out the logic of the frames. In a great many cases, metaphorical thinking is used as well. What cognitive semanticists have found is that we think in terms of systems of concepts, systems that fit together and make sense. In a discourse, our systems of concepts are used to make sense of what is said overtly.

When we apply this technique of analysis to political speeches, interviews, call-ins on talk shows, op-eds and editorials, think tank reports, letters to the editor, blogs, and so on, certain recurrent patterns of thought emerge—general modes of thought based on assumptions about what is the right thing to do. Some of this is conscious and overtly there in the language. But 98 percent of it is unconscious, unseen, but making sense of what is actually said.

Though the Old Enlightenment mischaracterized the human mind, Enlightenment values nevertheless wrought the foundations of American democracy. A New Enlightenment should likewise articulate America's original values, both conscious and unconscious, and extend them further in the same direction. America was founded and developed as a progressive country, and it is crucial that its values be reclaimed and extended to fit the needs of our century.

Conservatives have excelled at articulating their values and ideas. It is time for progressives to do the same. My job here is to unlock the cognitive unconscious, to take progressive thought off the leash and to draw an accurate picture of conservative thought for the sake of comparison. Radical conservatives have also excelled at carrying out hidden objectives that fit their values. Allowing hidden objectives to be seen is another benefit of cognitive science.

Conservatives and progressives do not just have different goals or values. They have very different modes of thought. Neither mode is obvious. The political mind has to be probed in depth to be understood. What we shall see is complexity: many Americans make use of both conservative and progressive modes of thought in their politics, but apply them to different areas in different ways. There are regularities, but there is no clear scale from left to right (or color spectrum from blue to red). There are no moderates—that is, there is no moderate worldview, no one set of ideas that characterizes a "center" or "moderation." People who are called "moderates" use conservative thought in some issue areas and progressive thought in others, without falling on any linear left-to-right scale. Indeed, many so-called moderates have no moderation at all, and are quite passionate about both their conservative and their progressive views. For example, consider Chuck Hagel, an antiwar conservative, and Joe Lieberman, a pro-war liberal. Both are called "moderates," but they have few beliefs in common and certainly do not share a single worldview.

The left-to-right scale that political pundits love is an inaccurate metaphor—and a dangerous one, for two reasons. First, it posits a political "mainstream," a population with a unified political worldview, which does not exist now nor has it ever. Because radical conservatives have so dominated political discourse in America over the past thirty years, conservative ideas are being passed off as "mainstream" ideas, which they are not, while progressive ideas are being characterized as "leftist" and "extremist," which they are not. Supreme Court justice John Paul Stevens, who was appointed to the Court as a conservative by Gerald Ford in the 1970s, is now considered a "liberal," though he says he has not changed his views. One can speak of left and right, as in left hand and right hand, or left hemisphere and right hemisphere of the brain, without any linear scale in between.

The very use of the left-to-right scale metaphor serves to empower radical conservatives and marginalize progressives. Here's why: what is really happening in the brains of Americans is that there are two very general modes of thought, one fundamentally progressive, the other fundamentally conservative. Each can be applied to—that is, neurally bound to—special cases, in all sorts of ways, as when Joe Lieberman applies his conservative mode of thought to Iraq and school vouchers, while applying his progressive mode of thought in other areas. Some people have no fixed binding of a mode of thought to an issue area, but may go back and forth, or not know what to think.

At the beginning of the 1970s, most Americans used the progressive mode of thought on most issue areas. *Roe vs. Wade* seemed settled, social security was secure, public education was a fixed institution, unions were strong, the separation of church and state was largely unchallenged, and taxation was understood as providing necessary government services. Since then, more people have been applying the conservative mode of thought to more issue areas, and the progressive mode to fewer, though the progressive mode is still widely used by the majority of Americans in most areas. Thus, polls show that most Americans agree with Democrats on most issues; though, for reasons we shall see, they don't vote accordingly.

At the same time, conservative modes of thought and language have come to dominate political discourse in the media. We can see this in the everyday use of conservative language and the ideas that go with it: *illegal immigrants*, not *illegal employers* or *illegal consumers*; *war in Iraq*, not *occupation of Iraq*; *surge*, not *escalation*; *supporting the troops*, not *squandering tax money*, and so on. Though the progressive mode of thought expresses the ideals of American democracy as seen in our founding documents, it has become less and less dominant in public discourse. The denial of habeas corpus, unrestricted tapping of citizens' phones, and routine torture have brought forth little discussion of the inalienable rights of life, liberty, and the pursuit of happiness.

Those who are thoroughgoing progressives hold to American democratic ideals on just about all issues. They are the bedrock of our democracy. But, when seen metaphorically on a left-to-right scale, the bedrock of our democracy is on one side—the "extreme left." The left-to-right scale metaphor makes it look like the bedrock of our democracy is "extreme." And conservatives have been characterizing defenders of traditional American ideals like civil liberties, the welcoming of immigrants, and public education as extremists.

Accordingly, the left-to-right scale metaphor creates a metaphorical "center" with about a third of voters located between the two "extremes"—even though their views vary every which way and don't constitute a single mode of thought at all.

Metaphor is a normal, and mostly unconscious, mechanism of

thought. It is sometimes harmless, and at other times can be used for good or ill. The left-to-right scale metaphor is not harmless. It is being politically manipulated to the disadvantage of American democratic ideals.

And yet the left-to-right scale metaphor is no concocted hoax. It is real as a metaphor; it is in people's brains. Even though it is grossly inaccurate, many people use it. My job here is to make you think twice about it, and then stop using it. If you can. It won't be easy. Thinking that way is a reflex. You *will* think in terms of the left-to-right scale. Try to catch yourself and stop. Overcoming misleading metaphors that are physically in your brain is never easy.

Progressive Thought and the Politics of Empathy

Behind every progressive policy lies a single moral value: empathy, together with the responsibility and strength to act on that empathy. Never forget "responsibility and strength," because there is no true empathy without them.

During the conservative reign we have seen what Barack Obama has called an empathy deficit—a failure to care, both about others and each other. Caring is not just feeling empathy; it is taking responsibility, acting powerfully and courageously. You have to be strong to care, and to act on that care with success.

The ethics of care shapes government. Care requires that government have two intertwined roles: protection and empowerment. Protection is more than just the army, police, and fire department. It means social security, disease control and public health, safe food, disaster relief, health care, consumer and worker protection, environmental protection.

Empowerment by the government is everywhere: highways and bridges, so you can go where you want to go and ship products; the Internet and satellite communications, to keep you in contact with the world; public education, to open the world up to you and to provide skilled workers to business; the banking system, to allow bank loans, whether you're buying a house or your company is buying another company; the SEC, to allow the stock market to function; the court system, to enforce contracts and protect patents. Nobody makes a dime in this country without being empowered by our government. There are no self-made men or women. It's a myth!

The role of progressive government is to maximize our freedom—and protection and empowerment do just that. Protection is there to guarantee freedom from harm, from want, and from fear. Empowerment is there to maximize freedom to achieve your goals.

Progressive government is, or should rightly be through protection and empowerment, the guarantor of liberty. That is what a life-affirming government is about.

Part of the genius of America came in the form of taxes, which used to be paid to the king of England before the Revolution. They were not abolished, but were instead directed toward protection and empowerment of the citizens of this country.

Corporations make use of government empowerment more than ordinary citizens. I drive my car on freeways; corporations send out fleets of trucks. I get a bank loan for my house; corporations get loans to buy other corporations. Corporations thus make compound use of government empowerment, and that is why they—and their investors—should be paying more, not less, than ordinary citizens for sustaining the empowering function of government.

Protection and empowerment are part of the moral mission of government. That is why governmental budgets are moral documents. Government is fundamentally different from business. The first responsibility of a business is to make money; the first responsibility of a government is to protect and empower its citizens. Businesses sell you hamburgers and TVs and rent you cars. The government is supposed to ensure that food and drugs and drinking water are safe; to maintain roads and bridges; to provide education; and to control the money supply to make sure that neither inflation nor unemployment gets too high.

When might the privatization of government functions be appropriate? When there is no moral mission involved, when the life-affirming role of government is not at stake. For example, suppose a government agency has a fleet of cars. It might be more efficient or economical to just rent them from Hertz or Avis. There is no moral mission involved. But when it comes to testing the safety of food or of drugs, a clear moral mission is involved: protecting the public. The danger in privatization is that the profit motive may intervene and undermine the moral mission. We have seen this repeatedly in cases where drug companies fake data on their tests for the sake of profits, which has lead to the death of people taking their drugs.

Empathy leads to recognizing that unfair and discriminatory treatment is a form of harm requiring government protection. This correlates with the idea that we are all equal, and that the denial of equality counts as harm. This is the moral basis of civil rights laws—voting rights laws, antidiscrimination laws, and so on. It is also the moral basis of labor law. The right to unionize, for example, recognizes the unfair advantage that employers have over employees in negotiating the conditions of their employment, and OSHA recognizes the need for worker protection.

Empathy is the basis for the concept of a fair and responsible market—a market whose job is to create wealth and distribute resources in such a way as to respect the protective function of government, sustain its empowering function, and treat everyone in the market as fairly as possible. Fairness means that employees should ideally be paid according to their work, their productivity, and their contribution to the society as a whole.

Empathy also forms the moral basis of class action suits, in which companies or government agencies that harm groups of citizens can be sued both for the harm caused and for "punitive damages" to give the companies an incentive not to harm the citizenry again. These are carried out in the civil justice system, which is like the criminal justice system except that the only punishment is monetary and that the detectives and the prosecuting attorneys are not government employees paid by taxpayers, but are instead civil justice attorneys—trial lawyers paid out of damages assigned by the courts. This means that civil justice attorneys tend to take only cases that they think they can win and where the harm is great enough that the damages will pay them for the time they spend on the case. The civil justice system is the last line of protection for the public against unscrupulous or irresponsible corporations.[2]

Perhaps the most important governmental protection is protection from the power of the government itself. That is why we have a system of checks and balances, with the power of government split between the legislature, executive, and judiciary. It is also why we have frequent elections. The idea is to avoid dictatorial powers via a balance of power and to avoid the exertion of unwarranted power for an unlimited amount of time. This is the moral basis behind the idea of the openness of government, so that governmental operations will be transparent and can be criticized when appropriate and prosecuted when necessary.

Empathy is also the moral basis of laws protecting citizens from abuse by the government. Habeas corpus—which protects citizens from being arrested without a charge, held without legal counsel or incommunicado, and with no requirement that the state show its evidence—is fundamental to our liberty. Also fundamental to liberty is the right of privacy and the need for the state to obtain a warrant stating reasonable cause before it can wiretap or get access to other private information.

Progressives have a range of attitudes toward the market. Some believe that it is possible for large corporations to function morally, for the public good, and to make that their highest priority, while making enough profit to thrive. Others believe that large corporations will almost always function to make money first and foremost. Their faith in markets rests on either tight governmental regulation or careful market construction for the public good.

But many progressives are keenly aware of, and tend to be suspicious of, corporations that lobby to serve their profit, not the public interest, and who will go with profit over the public interest when the chips are down.

Progressives also tend to favor small businesses over large ones, businesses with strong unions, and those where there is a lot of competition.

Progressives are hardly antibusiness. But they believe that government has a crucial moral mission to play—protection and empowerment, as we have observed, that in many cases inherently cannot be carried out by private enterprise.

It should be clear that empathy and responsibility are at the heart of progressive thought. But things are not so simple. Not all progressives are the same.

The Neoliberal Mode of Thought

Progressive thought today begins with empathy and responsibility, with government having the twin moral missions of protection and empowerment. What I will call "neoliberal thought" has the same moral basis, but overlays another mode of thought upon it. Neoliberal thought embraces the Old Enlightenment view of reason: it is conscious, logical, literal, universal, unemotional, disembodied, with the function of serving interests, one's own or those of others.

Neoliberal thought takes emotion as irrational and therefore ineffectual and weak, while it sees reason as rational, efficacious, and strong. Though it starts intuitively with an ethics of empathy and care, neoliberal thought tries to achieve care by setting up programs for the material interests of the disadvantaged, and to target the disadvantaged through programs for members of disadvantaged demographic groups (African Americans in the inner city, college students needing loans, children of lower-income families, middle-class workers, and so on).

The implicit moral intuition seems to be that empathy defines what counts as market success and failure. Where the market fails to provide for some demographic group, government should step in with an economically based program, either to restructure the market by law or to provide funding, either directly or through subsidies. But the concepts of empathy and of market failure are never discussed overtly. Indeed, there is no discussion in public discourse of what market failure or success is, how to tell when there is a market failure, and what to do about it.

The neoliberal mode of thought further assumes that lacks demonstrate needs. Accordingly, there is a focus on objective evidence for the needs of these programs via statistics showing lacks: things that can be objectively measured, facts and figures, surveys, statistics, presentation of evidence that, prima facie, is supposed to argue for the programs. For example, 47 million people lack health care, so-and-so many college students lack affordable college loans, a disproportionate number of African American young men are in jail for nonviolent crimes, and so on.

From the perspective of real reason, each such program is in principle highly commendable, providing that real reason is taken into account—providing that the "facts" really are objective (in the sense of being above prejudice); that the surveys take into account the cognitive unconscious—the frames and metaphors used in the survey instruments; that no presupposed content is hidden in the statistics; and that the evidence converges from multiple sources, as is required in science. In short, real reason is committed to realism—a realism that takes real reason itself into account. This is informed self-consciousness, and it is far more demanding than Old Enlightenment reason.

I mention this because neoliberals sometimes mistake real reason for relativism, because real reason recognizes that there are multiple ways in which the brain sees reality. I have previously criticized neoliberals for assuming that just citing facts and figures will carry the day politically, when what is needed is an honest, morally based framing of the facts and figures, showing their moral significance, and conveyed with the appropriate emotions and with words, images, and symbols that really communicate. When conservatives answer liberals' facts and figures with no facts or figures, but with their own morals-based frames presented with emotion and symbolism, their framing will win. Conservative frames will trump liberals' frameless—and hence meaningless—facts. That's one reason why neoliberals should pay attention to real reason and use frames that reveal truths and emotions that carry moral importance.

But the neoliberal mode of thought extends well beyond unframed facts and figures. Neoliberals' focus on Old Enlightenment reason leads them away from stating overtly the moral basis of their proposals, which flow from empathy and responsibility. Instead, they argue from interests—material interests of members of demographic groups—trying to reach the moral vision of empathy and responsibility from the interests of group members. The argument is: It is in our political interest to help others achieve their material interests. If we do that, they'll vote for us. The programs: reduced middle-class taxes; cheaper loans for college students; housing vouchers for the homeless; green jobs for inner-city African Americans; citizenship for immigrants without papers; protecting pensions for public employees; health care for children of the poor. All of these are commendable.

Their intuitive impetus is the morality of empathy. But the basis of the argument is group interests, not empathy. Why does this matter? Because political thought begins with moral premises, since all political positions are supposed to be correct. To get the public to adopt progressive moral positions you have to activate progressive moral thought in them by openly—and constantly—stressing morality, not just the interests of demographic groups.

Focusing on interests rather than empathy plays into the hands of conservatives in many ways: It allows them to criticize as "special interests" the groups whose interests are served. It angers people in demographic groups whose interests are not being served, and gives conservatives an opportunity to look moral, rather than just playing partisan politics. It fails to even state the progressive moral vision of empathy and responsibility, protection and empowerment. It gives support to the conservative version of the "free market" as the moral pursuit of self-interest that helps us all, because it activates in people's brains the idea of the morality of pursuing interests through the market. This helps conservatives fight against progressive values that are not materialistic—the arts, education for its own sake (not just for better jobs), environmental protection, and so on. And it leads to the use of the rational actor model in foreign policy, in which states are seen as people acting "rationally" to maximize their material self-interest.

The rational actor model in foreign policy hides the needs of real people—individuals who are poor, hungry, jobless, homeless, diseased, uneducated, being exploited, being oppressed. It takes empathy and responsibility toward people out of foreign policy, replacing it with state self-interest and the interests of our individual citizens with the "national interest"—GDP growth, corporate interests, military advantage, and so on. It leads to neoliberalism in foreign policy, in which "free markets" are seen as always creating wealth, which ought in theory to help everybody, but instead serve the interests of American and other multinational corporations over the needs and aspirations of real people.

Neoliberal thinking in terms of facts and figures on the one hand and serving the interests of demographic groups on the other also leads to "issue silos," the isolation of one issue from another—food and drug safety; children's health care; controlling military contractors—as if there were no general moral principle and political issue governing all of these. But there is: privateering (see chapter 7). Privateering is the destruction of the capacity of government to carry out its moral missions, together with the privatization of government functions with no public accountability and the enrichment of corporations at the public's expense.

Unfortunately, if you have to argue just on the basis of facts and figures, then the facts and figures about the lack of FDA food and drug inspectors have no overlap with the facts and figures about Blackwater security guards in Iraq, which have no overlap with the figures about children's health care. Neoliberal thought misses the overarching moral and political issue governing and connecting these and dozens, if not hundreds, of other cases.

Neoliberal policy think tanks therefore tend to be silos—cranking out issue-by-issue policies, while not addressing the deeper threats to our democracy, such as the threat of privateering. Their thought also leads to policy as technocratic solutions and "rational systems" to be instituted through legislation and implemented in government. The assumption is that the rational system of law, the enforcement of law, government regulation, and the courts will win the day. Meanwhile, conservatives have figured out ways to undermine all such strategies, by defunding or reassigning regulators, hiring lobbyists in government positions, letting corporate lobbyists write laws, refusing to enforce laws, and getting their judges into the courts. Let us call this "administrative undermining." Because Old Enlightenment reason creates issue silos, the general case of administrative undermining has not even been named, much less called a general threat to democracy and made an issue of. Old Enlightenment reason is not even up to the job of making the moral case that such general conservative policies as privateering and administrative undermining are threatening democracy.

Neoliberalism also has certain elitist tendencies that it cannot recognize as elitist. If you believe that reason is literal, logical, and universal and that your policies are based on reason, then those policies could not conceivably be elitist because every rational being would have to be in favor of the same policies because they would reason the same way. But if reason is really neither literal, logical, nor universal, then imposing policies from the top down, from policy think tanks to Congress and the courts, does smack of elitism. Even taking polls that frame policies from your perspective rather than from the perspective of others is a form of elitism that comes out with pronouncements like "Americans believe..." followed by your framing of the policy. And anything that smacks of elitism gives credence to the conservative charge that liberals are elitists.

Crucially, neoliberal thought cannot even recognize its own framing as framing. If Old Enlightenment reason is literal—if it always reflects the world directly and fits the rational structure of reality—then there cannot be any honest alternative framings. If you accept Old Enlightenment reason, then framing cannot involve real ideas and moral principles; it can only be about messaging; it can only be spin. The neoliberal failure to understand how brains and minds really work hides ideas and moral principles put forth by progressives who are not neoliberals.

Most dangerous of all, Old Enlightenment reason, being literal and universal, cannot recognize conservative framing as framing. Instead, it tends to take conservative language and concepts at their face value. If conservatives say there is a "war on terror," those following the neoliberal mode of thought will repeat "war on terror" and argue within the conservative frame. They may argue against conservative policy, but if they stay within the frame, they are activating and reinforcing the frame rather than challenging it and replacing it. The very idea that we think in terms of frames and metaphors is not merely foreign to neoliberal thought, it is inconsistent with it.

The political effect is that neoliberals tend to surrender in advance to conservatives, simply by accepting their frames.

Neoliberal reason, besides starting with self-interest, also depends on the idea of optimization: Let's get all we can get, even if it's not all that much. This is incrementalist thinking: better to get a little something now than nothing at all, even if it means accepting conservative framing. What's wrong with that? In some cases, everything. The question is whether the incrementalist solution will be a long-lasting one. Take health care. Insurance companies get their money by *denying* care, by saying no to as many people in need as they can get away with, while maximizing the premiums they get from healthy people. Health insurance will always work this way. It is not the same as care; "coverage," when you read the fine print, may not even include care. If neoliberal incrementalists establish a profit-maximizing insurance-based health care plan for the country, it will not be a step toward a system that eliminates health insurance companies. Instead, it will solidify their grip and make real health care reform that bypasses the insurance companies impossible. Incrementalism can lead to disaster.

The result again is that neoliberals often wind up not even stating, much less fighting for, the progressive moral position. The entire territory of the brain is left to conservatives. There is a difference between pragmatic compromise starting with progressive moral values, and pragmatic compromise conceding those values in advance, without those values even being stated, much less tested.

Perhaps the saddest case is neoliberal economics as applied to other countries. The best statement I have seen of the link between Old Enlightenment reason and neoliberal economics is given by Al Gore in *The Assault on Reason*:

> Adam Smith's *The Wealth of Nations* and America's Declaration of Independence were published in the same year. In both, men were understood to be units of independent judgment, capable of making decisions upon the basis of freely available information, the collective result being the wisest possible allocation of wealth (in the case of the former) and political power (in the case of the latter).
>
> Capitalism and democracy shared the same internal logic: Free markets and representative government were both assumed to operate best when individuals made rational decisions—whether they were buying or selling property or accepting and rejecting propositions.[3]

Gore goes on to point out that this view is disaster because money made in the market and political power interact in "incestuous ways."

But Gore's description follows from neoliberal thought based on Old Enlightenment reason. What we see there, first, is a misrepresentation of American democracy, which (as the historian Lynn Hunt has observed)[4] is rooted in empathy, in connecting viscerally with others (presumably via our mirror neuron circuitry and pathways to and from the prefrontal and posteromedial cortices, and elsewhere), allowing us to share experience with others and therefore to comprehend a common humanity as the basis of equality. That is the real moral basis of the Enlightenment. Gore's description, however, fits the neoliberal understanding, based on Old Enlightenment reason, used for the sake of self-interest both in business and politics. But just as you can't get to empathy from self-interest, you can't get to democracy from the market.

That has been the disaster of neoliberal economics as applied to the third world. Privatization without empathy eliminates the progressive moral capacities of government—protection and empowerment—and with it what made America a thriving democracy. In lacking empathy for the people of third world countries, neoliberal economics all too often leads to the corporate taking of their land, their water, their natural environment, their culture, their way of life, their dignity, and their freedom and safety.

Old Enlightenment rationality, applied to foreign policy and free trade, makes neoliberal economics sound fair to all, when it isn't.

Finally, there is the way neoliberal thought affects how campaigns are run. It buys into the metaphor of the left-to-right scale—with disastrous results.

Because neoliberals believe thought is literal and logical, they cannot make sense of the reality that people can simultaneously have two inconsistent worldviews and use them in different areas of life without even noticing. Universal reason says there is only one rational mode of thought. Anyone who argues against you must be either mistaken (in need of the facts), irrational (needing to have their reasoning corrected), or downright immoral. The belief in Enlightenment reason leads to the inability to recognize opposing worldviews, and hence to the left-to-right scale.

Accepting the left-to-right scale leads to the logic—and the claim—that to get more votes you have to move to the right. This actually has three counterproductive effects for progressives:

1. Giving up on policies that fit the progressive moral worldview and hence alienating your base;
2. Accepting policies that fit the conservative moral worldview, thus activating the conservative worldview in voters, which helps the other side; and
3. Not maintaining a consistent moral worldview at all, which makes it look as though you have no values.

The stability of neoliberal thought varies. Some people use all of it all the time. Some even define their very identity by it. Others dip into it, thinking that way regularly on certain issues or when pressured by a friend or colleague.

Neoliberal thought arises from the Old Enlightenment view of the mind. It is anything but a trivial matter, since it has important political consequences. One of the things cognitive science teaches us is that when people define their very identity by a worldview, or a narrative, or a mode of thought, they are unlikely to change—for the simple reason that it is physically part of their brain, and so many other aspects of their brain structure would also have to change; that change is highly unlikely.

For this reason one cannot simply expect a confirmed neoliberal thinker to look "rationally" at the evidence from neuroscience and cognitive science, follow his general tendency to respect science, and then change the way he thinks. The best we can hope for from confirmed neoliberals is that they will, because of their Enlightenment commitment to open-mindedness, keep reading and realize that their very mode of thought is at issue politically in case after case.

What is such an open-minded neoliberal to do? First, the

hardest part: Learn to think outside the Enlightenment—in terms of worldviews, frames, metaphors, narratives, and so on. Learn to argue powerfully and emotionally from the moral perspective of empathy and responsibility, protection and empowerment. Point out that this is the moral basis of our democracy, and argue on a patriotic basis. Give up on the left-to-right scale and on the idea of moving to the right to get more votes. Look for generalizations across issues. Support the development of think tanks and other policy shops that go across issues—in fact, develop issues from the moral system and the general role of government down to specific cases. Never accept conservative framings of the issues, even in arguing against them; offer your own. End support for neoliberal economics at the global level. If you have to compromise with conservatives, start the negotiations from your own moral position—empathy and responsibility, not neoliberal self-interest.

There are many cases where neoliberal thought coincides on policies with conservative thought. We shall soon see why.

Conservative Thought and the Politics of Authority

Conservative thought has a very different moral basis than progressive thought. It begins with the notion that morality is obedience to an authority—assumed to be a legitimate authority who is inherently good, knows right from wrong, functions to protect us from evil in the world, and has both the right and duty to use force to command obedience and fight evil. He is "the Decider." Obedience to legitimate authority requires both personal responsibility and discipline, which are prime conservative virtues. Obedience is enforced through punishment. In large institutions, there will be a hierarchy of authority, used, among other things, to maintain order. Loyalty is required to maintain the hierarchy. Freedom is seen as functioning within such an order: As long as you follow the rules laid down for you, you are free to act within that order. A sign on a military base in the American South in 2007 read, "Obedience Is Freedom!" As President James E. Faust of the Mormon church explains it, "Obedience leads to true freedom. The more we obey revealed truth, the more we become liberated."[5] And in the famous words of Rudy Giuliani, "Freedom is about authority."[6]

It is common for institutions to be personified. We understand churches as having beliefs, newspapers as having opinions, unions as making decisions, and country clubs as being uppity. In the law, corporations are legally "persons" with First Amendment and other rights. The same is true of the institution of the market. Progressives, as we have seen, believe that markets ideally should be moral and treat people fairly.

For conservatives, the market is seen metaphorically as an institution personified as a legitimate authority who makes rational decisions ("Let the market decide"), as imposing market discipline, and as rewarding discipline and punishing the lack of it. Prosperity is seen as a mark of discipline, which is in turn seen as moral, since discipline is required to obey moral laws and whatever is required by those in authority. By the logic of this system of thought, if you are not prosperous, you are not disciplined, and therefore cannot be moral, and so deserve your poverty. It follows that if people are given things they have not earned, they become dependent and lose their discipline and with it their capacity to obey moral laws and legitimate authority.

We can now see where neoliberals and conservatives converge. In conservative thought, people are born bad—greedy and unscrupulous. To maximize their self-interest, they need to learn discipline, to follow the rules and obey the laws, and to seek wealth rationally. The market imposes discipline. It works rationally by rules and laws, and requires disciplined rational thinking. It rewards those who acquire such discipline and punishes those who do not. The market, from this perspective, is fair and moral.

Neoliberal thought applies Enlightenment rationality to the market. Markets are ideally constructed to be fair and moral, though they may need government regulation to guarantee it.

Rational choice in a well-regulated market will lead to an optimal, natural distribution of wealth. Well-regulated markets, from the neoliberal perspective, are fair and moral.

In trade policy, neoliberals and conservatives often agree that what is uppermost is the "national interest," optimizing the overall wealth of the country as measured by GDP and corporate wealth—in competition with other countries who are trying to maximize their wealth. Here neoliberalism, like conservative free trade policy, is about maximizing American wealth. Neoliberal thought and conservative thought coincide.

Incidentally, this is anything but a new development.[7] Adam Smith's concept of the free market was originally a liberal proposal to free the poor and the powerless from economic oppression. As such, Smith's ideas were adopted into the French Revolution. Smith, for example, favored certain wage regulations: "When the regulation... is in favor of the workmen, it is always just and equitable; it is sometimes otherwise when in favour of the masters."[8] Smith argued against an inequitable division of wealth: "No society can surely be flourishing and happy, of which the far greater part of the members are poor and miserable. It is but equity, besides, that those who feed, clothe, and lodge the whole body of the people, should have such a share of the produce of their own labour as to be themselves tolerably well fed, clothed, and lodged."[9]

But by 1800, Edmund Burke and others had reframed Adam Smith's ideas as fitting the conservative worldview, arguing against government interference in what became a laissez-faire view of the free market.[10] Contemporary neoliberalism and radical conservatism continue these interpretations of what is meant by the "free market," with conservatives dominating the public debate.

The conservatives' market, as a moral authority in itself, is supposed to be "free" of outside interference—from the government. It is also seen as conferring economic freedom—freedom to make money in business any way you can. What progressives see as government protection (moral), conservatives see as government interference (immoral) that imposes restrictions on making profits. Regulations to protect consumers and workers limit profits; the civil justice system, which protects consumers, threatens profits in lawsuits; and taxation, which sustains our system of protection and empowerment, takes away profits. Conservatives rarely talk about government empowerment and act as if it does not exist—except in the case of corporate subsidies. Thus conservatives tend to be antiregulation, antiunion, against class action suits, and antitaxation.

Not only do conservatives not talk about the government empowerment of business, they also miss a central truth about deregulation, privatization, and corporations.

Under the Bush administration, Food and Drug Administration funding for the testing of prescription drugs was cut, resulting in the deregulation of significant prescription drug testing, and thus in the privatization of such testing, since it was then up to the drug companies. Wyeth, in the case of fen-phen, and Merck, in the case of Vioxx, misrepresented test results for the sake of profits, thereby causing thousands of heart attacks and many deaths.

The myth is that the deregulation or privatization of a moral mission of government eliminates government. But it doesn't. Large corporations also govern our lives—often making life-and-death decisions that affect us. Government isn't eliminated. It is just shifted from the public sector, where there is an ethic of protection and public accountability, to the private sector, where there is an ethic of profit and no public accountability. The principle here is the "conservation of government." Deregulation and privatization do not eliminate government; they only make it unaccountable and take away its moral mission.

But conservatives cannot admit this, because it would fly in the face of the idea of "free enterprise." The "free market" doesn't free us from government; it just gives us unaccountable government without a moral mission.

Now consider the Bush administration's doctrine of the "unitary executive." The doctrine claims unprecedented powers for the president and restricts the powers of Congress previously assumed under the idea of "checks and balances." For example, President Bush has used "signing statements" more than eight hundred times to either refuse to enforce a passage in a law passed by Congress or to interpret it to his liking. He has assumed the power to imprison citizens without charges, violating habeas corpus, our most important guarantee of freedom. He has permitted torture in violation of international law, and has assumed the power to wiretap citizens without a warrant. He has refused to allow Congress its traditional role of overseeing the executive branch, has challenged Congress's power to subpoena members of the executive branch to testify under oath, and has effectively made law through hundreds of executive orders. He has challenged the appointment of independent counsels. The "unitary" aspect of the unitary executive has been used to prevent any branch of government, such as the Environmental Protection Agency or the State Department, from carrying out its moral mission when it contradicts the will of the president. For example, the EPA was prohibited from suing the Defense Department to get it to clean up toxic waste at military bases. The claim of the "unitary executive" is that this would be like the president suing himself. It is a metaphor that defines a new and frightening "common sense" that can deny the moral mission of government.

Progressives have rightly seen such accrual of powers by the president as antidemocratic, violating the balance of powers specified in the Constitution and assuming powers akin to those of a dictator.

Conservatives have supposedly been against "big government" as restricting freedom and threatening the "liberty" of citizens. But except for figures like John Dean and Bob Barr, they have not objected to the doctrine of the unitary executive—to wiretapping without a warrant, to the suspension of habeas corpus, to the refusal to enforce selected provisions of the laws passed by Congress. Why should conservatives, who see themselves as defenders of liberty against an overly powerful intrusive government, not be outraged by the most powerful and intrusive government in our history? Indeed, why should they vocally support it?

The answer is clear. Conservative morality is the morality of obedience. For example, note what happened when Steven Bradbury, head of the Justice Department's Office of Legal Counsel, testified in July 2006 before the Senate Judiciary Committee. Senator Patrick Leahy (D-VT) asked whether the president was right or wrong on the Hamdan case—whether the president had the authority to void all normal legal protections and to set up military tribunals at Guantánamo. Bradbury's response: "The president is always right."

What is remarkable about this answer is that it is coming from a man whose job is supposed to be to tell the president what is legal and what is not. It is his job to determine whether the president is right.

Would a progressive president be "always right"? Hardly. The reason is that the authority of a progressive president would not be seen by conservatives as "legitimate," since such a president would not abide by the conservative moral system. For conservatives, their moral system comes first. It is the moral system that must be defended at all costs.

What we learn from cognitive science—from looking at the mode of thought used in current-day conservatism—is that George W. Bush is not himself the source of the authoritarianism of his administration. It is general conservatism—the mode of thought itself.

Take the example of health care. Former presidential candidate Rudy Giuliani framed health care as a commodity—like buying a flat-screen TV set. The market should take care of health care, he said. As in the case of flat-screen TVs, competition in the market should bring the price down.

But health care is a matter of protection, not a commodity. It is a matter of pain and suffering, of life and death. Many people die, or suffer terrible pain, for lack of adequate health care. No one dies for lack of a flat-screen TV. Protection is a moral mission, for the government, but not for business.

Take other forms of protection. Is police protection a commodity? Should you have to buy your police protection, say, from competing security services? Burglars? With guns? Sorry, you're not up to date on your premiums. You'll just have to let them rob you, or maybe kill you. Or fire protection? Is it a commodity? Sorry, your house will have to burn down. You didn't pay your premiums. Health care is just as much a matter of fundamental protection. It shouldn't be sold like insurance. The issue is not just a matter of cost, though one-third of the cost of private health care goes for profit and administration, while Medicare only spends 3 percent on administration and none on profiteering.

Administration? That's not just secretarial help, though the paperwork is considerable. To understand "administrative costs," a brief look at one of the old Nixon tapes is enlightening. Here is John Ehrlichman talking to Nixon:

> EHRLICHMAN: Edgar Kaiser is running his Permanente deal for profit. And the reason he can—the reason he can do it—I had Edgar Kaiser come in—talk to me about this and I went into it in some depth. All the incentives are toward less medical care, because—
>
> PRESIDENT NIXON: [unclear]
>
> EHRLICHMAN:—the less care they give them, the more money they make.
>
> PRESIDENT NIXON: Fine. [unclear]
>
> EHRLICHMAN: [unclear] and the incentives run the right way.
>
> PRESIDENT NIXON: Not bad.[11]

The "not bad" was said with an intonation of admiration—admiration for finding a way to make money by not providing health care, by denying health care. That is what most "administrative costs" are about. They are the costs of finding ways to deny people care. Like making money by not growing crops—a scam, but much worse, since getting payments for not growing corn does not result in people dying, or living in pain.

The question is: Why should Nixon have seen this plan as a good thing? Why didn't he react with outrage at anything so callous?

The conservative view of the market is only part of the answer. Edgar Kaiser was doing what conservatives think one is supposed to do—use your entrepreneurial skills to make money any way that's legal. Another part of the answer is the absence of progressive morality, the absence of empathy for the people getting hurt. Nixon was identifying with the entrepreneur, not with the people getting less medical care. That's a fundamental difference. Finally, there is the last part: individual responsibility. Everyone is supposed to be taking care of himself. Let the buyer beware. No one's forcing them to get their health care that way. Except that now, with HMOs, virtually all health care is like that.

What's wrong with Medicare for all? If we take the profit and "administration" out of health care and stop treating it as a commodity, enough money could be saved to cover everybody. But from a conservative perspective, it would be immoral: no one should have their health care paid for by anyone else, lest they become dependent, lose their discipline, and be unable to function morally.

But from a progressive point of view, there is a moral bottom line here: health is fundamentally life-affirming; denial of care when health and life are at stake is fundamentally life-denying.

Framing Comes Before Policy

The health care example shows something deep and important about the relation between framing and policy. If health care is framed as "health insurance," then it will be seen through an insurance frame, and the policy will fit that frame: it will be a business, with profits, administrative costs, premiums, actuaries, outsourcing, care criteria, denial of care to maximize profits, and many people not buying insurance even if it is required by law.

Whereas if health care is seen as protection—on a par with police and fire protection, food safety, and so on—then it becomes part of the moral mission of government, where the role of government is protection and empowerment, which in turn is based on a morality of empathy and responsibility. In this case, policy proposals will look more like Medicare for all.

Many people get policy and framing backward. Policy is about fitting frames—moral frames. The mistake is when people think framing is about selling policy. When a PR firm sells a policy honestly, the visual and linguistic framing of its ads should fit the moral framing of the policy. When the ads are deceptive, the deception is that the ads are linked to a supposed moral framing inconsistent with the one the policy is really based on. Either way, moral framing precedes policy.

In its moral basis and its content, conservatism is centered on the politics of authority, obedience, and discipline. This content is profoundly antidemocratic, whereas our country was founded on opposition to authoritarianism. Yet conservatism also lays exclusive claim to patriotism. There is a contradiction here. How do conservatives get around it?

The answer can be found in the word "conservatism" itself. Those who call themselves by that label typically say they are in favor of conserving the best of the past traditions. Yet contemporary "conservatives" are often quite radical, wanting to impose near-radical values where they had not been before, such as eliminating habeas corpus and other safeguards of liberty, eliminating checks and balances and supporting the powers of the "unitary executive," abolishing public education, and so on. Fiscal conservatism used to be seen as holding back on government spending, but today it means accumulating an astronomical deficit as a way to justify cutting social programs and government protections, while supporting militarism. That is hardly "conservative" in the traditional sense of preserving.

In place of the reality of conserving the best of the past—public education, the balance of powers, the separation of church and state, habeas corpus—many right-wing radicals have created mythical narratives governed by radical conservative values that they want to go "back" to. One such narrative is "originalism" in judicial decisions, where "meaning" is a supposed "original meaning." The "original meaning" is somehow always in line with radical conservative values. There is a narrative of the wonders of homeschooling when homeschooling is rarely all that good. There is the mythical narrative of America as an original "Christian nation," though many of the founding fathers were deists and a nation of Christians does not equal a "Christian nation." There is the narrative of war as noble, when it rarely has been. There is the narrative that corporate agribusiness is a return to the family farm, when it is actually destroying the family farm. There is the narrative of American exceptionalism, in which America is inherently good and has an evangelistic duty to spread its way of life—and when it fails or harms people, it is because it was betrayed from within by "defeatists," by cowards who would "cut and run," by "leftist extremists," and so on. Mythical narratives are the stuff of politics, and contemporary conservatism is rife with them.

Biconceptualism

Terms like "conservative," "liberal," and "progressive" do not, and cannot, do justice to the complex reality of our politics and our experience as humans. There are indeed two worldviews in use, general progressivism and general conservatism, as we have just discussed them, but they do not exist in separate spheres. Though many self-identified "conservatives" use the general conservative worldview in areas that matter for them, they may use the general progressive worldview in other areas. The converse is true about self-identified "liberals" and "progressives," who may be progressive on domestic policy and conservative on foreign policy, or conservative on economic policy and progressive on everything else.

Barry Goldwater, "Mr. Conservative," had the general conservative worldview for foreign and military policy and economic policy, but had the general progressive worldview about Native American rights, about religion, about gays in the military ("You don't have to be straight to shoot straight"), and about governing itself, where he believed in honest, open, and cooperative government as opposed to government by obedience. At the time, he was the most prominent example of the term "conservative," though pure "conservatives" today would see him as not nearly conservative enough because, though he was a conservative at heart, he was nonetheless a partial progressive in significant ways. That made him "biconceptual."

But what made him a biconceptual conservative and a partial progressive, rather than a biconceptual progressive and a partial conservative? The answer is identity. Goldwater identified himself with his conservative views. He took them as defining who he was. Identity is crucial to politics.

Biconceptualism is often unconscious. Many self-identified "conservatives" have many, many progressive views without being aware of it. How is this possible? How can contradictory political views go unnoticed?

To understand biconceptualism better, think for a minute of the case of Saturday-night and Sunday-morning value systems. The same person can happily and without a pang of conscience drink, smoke, gamble, carouse, and be adulterous on Saturday night, while genuinely adhering to the opposite values in church on Sunday morning. Brains make this possible.

Behind Biconceptualism

The brain mechanism of biconceptual thought is mutual inhibition, where both worldviews exist in the same brain but are linked to nonoverlapping areas of life. The activation of one worldview naturally inhibits the other. And the contradiction goes happily unnoticed unless the mistress shows up pregnant in church confronting the wife.

Political worldviews are like that, which is why there are so many biconceptuals. The brain makes possible such mutually inhibitory worldviews over different areas of life. Each is a coherent system of concepts in itself, and they coexist happily if they can be kept apart, like Saturday night and Sunday morning with mistress and wife never meeting.

But wait a minute! Isn't the guy with the Saturday-night and Sunday-morning values a hypocrite? Aren't his Sunday-morning values supposed to apply to Saturday night as well? And from the perspective of his Saturday-night values, wouldn't he see himself as a self-righteous dweeb on Sunday morning? How can he live with himself?

A "hypocrite" is defined relative to what we will call a value-consistency frame, in which values are supposed to be consistent and all-encompassing, the same ones used in all cases. If you have value consistency, you have "integrity," otherwise you are a "hypocrite."

Pure progressives and pure conservatives often consider biconceptual political leaders hypocrites when they apply different worldviews to different issues. But biconceptualism is simply a fact about brains. We are human beings and we had better understand what it means to be one. The "hypocrite" may not even notice the "hypocrisy" if his brain automatically and unconsciously switches back and forth depending on context.

Many progressives considered Bill Clinton a hypocrite for his support of NAFTA, which promoted the outsourcing of jobs and allowed the dumping of American corn on Latin American markets, impoverishing small farmers in those countries, and had no environmental or labor protections. But Clinton was a biconceptual on economic policy, looking at free trade through the eyes of Treasury Secretary Robert Rubin and Wall Street.

Many conservatives consider George W. Bush a hypocrite for his stand on immigration—for favoring the granting of citizenship to those who entered the country without papers, and for supporting a guest worker program. Bush claims to have empathy for hardworking Latinos trying to make a life in America, and he also has primary loyalty to business interests who need the workers.

The true biconceptual does not see himself as a hypocrite at all, since the switch is automatic and unconscious, and he or she does not apply different worldviews to the same issue area. The mistress and wife live in different houses. Area by area, there can be consistency of values. It's only when you go across issue areas that an inconsistency arises.

But isn't it simpler to live by a value-consistency frame?

In most cases, yes. If you have a single, all-encompassing worldview, you use the same basic values all the time. It's easier to be a total conservative or a total progressive.

But given a human brain, it can be almost as easy to be biconceptual—except that moral contradictions do occur and resolving them does take work by the brain, in particular the ventromedial prefrontal cortex. But if the contradiction is resolved unconsciously, which happens as Drew Westen has shown, it is not even noticed.[12]

A biconceptual may not have an utterly clear division between those areas that are understood in terms of general progressivism and those understood in terms of general conservatism. For example, some people don't know what to think about abortion and can see two sides of the issue. Such folks are said to "go back and forth on the issue."

Biconceptualism is made possible by the brain. First, there is mutual inhibition, which permits conflicting modes of thought, but only one at a time. Second, there is the difference between general modes of thought versus the special cases. Neural binding is the mechanism for applying a general mode of thought to a special case, say, applying general conservatism to health care, or applying general progressivism to global warming.

In many cases the bindings are long-term or permanent; sometimes they are short-term and may change. Someone who starts out being a conservative on an issue may change; that is, the neural bindings from the conservative mode of thought to the details of the issue may be replaced by neural bindings from progressive thought to the same issue. Someone who has no fixed binding between the abortion issue and either general progressivism or general conservatism is said to "have no opinion." Someone who has weak bindings to both might be said to be "confused."

The two worldviews are modes of reasoning, sometimes conscious, most often unconscious. They are general, above and across issue areas. General conservative reasoning and general progressive reasoning can occur on any issue—in economic policy, in foreign policy, on the environment, about social programs, about education and health care, about religion, and so on. You can pick out general conservative and general progressive reasoning when you look at arguments for or against particular positions, as we did earlier in the chapter.

Can there be authoritarian progressives? In a word, yes. One reason is that means and ends can function as different domains of experience. Thus one can have progressive ends but authoritarian conservative means. One can even, in the extreme, be an authoritarian antiauthoritarian. Imagine someone who runs an advocacy group that is antiauthoritarian in its goals, but runs the group itself in an authoritarian way. Certain union leaders may be hierarchical and punitive in their methods, but progressive in their aims. Indeed, the leader of any progressive organization can function like that. There is a name for people with progressive goals and conservative authoritarian means: militants!

How Can You Effect Change?

What is the brain mechanism whereby people who call themselves conservatives or independents come to have more progressive views?

Imagine a conservative who is biconceptual, already having partial progressive views. That means that he or she has both worldviews, mutually inhibiting each other, but with the conservative worldview generally stronger—with more receptors at the synapses, which makes the conservative worldview more likely to be bound to specific issue areas. If his or her general progressive worldview is activated more and more, then its synapses will grow stronger, and it will become increasingly likely that the progressive worldview will start binding to more issue areas.

How do you activate a biconceptual's progressive worldview? By getting him or her to think and talk about those issue areas where they are already progressive! That is, by finding areas where they already agree with you and talking with them about those areas, casting progressives as heroes, and by implication, conservatives as villains. Conservatives have done the equivalent for decades.

To change minds, you must change brains. You must make unconscious politics conscious. Because most of what our brains do is unconscious, you can't find out how people's brains work by just asking them. That is why neuroscience and cognitive science are necessary.

Neither progressives nor conservatives have described their views as I just have. What I have done is to look behind the veil of conscious thought to see the principles underlying the way both progressives and conservatives really reason, usually unconsciously.

This is bound to be controversial, and it should be. It is important to understand political thought. If that thought is unconscious, it is all the more important to understand it, since unconscious thought has a more powerful effect than conscious thought. When thought is conscious, you can discuss it, question it, try to counter it. When it is unconscious, it has free rein.

CHAPTER 3

The Brain's Role in Family Values

Why do certain people, most of them self-identified as conservatives, find certain acts of love—premarital, extramarital, or homosexual—more sinful than war or torture?

Why should a conservative living in the Midwest find it personally threatening when gays get married in San Francisco or Massachusetts?

Why doesn't a conservative government take better care of its veterans, and why don't veterans and their families rebel en masse?

Why do many progressives object to the death penalty on moral grounds, while not being opposed to abortion on the same grounds?

Why do progressives feel a sense of responsibility for righting the wrongs of past generations?

And why should we find progressive and conservative values and modes of thought outside of politics proper—in kindergartens, Little League coaching, churches, summer camps, and so on?

Why should political values and modes of thought pervade our society?

The analysis of chapter 2—the politics of empathy and authority—did not go far enough to explain all these apparent contradictions, or hypocrisies, some would say. To answer these questions and many others, we need to move to the study of family values, some of which I discussed in my book *Moral Politics*. Since writing that book I've encountered new research on the workings of the brain that sheds new light on the specific form of morality today called "family values."

I was drawn into the study of politics back in 1994 by a basic puzzle. As a progressive, I could not understand how the main conservative positions fit together: What does being for cutting taxes have to do with being against gun control? What does being against abortion have to do with being against environmental regulation? What does advocating for tort reform have to do with shunning gay marriage? What makes these positions fit together sensibly? I have opposing positions on all these issues. How do my views fit together?

The eighteenth-century view of the mind doesn't help here. But all these questions have straightforward answers when one looks at how the mind really works. What I discovered was that family values are absolutely central to American politics. But not in a direct literal fashion.

In chapter 2, I argued that American politics is based on an opposition of empathy and authority. That was a literal description, an oversimplified one that was stripped of deeper content. The content is metaphorical at a deeper level.

We all think with a largely unconscious metaphor: the Nation as Family. Every third-grader knows that George Washington was the Father of his Country. Nobody questions it. We all speak of the founding fathers. We send our sons and daughters to war, even if they are not our sons and daughters. We speak of Daughters of the American Revolution. We have Homeland Security. And conservatives complain that progressives want a "nanny state." And in other countries, there is Mother Russia, Mother India, and the Fatherland.

From my research on conceptual metaphor, I knew that we drew inferences about the metaphorical target using the metaphorical source. I reasoned that as there were two versions of what the nation should be like, there might be two ideal versions of the family mapped by the Nation as Family metaphor onto the nation. I worked backward: given the structure of the metaphor and the political differences, I hypothesized two idealized versions of the family that would correspond to two idealized versions of the nation. What emerged were two versions of the family—a strict father family that mapped onto pure conservative politics, and a nurturant parent family that mapped onto pure progressive politics.

Before going into them, it is worth clearing up some misunderstandings. These family models are idealized; they are mental models of idealized family life, mapped onto mental models of idealized national life. They may or may not have to do with how you were actually raised. Indeed, you may have rebelled against your upbringing, whichever it was.

As a cognitive scientist seeking to answer such questions, I was led to hypothesize these models. Such modeling using the best available hypothesis is standard in science. The models have turned out to explain a huge amount, and their explanatory power speaks volumes.

It should be noted that these models are descriptive not prescriptive. They do occur in people's brains. They are not something I am suggesting that people follow; people just do follow them. Newton, as a scientist, described how objects move; he had no power to make them move that way. The same is true here. American politics does use these models. All I can do is describe them. I have no power to make anyone think about politics using them. And no one else has the power to stop Americans from using them. They are an inextricable part of our politics. You may wish that other models were being used, and you may propose one or more of them. But you cannot impose some other model on people's brains.

The Strict Father Model

The strict father is the moral leader of the family, and is to be obeyed. The family needs a strict father because there is evil in the world from which he has to protect them—and Mommy can't do it. The family needs a strict father because there is competition in the world, and he has to win those competitions to support the family—and Mommy can't do it. You need a strict father because kids are born bad, in the sense that they just do what they want to do, and don't know right from wrong. They need to be punished strictly and painfully when they do wrong, so they will have an incentive to do right in order to avoid punishment. That is how they build internal discipline, which is needed to do right and not wrong. With that discipline, they can enter the market and become self-reliant and prosperous. As mature, self-disciplined, self-reliant adults, they can go off on their own, start their own families, and become strict fathers in their own households, without any meddling by their own fathers or anyone else.

Mapped onto politics, the strict father model explains why conservatism is concerned with authority, with obedience, with discipline, and with punishment. It makes sense in a patriarchal family where male strength dominates unquestionably. Authority, obedience, discipline, and punishment are all there in the family, organized in a package.

Why would someone in the Midwest genuinely feel threatened if gays in San Francisco are allowed to marry? The explanation is simple: there can be no gays in a strict father family; the gender difference and the role of masculinity are crucial. Suppose that kind of family—its values and its politics—defines who you are in everyday life. Suppose those values define your personality, not only how you function in your family but with your friends, in your business, in your church. Suppose that strict father marriage, with its version of masculinity, is a major narrative you live by. Then a threat to its legitimacy is a threat to your very being. Marriage isn't the real issue; the real issue is identity.

Why is it that conservatives, not progressives, tend to be against abortion? Think of some of the people who need an abortion: a woman who sees a conflict between motherhood and a career, or a teenager who has had sex outside marriage. In both cases, a decision by the woman on her own is an affront to the strict father. He is to determine whether his wife gives birth—and conservatives in many states have supported husband notification laws. The pregnant teenager has disobeyed her father and should be punished—and many states have parental notification laws.

There is a second reason as well. For the father to know right from wrong, there must be an absolute right and wrong, and that means that categories must be absolute. If category lines are fuzzy, it could be hard to tell if a rule or a law was broken. Absolute categorization requires essences, properties that define absolute categories. Though it took Aristotle to spell out how the theory of essences worked, he was simply noticing the everyday version in the cognitive unconscious. There is an unconscious but pervasive folk theory of essences, in which essences define strict categories. Essences in this folk theory are inherent, don't change over time, and are the causal sources of natural behavior.

The logic of essences is all over conservative thought. Take the concept of character. Why do conservatives dote on it? If you can train people to have the right (read "conservative") moral character, they will do the right things even when not told. As for babies, if they have the essence of a human being at birth, and if that essence cannot change, then they had the essence of a human being before birth... all the way back to conception. The folk theory of essence is not conscious. It just defines intuitive "common sense."

In a strict father family, it is assumed that the father merits his authority, and indeed, throughout conservatism, hierarchies of power and wealth are justified on "merit." Why should CEOs make so much more money than other employees? They deserve it.

Competition is crucial. It builds discipline. Without competition, without the desire to win, no one would have the incentive to be disciplined, and morality would suffer, as well as prosperity. Not everyone can win in a competition, only the most disciplined people, who are also the most morally worthy. Winning is thus a sign of being deserving, of being a good person. It is important to be number one! Strict father families often promote competitive sports and take them very seriously.

Why do conservatives want schools to teach to the test and make judgments on the basis of test scores? To determine merit—who deserves to move up into the stratosphere of merit versus who gets to serve people of merit. That should be determined by discipline, punishment, and obedience—learning answers by rote, with punishment for failing to do so as an incentive to be more disciplined.

Why are fundamentalist Christians conservative? Because they view God as a strict father: Obey my commandments and you go to heaven; if not, you go to hell. Well, I'll give you a second chance. You can be "born again." Now obey my commands (as interpreted by your minister) and you go to heaven; otherwise, you go to hell: authority, obedience, discipline, punishment. Note that "individual responsibility" is a hallmark of this view of religion—it is up to you and you alone as to whether you get into heaven.

This explains why James Dobson, the leading exponent of strict father childrearing, is a political conservative, a fundamentalist Christian, while at the same time being a laissez-faire free marketer and an advocate for the use of force in foreign policy.

If your very identity is defined with respect to a strict father family, where male-over-female authority rules, then the legitimacy of gay marriage can threaten your identity. So can anything that violates the strict father family, such as extramarital sex.

On the other hand, war and torture at a national level are carrying out the protective function of the strict father. Why torture? If your enemies are evil, you can—and may have to—use the devil's own means against them.

From a conservative perspective, individual responsibility means being willing to deal with the consequences of your own decisions. If you join a volunteer army, you get paid to fight, you know you may be killed or maimed, those are the chances you take, and you should be prepared to deal with the consequences.

That's why conservatives don't pay that much attention to injured veterans. Moreover, the veterans themselves often have a strict father, hypermasculine identity and follow the code of strict self-reliance. There are some who will not accept outside help, even if it means being homeless.

The Nurturant Parent Model

Progressives, correspondingly, have a nurturant parent model: two parents, with equal responsibilities, and no gender constraints—or one parent of either gender. Their job is to nurture their children and raise them to be nurturers of others. Nurturance is empathy, responsibility for oneself and others, and the strength to carry out those responsibilities. This is opposite of indulgence: children are raised to care about others, to take care of themselves and others, and to lead a fulfilling life. Discipline is positive; it comes out of the child's developing sense of care and responsibility. Nurturance requires setting limits, and explaining them. It requires mutual respect—a parent's respect for children, and respect for parents by children must be earned by how the parents behave. Restitution is preferred over punishment—if you do something wrong, do something right to make up for it. The job of parents is protection and empowerment of their children, and a dedication to community life, where people care about and take care of each other.

Here we see the politics of empathy emerging in the family. When mapped onto the nation, the result is the progressive politics of protection, empowerment, and community.

There is a reason why this model is gender neutral. Fathers can, and do, form deep positive attachments with their kids. They, as well as mothers, can do all the things required by the nurturance model. Conservatives, however, often parody this model by describing it as a mommy or nanny model, calling the Democrats the "mommy party" and speaking of the "nanny state." The same is often true of those who grew up with strict fathers and nurturant mothers. But it is a mistake. Nurturance is not gendered and requires strength.

This does not mean that conservatives are all literal strict fathers or were raised by strict fathers. It does mean that deep conservative values and modes of thought are strict father values and modes of thought. And so it goes for nurturant parents and progressives. Biconceptuals, who have both modes of thought in different arenas of life, may differ on what happens in their actual families. But it is common for the model used in one's family to be the model used to define one's identity.

The point is simple. Metaphorical thought is natural. We have a Nation as Family metaphor. We have two very different idealized models of the family, which are mapped by the metaphor onto two very different views of the nation. Our modes of moral and political thought are taken from these models.

Until about ten years ago, these were the substantiated models. A lot has been learned about the brain since then. What has been learned basically verifies these views, but extends them to explain a lot more.

Why should there be a Nation as Family metaphor, in our culture and in many others? Why, in America, do the strict and nurturant models apply not only to nations but to sports teams, businesses, classrooms, advocacy groups, dance troupes, bands, and groups throughout civil society? Why are moral systems organized along these lines? How does a metaphor organize a system of values and a mode of thought?

The Brain's Role in Metaphorical Thought

Metaphors are mental structures that are independent of language but that can be expressed through language. Metaphorical thought is ordinary, and mostly unconscious and automatic. Indeed, it is so unconscious and automatic that the basic way it works was discovered only three decades ago. We will start with some simple examples.

When we say that prices are rising, we do not mean that they are literally going upward. We are understanding quantity in terms of verticality, where an increase in quantity is understood in terms of motion upward. We then use words for motion upward to indicate an increase in quantity and words for motion downward to indicate a decrease in quantity: Prices fell. The stock hit bottom. The temperature rose.

When we speak of a warm person or a cold person, we are usually not referring to body temperature, but to how affectionate they are. When we speak of reaching the end of project, or being bogged down writing a book chapter, we are not literally referring to motion and impeded motion, but rather to achieving some purpose or having trouble doing so.

We think and talk using thousands of such conceptual metaphors, mostly without awareness. Complex metaphors are made up of a number of simple ones, called primary metaphors. Primary metaphors arise spontaneously, usually during childhood, when two different parts of our brains are activated together during certain experiences. For example, when we are children, we are held affectionately by our parents and feel warmth. Whenever we pour water into a glass, the level goes up; whenever we pile more things on a table, the level goes up. This experience occurs over and over, every day of our lives.

Two different parts of our brains—one characterizing verticality and the other quantity, or one characterizing temperature and the other affection—are activated together, day after day. Activation spreads outward along networks of neurons from those two brain centers, and eventually two paths of activation meet and form a single circuit linking those two areas of the brain. As neuroscientists say, "Neurons that fire together wire together." As the same circuit is activated day after day, the synapses on the neurons in the circuit get stronger until a permanent circuit is formed. This is called neural recruitment.

The idea of "recruitment" is this: we have billions of neurons in our brains, each taking input from and giving output to between a thousand and ten thousand other neurons. That's trillions of connections. If you trace through all possible pathways, the number is astronomical. But most of those possible pathways are not doing anything useful. For that, there has to be sufficiently strong activation flowing from neurons in one area in the brain along that pathway to neurons elsewhere in the brain. For that to happen, the synapses along the route must all be strong enough to relay a strong signal. "Strong" for a circuit means that there must a large number of receptors for neurotransmitters at each synapse along the route. But most pathways are not like this. Many possible pathways can only be weakly activated if at all, since the synapses along them are not all strong enough to pass a signal over the whole route.

"Recruitment" is the process of strengthening the synapses along a route to create a pathway along which sufficiently strong activation can flow. The more neurons are used, the more they are "strengthened." "Strengthening" is a physical increase in the number of chemical receptors for neurotransmitters at the synapses. Such a "recruited" circuit physically constitutes the metaphor. Thus, metaphorical thought is physical.

Because temperature is publicly discernible, while affection is not, the temperature synapses fire more often and so are stronger. As a result, activation will flow from temperature to affection, and not in the opposite direction. That is why words for temperature are used for affection ("She warmed up to me") but not the reverse. We cannot say, "The soup got more affectionate," meaning it heated up on the stove. The same is true for hundreds of primary metaphors.

Such a circuit is called a neural mapping. The standard notation for such metaphorical mappings is of the form: Affection is Warmth. This is a name for the metaphorical mapping, not the mapping itself. The name is written in English. The mapping it names is neural in character.

Such simple metaphors can then be combined via neural binding to form complex metaphors. For example, a common metaphor for time in this culture (but not all) is that the Future is Ahead and the Past is Behind. Prices on the stock market are seen as moving forward (from past to future), upward (increasing), or downward (decreasing), which is a complex metaphor combining More is Up and the Future is Ahead. Thus a sentence like "The market reached a high of 1400" is an instance of the neural binding of those two metaphors.

The Brain and Governing Institutions

Most people's first experience with governance is in their family. Your parents govern you: they tell you what to do, what's good for you and bad for you, and what's good for the family; they may dole out an allowance; and they have expectations of you: make your bed, eat your dinner, take out the garbage, do your homework.

An "institution" is a structured, publicly recognized social group that persists over time. "Governing" is setting expectations and giving directives, and making sure they are carried out by positive or negative means. In a family, the means of making sure they are carried out are, positively, by expressing affection, social pressure, fulfilling desires, or instilling pride; and, negatively, by withdrawing affection, social isolation, denying desires, instilling guilt or shame, or physical force.

In short, your early experiences of governance and family life co-occur, as follows:

The institution is the family. A governing individual is a parent. Those governed are other family members.

This co-occurrence gives rise to an extremely important primary metaphor: a Governing Institution is a Family. We see this metaphor alive in many special cases, where organizations, from businesses to sports teams, are referred to as families, and reason about themselves in family terms. When the metaphor applies to the nation and the national government, there are a number of special cases. Here are the basic ones:

The Institution [the Nation] is the Family
The Governing Individual [the Government] is a Parent
Those Governed [the Citizens] are Family Members

There is another important special case:

The Institution [the Nation] is the Family
The Governing Individual [the President] is a Parent
Those Governed [the Citizens] are Family Members

And there is still another special case:

The Institution [the Government] is the Family
The Governing Individual [the President] is a Parent
Those Governed [the Government Officials] are Family
    Members

These variations appear throughout politics. Back when Bob Dole was Senate majority leader, Democrats defeated his proposed balanced budget amendment by one vote. He was furious, and went on TV railing against people who think "Washington knows best." *Washington*, of course, stood for the government. And "__ knows best" comes from "Father knows best." Dole was seeing the government as the meddling strict father interfering in the lives of his grown children. Tens of millions of people heard the speech on TV, and they understood it. That use of the metaphor was clear.

Bush's use of the unitary executive principle is a case where the institution is the government, the president is the strict father, and government officials are family members. Bush's claim that, as a wartime president, he can wiretap citizens at will is the case in which the Nation is the Family, the President is the Parent, and the Citizens are Family Members.

There are many other special cases throughout society. As children, we have experiences with various governing institutions—

communities, churches, classrooms, teams, stores, clubs, camps, Boy and Girl Scout troops—each with its expectations and typical directives, and positive and negative forms of enforcing them. But the family is the one that we have the most, and most powerful, experiences with. Each of the others can be conceptualized as a family.

Moreover, the most prominent governing institutions—teams, communities, armies—can give rise to other metaphors for governing institutions: as teams, communities, and armies. These can all be applied to, say, businesses. Is your business conceptualized and treated as a family, team, community, or army? In general, family has the most powerful pull—and might be avoided for that very reason in certain institutional settings.

It is common to understand many governing institutions in family terms. Priests in the Catholic Church are called "father." Parishioners in the same church are sometimes called "brethren." The ladies' group in a synagogue is called a "sisterhood." Squadrons in the army are called "bands of brothers"—and Pat Tillman's death at the hands of one of his army "brothers" was technically called "fratricide."

Whatever your family at home is like, you may experience either strict or nurturant governance in other institutions. Just as we had some teachers who were strict and others who were nurturant, the same applies with coaches of Little League teams, ministers, store managers, policemen, and so on. Given such a range of experiences, it is no surprise to find biconceptualism in our political lives.

What Is Not Mapped

The neural theory of metaphor explains why we commonly conceptualize governing institutions as families and what the variations are. The theory also explains what is not mapped. The neural mapping occurs between the Family frame and the Governing Institution frame. The frames are cognitive models of families and institutions in general—not necessarily your family.

In the Family frame, young children are typically dependent and lacking adult judgment. This is not true of members in the Governing Institution frame. In the brain, contradictory properties are mutually inhibitory: the activation of one inhibits the other. Because of the mutual inhibition, these two properties of children in the Family frame cannot be mapped to the properties of members in the Governing Institution frame, where in most special cases it is assumed that members are independent and mature adults. Such a neural mapping could not override the mutual inhibition of inconsistent properties. It would be a physical impossibility. That is why the special cases of the Nation as Family metaphor do not treat citizens as dependent children lacking mature judgment, but only as family members with no further specifications.

I bring this up because libertarians commonly misunderstand how conceptual metaphor works and what this analysis is about. They seem to think I am proposing that politics should work that way, when I am actually describing how it does work in the cognitive unconscious. Secondly, they protest that in libertarian politics, citizens are treated as mature adults, not children. The same is true in all the Nation as Family models because of the nature of neural mappings.

Another common mistake is thinking that one can propose just any model at all for politics and have it accepted. For example, some folks who don't like the family-based models think that we should adopt other metaphors: the nation as community, or team, or collective. But the family metaphor has a much stronger basis in experience than other models, and our brains form that mapping more readily and much more strongly. The others are hard to establish. This one is hard to get around or overcome. Brains have certain kinds and amounts of plasticity, but they are not infinitely plastic.

This is not a metaphor that I, as a cognitive scientist, like or dislike. It just is. That neural mapping exists just like gravity exists and species exist. I didn't create the metaphor. I'm just describing it.

We do sometimes have ways to make metaphors real—by turning them into institutions or by restructuring institutions. There are business gurus who make a lot of money advising companies to change their organizing metaphors. There is a small number of metaphors for cooperative groups as we have just seen: they can be families, armies, factories, communities, teams, play groups, and so on. The gurus may advise companies structured as armies or factories to reorganize as communities, or companies organized as communities to reorganize as teams, or companies that have teams to turn them into play groups in big rooms with blackboards and toys. In general, governing institutions have to have a function, a culture, and a structure—often adapted via metaphor from other institutions. Within a business, it is sometimes possible to change the metaphor and thus change the culture of the business, though not without difficulty.

For example, the civil service bureaucracy in the federal government was a replacement for the old spoils system, where elected officials got jobs for their friends, who then took bribes. The civil service was designed on the factory metaphor, with officials like replaceable cogs in a big machine—with well-defined jobs as part of a large machine, and well-defined career paths.

The government as factory succeeded in replacing the spoils system, but in too many cases lacked responsiveness to the public, as well as efficiency. The Reinventing Government movement of the 1990s was an attempt to model government on service industries so as to better "serve" the public. The metaphorical question asked was, "Who is the customer?"—asked so as to find out the "customer's" needs and desires, and provide better "customer service" for the public. The idea had limited successes, where retirees were not replaced and budgets could be cut, and where the notion of a "customer" made some sense in an organization with fewer employees.

But many government agencies are not there to serve customers, but rather have the moral mission to protect and empower
the public—to preserve the environment and save endangered
species, to protect the health and safety of workers, to make sure
food and drugs are safe, to help create an educated populace, to
advance scientific research, to build and maintain a public infrastructure, to promote the arts, to help people when natural disasters strike, and so on.

Under the Bush administration, the moral mission of government changed. Strict father morality was introduced throughout.
The president, as strict father, was seen as always right and to
be obeyed, with rewards for obedience and punishments for dis-
obedience. The concept of accountability changed: the president
and the government were no longer accountable to the people.
Instead, underlings became accountable to those higher in the
hierarchy. When things went wrong, the lowest accountable person was punished, not the highest, as in Abu Ghraib.

Government became an instrument to use public funds, man-
power, and property to serve the needs of private business and
other supporters. Lobbyists came in to run government agencies,
and later left for lucrative jobs in private industry. Functions of
government were eliminated and privatized so as to provide private profits at public expense—even intelligence-gathering and
military functions. Public lands were seen as resources for private
gain. A form of corruption returned, with overt bribes largely
being replaced by implicit guarantees of lucrative jobs with companies helped financially by public officials, although there were
overt bribes as well, as in the Abramoff scandal.

The changes will be hard to reverse. It is easier to disman-
tle a civil service built over a century than to put one together.
Once public funds that used to go for government protection
and empowerment are delivered into private hands, it is hard
to get them back, if possible at all. Once government capacities
are destroyed and private companies—Blackwater, Halliburton,
CH2M Hill, and others—are becoming the only alternatives for

carrying out those functions, it is difficult to rebuild government capacities. What has happened is that corporations have become private governments—they govern us, but without accountability, and we pay for them, and will be paying more in the future, not at prices set by legislation (taxes) but by what the market will bear.

The country is largely unaware that the moral foundations of our society are now being, and to a large extent have already been, surreptitiously changed in a major institutional and material way.

How did this happen? Because the public has been largely unaware of the moral models governing our politics, since they are part of the cognitive unconscious. The media has similarly been unaware. And progressives have been unaware.

CHAPTER 4

The Brain's Role in Political Ideologies

Our moral narratives have two parts, both of which are physically in our brains. The first is the dramatic structure of the narrative, with roles like hero, villain, victim, helper, and so on performing actions and undergoing effects. The second is the emotional structure, what Damasio has called "somatic markers," linking the dramatic structure to positive and negative emotional circuitry. They provide the emotional texture of simple narratives. Because they are neurally bound, the emotional structure of the narrative (anger, fear, relief) is inseparable from the dramatic structure (villainous action, battle, victory).

And when simple narratives are neurally bound together into complex narratives, simple emotional textures become emotionally very complex. As we have just seen in the case of metaphor, what is complex for us to explain is part of the learned structure of the brain that is easy for the brain to use.

Narratives are brain structures that we can live out, recognize in others, and imagine, because the same brain structures are used for all three kinds of experiences. Moral narrative is physical through and through.

The Brain's Morality

Morality is fundamentally about well-being—the well-being of oneself, others, and the groups one belongs to: family, community, business, nation. Our feelings of well-being and ill-being correlate with the activation of the positive and negative emotional pathways. Our brains are wired to produce experiences of well-being and ill-being. These are linked to sites in the forebrain, the prefrontal cortex, which embody our ability to make moral judgments and do moral reasoning, both conscious and unconscious. The mechanisms for moral judgments in the brain are bound to the mechanisms for positive emotions (well-being) and negative emotions (ill-being): joy and satisfaction versus anger, fear, anxiety, and disgust.

Primary metaphors, as we have seen, arise when two different kinds of experiences regularly occur together and activate two different brain areas at the same time, over and over. As it turns out, our experiences of well-being and ill-being correlate regularly, especially in childhood, with many kinds of other experiences. In general, if an experience of well-being regularly occurs together with another experience, X, then there will be a reasonable probability that we will acquire a metaphor of the form Morality is X.

For example, we typically feel disgust when we eat rotten food and good when we eat pure food. This leads to the conceptual metaphor Morality is Purity; Immorality is Rottenness. We commonly feel fearful in the dark and relieved and happy when it becomes light out. This leads to the conceptual metaphor Morality is Light; Immorality is Darkness.

The result is that we learn an extensive system of mostly unconscious primary metaphors for morality and immorality just by living normally in the everyday world, within a culture and a family. We just live. Our brains do the work. As a result, from the time we are children, we go around with a whole system of metaphorical thought for what is right and wrong. Such metaphorical thought actually governs moral thought and action, especially in politics, as we shall see.

Moreover, if a correlation between experiences occurs widely around the world, then the corresponding conceptual metaphor for morality should occur widely around the world. So far as we have be able to determine, this seems to be true.

One of the most widespread metaphors for morality is what I

have called Moral Accounting. It is based on a simple fact about well-being: you are better off if you have the things you need than if you don't.

This gives rise to the metaphor Well-Being is Wealth. When we speak of "poor Harry," we generally do not mean that he lacks wealth, but that he is unfortunate, that he lacks well-being. When we speak of a rich life, we are not talking about money, but about a life filled with experiences that produce well-being.

Suppose you do something to help me, to increase my well-being. Metaphorically, according to Well-Being is Wealth, increasing my well-being is like giving me money. I can say things like, "I'm in your debt," or "How can I ever repay you?" Principles of very basic accounting and the concept of paying debts, when combined with the Well-Being is Wealth metaphor, provide a rich and widespread way of understanding what moral action is.

Suppose you do something to harm me. Metaphorically, decreasing my well-being is incurring a debt. There are a number of alternatives. If I decide on retribution, I can say, "I'll make you pay for that!" As I exact retribution, I can say triumphantly, "Payback time!" If convicted of a crime and sent to prison, you can "pay your debt to society."

Alternatively, I can decide on restitution and say, "You owe me!" Or I can balance the moral books by taking revenge—taking something of value from you. Another possibility is forgiveness: canceling the debt.

Moral Accounting is also the basis of the philosophy of utilitarianism—the greatest good for the greatest number. Utilitarianism is the metaphor taken literally: it provides an arithmetic of goodness. The famous case for it goes like this: You are a rail-yard switchman who sees a runaway train about to kill five people. You can save them if you switch the train to another track. But that track has a person on it who will be killed if you switch the track. The moral dilemma: Do nothing and five die. Switch the track and five are saved, but one dies as a direct result of your action. One dead or five dead, you make the choice. Moral arithmetic.

Because there are many forms of well-being and ill-being that we normally experience, there are correspondingly many metaphors for morality. Below is a table listing a number of them. Each entry contains a statement of the form "You are better off if you can *X*," a conceptual metaphor roughly of the form Morality is *X*, and, where appropriate, some linguistic examples.

You are better off if...	*Morality Is...*	*Linguistic Examples*
You are better off if you can stand upright than if you cannot	Morality is Uprightness Immorality is Being Low	An upstanding citizen High moral standards Above reproach A low thing to do Underhanded Stoop to that A snake
You are better off if you are functioning in the light than in the dark	Morality is Light Immorality is Darkness	Snow White The Prince of Darkness White hats Black hats A white knight Black-hearted
You are better off if you eat pure food than if you eat rotten food	Morality is Purity Immorality is Rottenness	Pure as the driven snow Purification rituals A rotten thing to do That was disgusting Tainted by scandal Stinks to high heaven
You are better off if you are strong than if you are weak	Morality is Strength Immorality is Weakness	Stand up to evil Show your backbone A flip-flopper—no backbone

You are better off if you are healthy than if you are sick	Morality is Health Immorality is a Disease	Terrorism is spreading The contagion of crime A sick mind Exposed to pornography
You are better off if you are physically attractive than if you are not	Morality is Beauty Immorality is Ugliness	A beautiful thing to do It's getting ugly around here
You are better off if you are treated fairly than if you are not	Morality is Fairness Immorality is Unfairness	An unfair labor practice A fair market Fair trade
You are better off if you know the truth than if you don't	Morality is Honesty Immorality is Deceit	He cheated on his wife Make an honest woman of her
You are better off if you are happy than if you are miserable	Morality is Happiness Immorality is misery	A happy coincidence A miserable thing to do
You are better off if you are with your community than if you are not	Morality is following a path Immorality is deviating Morality is staying within boundaries Immorality is transgression	A sexual deviant The path of righteousness A transgression You crossed the line Follow the Ten Commandments
You are better off if you are cared for than if you are not	Morality is Caring Immorality is Not Caring	He's a caring person You don't give a damn about anyone

You are better off if...	Morality Is...	Linguistic Examples
You are better off if, as a child, you obey your parents than if you don't	Morality is Obedience Immorality is Disobedience	Obey the law Don't defy the law He's guilty of insubordination He's misbehaving She's resisting authority
You are better off if you have discipline than if you lack discipline	Morality is Discipline Immorality is Lack of Discipline	He just can't control himself He shows no self-restraint
You are better off if you are free of oppression than if you are not	Morality is Freedom Immorality is Oppression	Throw off your chains! Let my people go
People are better off if others are generous than if they are selfish	Morality is Generosity Immorality is Selfishness	A giving person What a miser!
You are better off if you don't challenge those with more power than you than if you do	The Moral Order Morality is Maintaining Order Within a hierarchy of power	A society in chaos Law and order Uppity

There are more, but I think you get the idea.

The last of these, the Moral Order metaphor, deserves special comment. The logic behind the metaphor is this: since we owe everything we are—our very existence—to the workings of nature, nature is seen as moral. In short, over history, natural hierarchies of power emerge. Since they are natural, and nature cannot be immoral, traditional hierarchies of power are moral.

According to the logic of the metaphor, to find out who is most moral, look at who has been, over history, most powerful in the hierarchy: God above Man, Man above Nature, Adults above Children, Western Culture above Non-Western culture, America above other nations, Men above Women, Whites above Non-whites, Straights above Gays, Christians above Non-Christians (or majority religion over minority religion). Not a pretty metaphor, but an all too common one.

It has been the basis for discrimination, and even mass murder, when those lower in the hierarchy are seen as lesser beings or even nonhuman. Today it is the basis for racism, sexism, homophobia, anti-Semitism, genocide, ethnic cleansing, and the hunting of species into extinction. In earlier days, it was the basis for notions of nobility—a most powerful king, and a hierarchy of warlords known as "nobles," so called because their power and wealth was seen as a sign of morality and hence purity and inherently deserved social status. Even the Great Chain of Being had a version of this in which, say, the lion, the most powerful of predators, was known as the "king of beasts" and portrayed as noble.

An important reaction against this metaphor often goes unrecognized: the Reverse Moral Order metaphor, the idea that the oppressed are more moral than their oppressors. We see this, for example, in arguments defending suicide bombing or extreme violence by those who are oppressed.

The Bodily Nature of Morality

Metaphor is not just a matter of words. We think metaphorically. All thought is brain activity, and the neural theory of metaphor explains why we have the primary metaphors we do. Primary metaphor arises from embodied experience, from two experiences that regularly occur together. It should not be surprising then that metaphors can have behavioral effects.

Chen-Bo Zhong and Katie Liljenquist have shown in a set of remarkable experiments that the Morality is Cleanliness metaphor affects the behavior of subjects: a threat to one's moral purity induces the need to cleanse oneself literally. Purification rituals in cultures around the world and lyrics like "Wash your sins away in the tide" suggest this, but the experiments have confirmed it.[1]

The experimenters asked students to recall either an ethical or unethical behavior in their past. Students who remembered their own unethical behavior were more likely to act as if they felt unclean. On a word-completion task that followed, the "unethical memory" students were more likely to say that the unfinished word "W__H" was "WASH" instead of "WISH," and that "S__P" was "SOAP" instead of, say, "STEP."

In a second experiment, students were told that the study was to determine if handwriting was linked to personality. Some students copied out stories of ethical behavior (helping a coworker); others, stories of unethical behavior (sabotaging a coworker). They were then asked to rate the desirability of various products. Some were cleansing products (Crest toothpaste, Dove soap, etc.) and others were not (Post-it Notes, Energizer batteries, etc.). Those who copied out unethical stories rated cleansing products much higher than noncleansing products. In another version, students were asked to take as a free gift either a pencil or an antiseptic wipe. Those who wrote of the unethical deed were twice as likely to take the antiseptic wipe.

The conceptual metaphor Immorality is Disgust also has physical effects. Physical disgust and moral disgust lead to similar facial expressions and physiological activation (lower heart rates and clenching of the throat), and recruit overlapping brain regions in the lateral and medial orbitofrontal cortex.[2]

Similar results have been found for the conceptual metaphor Morality is Generosity, Immorality is Selfishness. Jorge Moll and Jodan Grafman, neuroscientists at the National Institutes of Health, scanned the brains of volunteers who were told to think about one of two scenarios: donating a sum of money to charity, or keeping it for themselves. The volunteers thinking about helping others more than themselves showed increased activity in the neural pathway for positive emotions involving the limbic system—usually associated with the pleasure of eating or sex. The sense of pleasure correlates with the production, when activated, of the neurotransmitter dopamine. In short, when we do good, we feel good—we feel a sense of well-being.[3]

In addition, mirror neuron and associated research tells us that we are born with a capacity for empathy. Configurations of face and body muscles correlate with emotions through a two-way pathway via the insula, to the reward and punishment centers in the limbic system: we have facial expressions for happiness, sadness, anger, disgust, and so on. Via mirror neuron circuitry, we can feel what it is like to have those muscular configurations. That means that you can not just sense the musculature of someone else experiencing emotions, you can also feel what someone else feels; that is, you can feel the emotions that go with the musculature. We have the physical capacity to feel the joy and pain of others in ourselves physically. There is a neural mechanism that says in your very nervous system: You will feel better if you do unto others as they would have you do unto them.

In addition, the mirror neuron system (in the right inferior frontal gyrus and the bilateral inferior parietal lobes) is more active during the preparation of complementary joint actions than during the preparation for imitative actions. In short, we are not just pre-wired for empathy, but for cooperation.[4]

The Visceral Force of Empathy

The metaphors for morality arise from bodily experiences of well-being. They are not "mere" metaphors, not extraneous; they are neither arbitrary nor disposable. They tell us what the heart of morality is.

Empathy is at the center of the progressive moral worldview. When Hurricane Katrina hit New Orleans and scenes of drowning and suffering victims were shown on TV, the result was massive empathy on a national scale. Americans sent money, volunteered to help, and hundreds of thousands offered their own homes to house the victims. The nationwide empathy had a political effect:

the Bush administration was seen as callous and uncaring, and it marked the turning point for the administration's political popularity.

The effect of empathy is powerful. During the Vietnam War, the TV pictures of wounded soldiers and coffins coming home day after day helped to turn Americans against the war. More recently, such pictures have been banned by the Bush administration since the beginning of the Iraq War. But as the violence in Iraq increased, pictures of dead and maimed Iraqis filled our TV screens, again with an empathic effect increasing the unpopularity of the war. The scandal at Walter Reed Hospital, with pictures of mistreated wounded veterans, aroused empathy once more, again bringing down even further the Bush administration's popular support.

As the Walter Reed scandal unfolded in March 2007, there appeared in the journal *Nature* the results of a remarkable study about the power of empathy. It pointed out that conscious rational decision-making is centered in the frontal lobes. That includes moral decision-making of a purely calculative nature, based on utilitarianism—the greatest good for the greatest number, for example, deciding in the abstract that one person should be sacrificed to save five others. However, the study showed very different results when the moral decisions involved direct one-on-one physical interaction where empathy was aroused—smothering a crying baby or pushing someone in front of a train to save other lives. There, for normal people, empathy interfered with any abstract moral calculus, either overriding it or raising serious moral qualms.

The locus of empathic decision-making, the study revealed, is the ventromedial prefrontal cortex. People who have had brain injuries or strokes in that region, however, showed no such qualms. They treated the one-on-one direct contact cases just like the utilitarian moral calculus cases, even when it involved suffocating a baby. Empathy is normal, and it takes a special education (such as basic training in the army), a special heartlessness, or a brain injury to disengage it.[5]

In short, empathy is morally powerful, and its political power seems to arise from its moral force, which in turn is a consequence of brain structure—of the fact that we have mirror neuron circuitry linked via neural pathways to the emotional and other regions of the brain central to empathy.

Here is where the brain gets interesting for politics. Morality is about right behavior, behavior that leads to well-being. The metaphors for morality are grounded in a wide variety of experiences of well-being. Each such metaphor characterizes one idea of what right behavior is about; for example, Care, Obedience, Discipline, Fairness, Order, Cleanliness, Purity. But instead of a random system of utterly different conceptions of morality, our brains organize these views of what is right into two systems of moral and political thought. What makes this possible?

A brain is a physical system. It works by least-energy principles, like any other physical system. Given two possibilities in a given situation, it will take the least-energy path in that context. That is called the "best fit" property of neural systems. The brain always seeks a local best fit. Think of it this way:

Suppose neuron A is connected to neurons B and C.

B and C are mutually inhibitory; the firing of one tends to inhibit the other to some extent, depending on the strength of the firing.

B has a lot of receptors at the synapse with A, while C has few receptors at its synapse with A.

A fires, releasing the same amount of neurotransmitters into the gap where both synapses are.

The large number of receptors at B's synapse will pick up more chemical input (from neurotransmitters) than the small number of receptors at C's synapse.

Thus, B is more likely to fire than C, for simple physical reasons, and the more it fires, the more receptors build up at the synapse. And for the same reason, B will tend to fire more strongly than C, and to inhibit the firing of C.

Now suppose that neuron C also takes input from neuron D, and that the synapse on C, where C links to D, has a lot of receptors.

So if D and A fire at the same time, C's firing is determined by the input from both A and D. Think of D as supplying a "context." Then C's probability of firing and its strength of firing in that context may be greater than B's. In that case C will tend to fire and inhibit the firing of B. Context matters.

This is greatly oversimplified, of course. What it important is that such a situation can have political ramifications. Suppose A, B, C, and D are not single neurons, but rather complex circuits within conceptual systems. Suppose B and C characterize strict and nurturant morality respectively—the moral worldviews of general conservatism and general progressivism—within the brain of a biconceptual, someone who has both general models structured so that one inhibits the other. Suppose that A stands for the circuitry characterizing the idea of the "war on terror." Without additional context, it will tend to activate B, the conservative authority-based worldview, and with it support for conservative policy and the Bush administration.

Now suppose that D is Hurricane Katrina, which strongly activates C, empathy and the progressive empathy-based worldview and antipathy toward Bush and conservatives, while inhibiting the conservative authority-based worldview and inhibiting support for conservatives and Bush.

This is a guess at what happened in the brains of many Americans during Katrina, when empathy for the victims arose and support for Bush and conservatives fell precipitously.

I would guess that something similar happened during the Terri Schiavo case. Empathy went not to Terri, who had been brain-dead for many years, but to the responsible family members who bore the burden of difficult decisions. When conservatives tried to interfere with the family's deliberations, they generated empathy toward Terri's husband and antipathy toward the president and other conservatives. And I would guess that the same happened in the Walter Reed Hospital scandal, when the horrible treatment of veterans generated empathy toward them and antipathy toward the conservative administration.

There is a moral here for progressives: The more they can activate empathy in the public, the more support will be available to them and the worse conservatives will do. Correspondingly, the more conservatives can generate fear in the public, the more support they will generate, and the more that will inhibit support for progressives.

If this is true, then progressives should be talking more about their moral worldview—about empathy, responsibility, and hope—rather than accepting fear-based frames to think and talk within. Instead of moving to the right and activating the conservative worldview, stay without your own moral universe and activate the progressive worldview.

The primary metaphors for morality include Morality as Strength, Fairness, Order, Cleanliness, Purity, and so on. They are learned automatically and are general. They are not specific to the family.

At the heart of the nurturant and authoritarian models of the family are two central metaphors of morality: Morality is Care and Morality is Obedience to Authority. They are fundamentally what the nurturant parent and strict father models are about.

Other metaphors for morality happen to "fit better" with one of these family models than with the other. Let us begin with a simple example. Intuitively, Morality is Strength fits well with Morality is Obedience to Authority, since an authority requires strength to command obedience. It sounds simple enough, but the neural mechanism required is interesting.

The concept of strength is independent of the concept of obedience to authority. But strength may be required to force obedience, and you learn a frame in which strength is used to command obedience.

Whenever literal obedience to authority is activated as a concept, that frame receives some activation, linking strength to the exercise of authority. When that frame is not activated, the concept of strength functions independently. That frame linking strength and obedience to authority defines a "fit" of one concept to another. It is easier to activate strength with obedience than obedience by itself.

That "fit," therefore, also occurs between the metaphors Morality is Obedience and Morality is Strength. Though the metaphors arise independently, since they come from different experiences, the self-organizing function of the brain unites them as part of the same metaphor system.

Why should masculinity be a political issue? Why should Harvey Mansfield, the conservative Harvard government professor and hero to neoconservatives, write a book called *Manliness*? Why should conservatives be trying to feminize Democratic male candidates and officeholders?

Why should conservatives be pushing for long sentences for nonviolent drug offenders? Why should they support a three strikes law? And why should they, at the same time, support President Bush's commutation of Scooter Libby's jail sentence?

The answers to these and many other political questions come out of the primary metaphor that a Governing Institution is a Family plus the structures of the strict father and nurturant parent families. The family structure organizes ideas that, in principle, could be separate in politics. But because the family structure is mapped onto politics, the ideas that come together in the family structure are projected as a whole onto politics.

Masculinity is a good example. It is vital in a strict father family, where there is a strong gender differentiation and paternalistic male values are central. The strict father, to be effective, cannot be effeminate or weak. He must act like a "real man."

And why are conservatives punitive? It is assumed, in a strict father family, that the only way to teach a child right from wrong is to punish him for doing wrong. The lack of punishment is seen as a moral failing of the strict father. Moreover, the point of punishment—that is, physical "discipline"—is to get children to discipline themselves mentally so that they will do what the father says, to do right not wrong. Such discipline is seen as the only way to produce moral people.

Drugs are seen as taking away discipline, and hence taking away the capacity to be a moral person and the capacity for self-reliance. Drug addicts are also seen as leading others to take drugs, and hence leading to the immorality and lack of self-reliance of others. For this reason, conservatives see taking drugs as a serious offense against their moral system, even though the person taking drugs may not be violent or otherwise criminal. Since a refusal to punish for an offense is seen as a moral failing by a conservative, conservatives insist on strict punishment for nonviolent drug offenders. This is reinforced by the Moral Order metaphor whenever the offender is nonwhite, an immigrant, or a poor person.

Scooter Libby, on the other hand, was seen as upholding the authority of the president, and his crime was not seen as a real crime. Indeed, he was seen as holding up the moral system, since the strict father system depends on the unquestioned authority of the strict father. Libby was loyal. And loyalty to the strict father is loyalty to the moral system itself, and is seen as a virtue, not an offense.

What is happening here is that the strict father family as a cultural entity binds together elements of a family-based moral system: masculinity, strength, obedience, discipline, punishment. Metaphors preserve inferences as much as possible. And so the way that these elements of a family-based moral system fit together is preserved under the metaphor of a Governing Institution is a Family.

The bottom line: the existence in American culture of two very different models of the family, in the presence of the primary metaphor of a Governing Institution is a Family, gives rise to two very different ways of conceptualizing governing institutions—including different moral worldviews and modes of thought. These arise unconsciously.

When they remain unconscious, there can be serious political effects.

The Brain and Biconceptualism

The two modes of thought described so far are quite general, and versions of both have been found in just about everyone studied. We all have both progressive and conservative worldviews, applied in different areas and in different ways.

Neural binding—the binding of a general worldview to a specific issue area—makes this possible. We saw some of this in chapter 2. Suppose the issue area is religion. Progressive Christianity sees God as a nurturant parent, and imposes the nurturant moral view on the institution of the church and on what it means to be a good Christian: you have empathy for people who are poor, sick, hungry, or homeless, and you act politically to help them.

A conservative fundamentalist Christian might well have the opposite views on all these issues, with God as a strict parent, threatening the punishment of eternal damnation for violating God's commandments as interpreted by the clergy.

Then there are the biconceptuals. The National Council of Evangelicals believes in a strict father God who rewards with heaven and punishes with hell, in the absolute truth of the Bible, and in the right to proselytize. But recently it has been taking seriously those progressive parts of the Bible calling for good stewardship of the earth and fighting global warming, for antipoverty programs and health care, and for putting an end to torture. It has both strict and nurturant worldviews, and applies them in different areas.

There are self-identified conservatives who are indeed conservative on family values, gun control, and fundamentalist Christianity, but who are progressive in a number of areas: they love the land, like to hunt and fish, hike and camp. They resent big corporations exercising mineral rights by building oil rigs, installing mine shafts, and digging open-pit mines on their ranches, and in the process poisoning their wells and ponds and streams, interfering with ranching, and leaving an unsightly mess. They want progressive communities, where officials care about people, act responsibly, openly, and honestly, and where people care about each other, cooperate, and do community service.

In short, contextual "best fit" plus neural binding allows general progressive and conservative worldviews to be applied to specific cases in different ways—and sometimes in opposite ways. What is preserved in such binding to specific issue areas are the values and modes of reasoning brought to bear on such issues.

Then there are the independents and swing voters, who are biconceptuals with both progressive and conservative modes of thought at the general level, but who do not have fixed neural bindings to all specific issue areas. They may "go back and forth" on issues.

It should be remembered that "best fit" does not always mean perfect fit. For example, the general conservative worldview can be fitted to the issue area of immigration in a number of ways, depending on which priority is chosen:

1. Business interests, which require a continuing supply of cheap labor;
2. Law-and-order enthusiasts, who see legalization of immigrants without papers as "amnesty" for criminals;
3. Racists, who want to keep America as "pure" as possible; and so on.

Numbers 2 and 3 are consistent, allowing some racists to hide their racism under a banner of law and order. Numbers 1 and 2 are not consistent given the realities of American life. At this writing, no compromise has been figured out. The result is a schism on this issue, even among pure conservatives.

Do disagreements on these issues mean that conservatism is breaking down? Not at all. Each position is a conservative position. It's just that there is wiggle room within conservatism, as there is within progressivism. Disagreements about how to apply general conservative thought to specific issue areas are common.

That does not imply that conservatism is breaking down—quite the contrary.

Nor does it mean that progressivism is breaking down when progressives have disagreements about priorities. Should open-pit coal mines be banned on environmental grounds with miners losing jobs, or should the miners' jobs be protected over the environment? One can be both for the environment and for jobs as a progressive, and still face the dilemma, because it is not about progressive versus conservative values. On the other hand, one may be supporting the coal mines to protect corporate profits, not jobs. Then it does become a matter of progressive versus conservative views. Reasons matter.

The Brain's Politics

Politics is about real-world power and the way we understand morality. The bitterness in politics is partly about who has power and patronage and the control of money and resources that goes with political power. But the wider and deeper emotionality and bitterness is about morality, about whose moral system will rule. That is what public political discourse is mainly about. And public discourse has an enormous effect upon the outcome of elections.

For the most part, moral worldviews are within the cognitive unconscious. They are not discussed openly in public discourse. But cognitive science and neuroscience allow us to better understand what the shouting is about. The question now is what to do about it.

PART II

POLITICAL CHALLENGES FOR THE TWENTY-FIRST-CENTURY MIND

An Approach to Social Change

Understanding the brain, and how conservatives achieved brain change over the past four decades, leads to important conclusions of how progressives can use that knowledge to move America back to fundamental American values and democratic institutions.

Most Americans are biconceptual, in one way or another. That is, they have both progressive and conservative modes of thought mutually inhibiting one another; the use of one shuts off the use of the other. And each mode of thought is neurally bound to—that is, applies to—different areas of life. Thus you can think progressively on domestic policy and conservatively on foreign policy. Or you can be progressive in every active area of life and politics, while using conservative modes of thought only culturally, say, to understand movies, TV, and novels.

What conservatives did was to use language, ideas, images, and symbols repeatedly to activate the conservative mode of thought and inhibit the progressive mode of thought in individuals who had both. This increased the synaptic strength of the neurons in the circuitry characterizing conservative thought, and did the opposite to progressive thought. The relatively greater activation strength of the conservative mode of thought increased the likelihood of its being neurally bound to conservative framings of particular issues. This gradually made people more and more conservative, though in most cases not wholly so.

Progressives can reverse the process. Many people who call

themselves conservatives or independents actually have progressive views already on many issues, if not all. You can use progressive language, ideas, images, and symbols repeatedly to activate the progressive worldview in people who have both worldviews, so that the progressive mode of thought is strengthened and the conservative mode weakened. The idea is to move biconceptuals to progressive framings of issues by activating the progressive mode of thought they already have. You can talk to biconceptuals about issues where they are already progressive—say, about love of the land, or progressive religious values (caring about the poor, the sick, and the oppressed), or progressive community values (neighbors caring about and helping neighbors).

What is most powerful is calling upon empathy and truths that are "obvious" once they are framed honestly.

What to Do

"What can I do?"

There is nothing more frustrating than knowing what is wrong yet not knowing what you can do about it. There are, of course, the obvious things. You can write letters to your representatives, to the editors, to blogs. You can volunteer in campaigns, canvass your district, go door to door, raise money, get out the vote, talk to your neighbors, contribute to causes and advocacy groups. And you can organize others.

Most of these activities involve communication, to Congress, to readers of newspapers and blogs, to your neighbors, to advocacy groups. Once you are engaged, "What can I do?" becomes "What should I say?" And what you should say depends on the ideas you are trying to communicate.

Part I characterized the problem you are facing. But knowing isn't enough. You have to apply what you know. That's the challenge. Part II illustrates with a group of examples how to apply that knowledge in a New Enlightenment:

- A new consciousness: There is a New Enlightenment consciousness, a basic stance toward each other and the world.
- Dealing with traumatic ideas: An idea can be introduced under conditions of trauma and then repeated so often that it is forever in your synapses. You need to find ways both to inhibit it and to provide alternative modes of thought.
- Framing reality: Sometimes you have to construct a conceptual frame and a name when there are none, so that an important truth can be seen.
- Overcoming fear of framing: If you are not careful, you can fall into conservative framing traps. The way out takes courage.
- Confronting stereotypes: Stereotyping is powerful force. You need to recognize it and to confront it.
- Finding the right targets: Accountability has opposite meanings for conservatives and progressives. Progressive accountability—accountability of authorities to the public—must be anticipated and insisted upon in every instance.
- Framing precedes policy: The relationship between frames and policies is quite often misunderstood. Framing precedes policies, and sometimes policies can evoke very general frames.
- Recognizing contested concepts: Our most precious ideas— freedom, equality, fairness, opportunity—are contested. That is, they each have a very general shared version, too general to be of much use. And then they have progressive and conservative versions, which most people are unaware of. You have to make the progressive version of these concepts uppermost in the public mind. Otherwise you will put conservatives at an advantage in public discourse.

These are among the challenges presented by the twenty-first-century mind.

Remember, you are not alone. There is power in numbers. If hundreds of thousands of people are saying the same things—ideas that are based in American values, that ring true, and that stimulate positive emotions—those ideas become powerful. Democracy is anything but private.

It also takes patience. Change does not come overnight. Say things not once, but over and over. Brains change when ideas are repeatedly activated.

CHAPTER 5

A New Consciousness

A New Enlightenment comes with a new consciousness, a basic stance toward each other and the world. It requires the realization that empathy and responsibility are at the heart of the moral vision on which our democracy is based, an understanding of real reason, and a comprehension of systemic causation: of our connection to the natural world and to each other. It also demands that we cultivate empathy, responsibility, self-reflection, and a sense of connection, together with a full life based on them. As a consequence, it is an ecological consciousness in the broadest sense: empathy and systemic causation focus on our connections to each other, to all living things, to the communities and institutions in which we find fulfillment, and to the natural world that permits and sustains life. It is a consciousness of ultimate value—what some call "sacred" or "spiritual," and others call "humanistic." Labels aside, it is the consciousness required of the New Enlightenment.

We begin with the biology of empathy. Our mirror neuron circuitry and related pathways are activated when we act or when we see someone else performing the same action. They fire even more strongly when we coordinate actions with others—when we cooperate. Mirror neuron circuitry is connected to the emotional regions of our brains. Our emotions are expressed in our bodies, in our muscles and posture, so that mirror neurons can pick up visual information about the feelings of others. Our mirror neuron circuitry and associated pathways connect us both physically and emotionally with others, allowing us to feel what others feel. In other words, they provide the biological basis of empathy, cooperation, and community. We are born to empathize and cooperate.

That does not mean that we are not also born to achieve our purposes by trying to control our environment, including other people. We have biological mechanisms for purposeful action and control as well as empathy. We also have neural structure in our forebrains—the so-called super-mirror neurons—that are thought to modulate the response of the mirror neurons. They have just begun to be studied, but they may be brain structures that can make us insensitive to—or more sensitive to—the suffering of others.

These biological tendencies show up in the politics of empathy and of authority—the deep bases of progressive and conservative thought. Both tendencies are present in us all.

The historian Lynn Hunt has studied the history of perhaps the most central ideas in the founding of America, written by Jefferson in the Declaration of Independence:

> We take these truths to be self-evident, that all men are created equal, that they are endowed by their Creator with certain unalienable rights, that among these are life, liberty and the pursuit of happiness.

Hunt shows that these truths were not always self-evident.[1] She argues that it took a century after the Enlightenment for these ideas to become "self-evident" and that the mechanism was the arousal and cultivation of empathy with those in other social groups, apparently via what we now understand as mirror neuron circuitry and associated pathways, through novels, art, and other cultural media. Empathy, she argues, was the historical basis of our democracy. That is consistent with what I have found by studying the moral worldview that makes sense of our most treasured ideas.

American democracy was founded on the politics of empathy and responsibility, with the role of government being protection and empowerment. From these flow the progressive ideals of equality, freedom, fairness, opportunity, general prosperity, accountability, and so on.[2]

We also start with real reason: It is largely unconscious and appropriately emotional. It is embodied, and the way it is embodied gives rise to frame-based and metaphorical thought.

Mutual inhibition and neural binding give rise to biconceptualism: the reality that we may have both progressive and conservative modes of thought, but use them in mutually exclusive ways over different issue areas. As a result, there may be people who identify themselves as conservatives but have progressive values in many issues: being good stewards of the environment, having a nurturant view of God, running a business that is consistent with the public good in all ways, and wanting to live in a progressive community where people care about and take care of each other. Progressives can connect with such folks if they address areas of common values.

As conservatives have taught us, social change involves many changes: material changes like war, the distribution of wealth, and the state of the environment; institutional changes like the constitution of the Supreme Court, the destruction of governmental capacities, and corporate consolidation; media changes, as in the control of radio, TV, and newspaper outlets. But the change that laid the groundwork for all of them was brain change: an extension of strict father morality to area after area, with corresponding alterations in public discourse.

A change back to democratic ideals and forward to an ecological consciousness will require brain change as well. Mutual inhibition and neural binding are central to understanding how such a change would work. Most Americans have both strict and nurturant worldviews in their brain, with each neurally bound to certain issue areas. Social change requires activating the nurturant, progressive worldview so that more issue areas in more brains will be bound to—and, hence, instances of—that worldview.

That is the mechanism. The means are language, images, and narratives that positively activate the progressive worldview, while acting negatively to inhibit the effect of the conservative worldview.

Our democracy is presently being threatened by the politics of obedience to authority, the very thing that democracy was invented to counteract. The politics of authority is succeeding because conservatives have been activating their ideas in the brains of the public, while finding ways to inhibit the use of progressive modes of thought. Progressives failed to uphold the spirit of American democracy by activating the ideas of empathy, responsibility, protection, and empowerment in the brains of their fellow Americans, thus allowing the basis of our most sacred principles to fall by the wayside and leaving the field open for conservatives. We must change this. Democracy is too important to leave the shaping of the brains of Americans to authoritarians.

There is a lot to be done: electing better political leaders, refurbishing democratic institutions, preserving our environment, constructing a more democratic economy, educating future leaders, informing the media. But all this will require changing minds, and hence brains. The capacity for empathy is there. It must be cultivated if democracy is to revive and flourish.

Ecological Consciousness

The biology of empathy allows us to comprehend our connection to each other, to other living things, and to the physical world that supports life. The twenty-first-century mind allows us to comprehend how embodied experience shapes thought, what worldviews are, and how our comprehension of the world is frame- and metaphor-dependent. As we shall soon see, it also shows that the very idea of economic man is based on metaphors that don't fit reality very well. Indeed, the reality of global warming, environmental health, and species death, as their consequences settle in, require a new view of what it means to be a human being: ecological consciousness.

It too often takes the evanescence of life to make us appreciate
or even notice it. As species die, we finally learn of their wonders.
As the Arctic melts, we admire the magnificence of its frozen
whiteness. As fish get contaminated with mercury and stocks die
out, and rivers, lakes, and streams get too polluted to eat the fish,
we miss what we once had. As midwestern pesticides wash down
the Mississippi and into the Gulf, killing sea life in a huge area,
we wonder about the future of Gulf prawns. As the air gets more
polluted and asthma rates go up, I think of my granddaughter,
who has asthma at six. I stand on the pier and wonder how much
of my hometown will be swallowed up if the Arctic—only ten
feet thick—melts fully and sea levels rise twenty feet. I listen for
frogs I don't hear and look for butterflies I don't see. And I wonder what country my fruit is from and whether it is laced with
unnamed chemicals.

The reality of global warming and global industrialization,
even of food, focuses our empathy—on native plants, on organic
food, on chickens that should not be in factory cages and shot
up with antibiotics, on the few salmon left to spawn, on whatever bees remain. Global warming, chemicals everywhere, plus
empathy breeds awe at the wonder and diversity of life, even as it
disappears.

Economic man produced global warming and chemical chickens. The unbounded pursuit of self-interest that was supposed
to be moral, was supposed to produce plenty for all, is bringing
death to our earth. If it continues, half the species on the planet
will die within a century. Economic man was an idea—a claim
about human nature. Empathy and real reason, as we shall see,
reveal its fallacies. They also reveal how ideas can be destructive.

A New Enlightenment will shift the entire perspective from how
to raid our environment for profit to how to live within it safely.
Instead of asking about a policy proposal—what are the economic
gains and what are the costs?—we must ask other questions first.

The Questions

What are a policy's empathetic consequences—how does it affect all that we are connected to? How does it affect the natural world? Does it sustain life, or does it harm life? How am I personally connected to its consequences, as a human being? What, if anything, makes it beautiful, healthful, enjoyable, fulfilling? What causal system does it fit into? How will it affect future generations? Is it fair and does it make us more free? Will it lift spirits, and will we find awe in it?

The questions mostly don't sound political at first, but they bear on political policies overall. This kind of ecological consciousness is fast becoming the consciousness of the progressive base of the Democratic Party, and it is spreading among young people. The Nobel Prize for Al Gore and the UN Intergovernmental Panel on Climate Change was not for a movie and a report. It was for shaping and accelerating the coming change in how we view the world.

Why should the farm bill become the food bill? When we ask those questions, we get the answer.

Why should we invest massively in a non-carbon-based, sustainable energy system? Ask those questions and you get the answer.

Why should we have a foreign policy centered on people rather than just on states? What should our trade policy be? What should education be like? What kind of health care system should we have? Why should we support the arts? Why is Net neutrality important? Ask those questions and the answers pop out at you.

A New Enlightenment will renew progressive values, and in doing so it will go beyond the liberalism of the Old Enlightenment. It will ask different questions, and that will mean different answers.

Ecology is not just a science about the natural world outside of people. It is a moral concern based in empathy; that concern leads to the science of natural systems and how systemic cau-sation works—in the natural world to be sure, but also in the interpersonal world, the social world, the business world, and the political world.

We are not just adding another dimension—the brain and the mind—to our understanding of politics. Real reason tells us why we must take part in politics, why the earth depends on it, and how we can act more effectively and urgently.

A deep ecological consciousness is also a spiritual conscious-ness: it encompasses our deepest connections to the world and to each other, it is fundamentally moral, it acknowledges gratitude, and it evokes awe every day. Real reason is emotional, and an ecological consciousness has awe as its central emotion.

When that ecological consciousness is violated, righteous anger is the appropriate emotion, and responsible organizing is the appropriate reaction. A true ecological consciousness must be lived.

CHAPTER 6

Traumatic Ideas:
The War on Terror

A misleading and destructive idea can be introduced under conditions of trauma and then repeated so often that it is forever in your synapses. It won't just go away. We need to inhibit it, get around it, and provide alternatives.

For a few hours after the towers fell on 9/11, administration spokesmen referred to the event as a "crime." Indeed, Colin Powell argued within the administration that it be treated as such. This would have involved international crimefighting techniques: checking bank accounts, wiretapping, recruiting spies and informants, engaging in diplomacy, cooperating with intelligence agencies in other governments, and, if necessary, undertaking limited "police actions" with military force. It would result in charges, trials, evidence, and determination of innocence or guilt in a court of law. Terrorists would be seen as criminals, not as heroic soldiers, by those they claim to represent. Indeed, such methods have been the most successful so far internationally in dealing with terrorism, and have been adopted with success in Britain.

But the crime frame did not prevail in the Bush administration. Instead, a war metaphor was carefully chosen: the "war on terror."

Synapses in the brain change most readily and dramatically under conditions of trauma, and 9/11 was a national trauma of the first order. It allowed the Bush administration to impose the powerful "war on terror" metaphor and make it stick.

Literal wars, unlike metaphorical ones, are conducted against armies of other nations. They end when the armies are defeated militarily and a peace treaty is signed. Terror is an emotional state. It is in us. It is not an army. You can't defeat it militarily and you can't sign a peace treaty with it.

"War on terror" means war without end. It was used by the Bush administration as a ploy to get virtually unlimited war powers—and further domestic influence—for the president. How? Because the mention of "terror" activates a fear response, and fear activates a conservative worldview, in which there is a powerful leader, willing to use his strength, who offers protection and security.

The war metaphor was chosen for political reasons, and first and foremost for domestic political reasons. The war metaphor defined war as the only way to defend the nation. From within it, being against war as a response was to be unpatriotic, to be against defending the nation. Shifting from "terror" to "terrorists" still preserves the war metaphor.

The war metaphor put progressives on the defensive. Once it took hold, any refusal to grant the president full authority to conduct the war would open progressives in Congress to the charge of being unpatriotic, unwilling to defend America, defeatist—traitorous. And once the military went into battle, the war metaphor created a new reality that reinforced itself.

The war metaphor allowed the president to assume war powers, which made him politically immune from serious criticism and gave him extraordinary domestic power to carry the agenda of the radical right: Power to shift money and resources away from social needs to the military and related industries. Power to override environmental safeguards on the grounds of military need. Power to set up a domestic surveillance system to spy on our citizens and to intimidate political enemies. Power over political discussion, since war trumps all other topics. In short, power to reshape America to the vision of the radical right—with no end date.

Moreover, the war metaphor was used as justification for the invasion of Iraq, which Bush had planned since his first week in office. Frank Luntz, the right-wing language expert, recommended referring to the Iraq War as the main front in the "war on terror"—even when it was known that Saddam Hussein had nothing to do with 9/11 and indeed saw Osama bin Laden as an enemy. Fox News used "war on terror" as a headline when showing film clips from Iraq. Remember "weapons of mass destruction"? They were invented by the Bush administration to strike terror into the hearts of Americans and to justify the invasion. Remember that the Iraq War was advocated long before 9/11 and promoted as early as 1997 by the members of the Project for the New American Century, who later came to dominate in the Bush administration. Why?

The neoconservative strategy was to use the American military to achieve economic and strategic goals in the Middle East: to gain control of the second-largest oil reserve in the world; to place military bases right in the heart of the Middle East for the sake of economic and political intimidation; to open up Middle Eastern markets and economic opportunities for American corporations; and to place American culture and a controllable government in the heart of the Middle East. The justification was 9/11—to identify the Iraq invasion as part of the "war on terror" and claim that it is necessary in order to protect America and spread democracy.

Domestically, the "war on terror" metaphor has been a major success for the radical right. Bush was returned to office in 2004 and the radical right got its Supreme Court justices, right-wing judges were appointed throughout the country, and the government was filled with right-wing appointees, able to realize their domestic goals far removed from foreign wars. Social programs are being gutted. Deregulation and privatization are thriving. Even highways are being privatized. Taxpayers' money is being transferred to the ultra-rich, making them richer. The environment continues to be plundered. Domestic surveillance is in place. Corporate profits have doubled while wage levels have declined. Oil profits are astronomical.

The metaphor is still in place. We are still taking off our shoes at the airports, and now we cannot take bottled water onto planes. Airport "security" really tells us we should be afraid. The very mention of the "war on terror" over and over evokes fear—unconsciously if not consciously. The Republican presidential candidates in 2007 repeated the phrase over and over. They were selling fear. Rudy Giuliani's very candidacy was based on the metaphor, on the claim that he could "fight it" more effectively than anyone else. John McCain comes on just as strong. Mitt Romney wanted to fight it with more torture—two Guantánamos!

The "war on terror" metaphor is still the staple of right-wing politics at home.

Neuroscience and the "War on Terror"

How did the "war on terror" metaphor get established as the idea to characterize our Middle East involvement? Neuroscience tells us that ideas are physically instantiated as part of our brains and that changes occur at the synapses. Such synaptic changes, called long-term potentiation, occur under two conditions—trauma (where there is especially strong neural firing) and repetition (where neural firing recurs). September 11 was a national trauma, and the "war on terror" was introduced under conditions of trauma, then repeated over and over for years. The result was that the metaphorical idea became physically instantiated in the brains of most Americans.

Neuroscience also tells us that you can't simply erase such changes. You can add a structure that might bypass the "war on terror" idea, or perhaps inhibit its activation, or add a modifying structure—perhaps even one that delegitimizes it. But you can't just get rid of it at will. Poof! "War on terror" be gone!

Moreover, when an expression like "war on terror" becomes a fixed part of your brain, you tend to use it *reflexively*, not *reflectively*. As we have seen, reflexive use is like a reflex, like the automatic movement of muscles you use when you ride a bicycle. You don't—and can't—control every muscle, one by one, as you ride the bike. You learn to ride, and then your brain and body take over, unconsciously controlling your movement.

Similarly, when you speak, you mostly just talk without consciously controlling every word, every grammatical structure, every inference. Your brain just takes over and works below the level of conscious control. Similarly, when you are listening, you usually just hear and understand, reflexively, without conscious *reflection* on every word. Part of the power of political language is that the ideas expressed are processed reflexively. You can't notice most of what you are thinking most of the time!

Reflective cognition—thinking about your thoughts—requires a conscious examination. Conscious reflection requires two levels of understanding—not just the conscious level of what you are thinking about, but also an understanding of unconscious thought.

I am suggesting a conscious discussion of the "war on terror" metaphor as a metaphor—a manipulative metaphor designed for conservative power. Openly discussing the war metaphor as a metaphor would allow the case to be made that terrorism is most effectively treated as a crime—like wiping out a crime syndicate—not as an occasion for sending abroad more than a hundred thousand troops and perpetrating massive bombings that only recruit more terrorists.

Finally, openly discussing the war metaphor as a metaphor would raise the question of the domestic effect of giving the president war powers, and the fact that the Bush administration has shamelessly exploited 9/11 to achieve the political goals of the radical right—with all the disasters that has brought to our country. It would allow us to name right-wing ideology, to spell it out, to look at its effects, and to see what awful things it has done, is doing, and threatens to keep on doing. The blame for what has gone wrong in Iraq, in New Orleans, in our economy, and throughout the country at large should be placed squarely where it belongs—on a right-wing ideology that calls itself "conservative" but mocks real American values.

Metaphors cannot be seen or touched, but they create massive effects, and political intimidation is one such effect. What would I like to have seen on September 12 or 13, 2001? Here is a dream:

Congress, the citizenry, and the press rising up and shouting, "Wait a minute! That's a metaphor that doesn't fit. You don't go to a war on an inappropriate metaphor." Media journalists recognizing that the repetition of "war on terror" is an attempt to change their brains and the brains of the citizenry, and thereby grab enormous unwarranted power, both internationally and domestically. The honest media (excepting, for example, Fox News and Clear Channel) refusing to use the words "war on terror." Masses of citizens writing to their congressional representatives to resist the metaphor. Viable candidates for the presidency raising the issue.

This is not entirely a pipe dream. Recently (in the spring of 2007), John Edwards actually took on the "war on terror" metaphor as a metaphor on national TV during a presidential debate. And on May 23, 2007, at the Council on Foreign Relations, Edwards said:

> It is now clear that George Bush's misnamed "war on terror" has backfired—and is now part of the problem.
>
> The war on terror is a slogan designed only for politics, not a strategy to make America safe. It's a bumper sticker, not a plan. It has damaged our alliances and weakened our standing in the world. As a political "frame," it's been used to justify everything from the Iraq War to Guantánamo to illegal spying on the American people. It's even been used by this White House as a partisan weapon to bludgeon their political opponents. Whether by manipulating threat levels leading up to elections, or by deeming opponents "weak on terror," they have shown no hesitation whatsoever about using fear to divide.
>
> But the worst thing about this slogan is that it hasn't worked to defeat terrorism. The so-called "war" has created

even more terrorism—as we have seen so tragically in Iraq. The State Department itself recently released a study showing that worldwide terrorism has increased 25 percent in 2006, including a 40 percent surge in civilian fatalities.[1]

As Edwards says, by framing this as a "war," we have walked right into the trap that terrorists have set—that we are engaged in some kind of clash of civilizations and a war against Islam.

The war metaphor has also failed because it exaggerates the role of only one instrument of American power—the military. This has occurred in part because the military is so effective at what it does. Yet if you think all you have is a hammer, then every problem looks like a nail.

There's an emerging consensus inside the armed forces that we must move beyond the idea of a "war on terror." The commander of the U.S. military's Central Command recently stated that he would no longer use the "long war" framework. Top military leaders like retired general Anthony Zinni have rejected the term. These leaders know we need substance, not slogans; leadership, not labels.

The question is, what should replace the "war on terror"? At the annual meeting of the World Affairs Council in 2007, former secretary of defense William Perry pointed out the metaphorical nature of the term and suggested banning it from serious discourse about national security. As if he could.

Unfortunately, it has been more than a bit too little too late. The metaphor is set in the synapses of brains all over America. And because his attempt didn't catch on immediately, even Edwards has largely dropped it, mistakenly calling the "war on terror" a "bumper sticker" now and then, trivializing its power and hiding its domestic intent.

Such a considerable change of brains can't happen from a speech or two on the stump or at a conference, especially since the conservative message machine and the Republican presidential candidates will go on repeating it. You can't just ban it. But you can make a public issue of it, partly with ridicule and partly with moral outrage. But the discussion, the ridicule, and the outrage cannot just be a one-shot event. It must persist, and must be done across the country over and over until no one will use the phrase for fear of being ridiculed or evoking extreme anger.

This would require civic participation throughout the nation.

It won't happen.

Old Enlightenment reason is too strongly entrenched in the Democratic Party, not just the political leaders, but the consultants and staff, the pollsters, the strategists, the ad agencies, even the donor community. The idea of building a sustained campaign to communicate truth and change how Americans think is unthinkable to Democrats at this point.

The military occupation in Iraq is going so badly that the Democrats might just win a big electoral victory in 2008. The broader question is, will they have changed the minds, and hence the brains, of Americans in any deep way, not just on terrorism, but on what the values of our country are and how the nation should be run?

CHAPTER 7

Framing Reality: Privateering

When an important truth is unseen because it is unframed and unnamed, you may have to construct a conceptual frame and a name, so that the important truth can be seen.

We think using conceptual frames. Words name elements of those frames. Without frames and names, it is difficult to think and talk about truths. A step toward a New Enlightenment is to recognize when frames for important truths are missing in public consciousness, and when we lack the needed words. Our job then is to construct the frame and to assign names, so that the phenomenon can be talked about openly.

To begin to shift the terms, I'd like to describe a widespread conservative practice that has not previously had a name and, being nameless, has not been publicly aired or even noticed as a single practice. I call it "privateering." You can think of it as a blend of "privatization" and "profiteering." The word previously existed with a related meaning, but has mostly gone out of use.

Privateering is a special case of privatization in which the capacity of government to carry out critical moral missions is systematically destroyed from within the government itself, while public funds are used to provide capital for private corporations to take over those critical functions of government and charge the public a great deal for doing so, while avoiding all accountability.

This not only strikes at the moral mission of government to protect and empower its citizens, but threatens to destroy democracy itself. It involves a collaboration between privateering corporations and privateering enablers who have governmental powers of some kind. It can occur at any level of government, but the most pernicious effects are at the federal level. And it is a result of conservative ideology being carried out successfully under the public radar screen.

The Privateering frame has the following components:

- Privateering enablers: Those in the government who act to destroy the government's ability to carry out some aspect of its moral mission of protection and empowerment.
- Surreptitious dismantling acts: Acts, usually below the public's awareness, that destroy a crucial governmental capacity. For example, budget cuts, executive orders, signing statements, reassignment of regulators, purposeful lack of enforcement, putting corporate lobbyists in charge of government agencies, appointing conservative judges, arranging for no-bid contracts, and so on.
- Privateers themselves: Corporations that fill the gap in some critical governmental capacity, often using public money to provide capital to take over those functions. The money commonly comes in the form of either lucrative government contracts or subsidies. Privateers tend to make considerable profits, paid for by the public, for doing governmental tasks that are vital but that government can no longer perform. There is typically little competition among privateers, so prices are high—whatever the market will bear.
- Surreptitious privateering: Working in coordination with enablers to make privateering possible, often via lobbying or personal connections.
- Transferred functions: Those critical moral functions of government that are transferred to privateers. Examples include: military functions; intelligence functions; monitoring food, drug, and product safety; interrogating prisoners; disaster relief; and educating the public. The privateers are not accountable to the public to carry out these functions well.

Negative effects have included the murder of civilians in Iraq; intelligence failures; poisoning the public via foods, drugs, and consumer goods; carrying out torture; letting people drown; and the resegregation of schools.

The primary mission of corporations is to maximize profits for their stockholders and executives, not to carry out the moral missions of protecting and empowering citizens. They are accountable to their stockholders, not to the public. It is inevitable that, when conflicts between the public good and corporate profits arise, the public good suffers.

In privateering, the public becomes a captive market. For crucial services, corporations can charge whatever the market will bear. In emergencies, the government itself—that is, the taxpayers—may have to pay exorbitant prices for those services, and many may not be able to afford them.

Privateering is a means of transferring wealth from ordinary taxpayers to wealthy investors, making the wealthy much wealthier, while robbing ordinary people of the security and opportunity that government should provide.

Democracy is the first casualty of privateering. Our lives are being governed more and more by private corporations. We have not elected them, cannot turn them out of office or make them accountable to us. Each act of privateering robs us of a portion of democracy.

The ultimate result could be a nightmare system of nondemocratic government, where proper government has been destroyed, where the moral mission cannot be depended upon, where there is no public accountability, where prices are exorbitant, and where the public must either pay those prices for untrustworthy services or go without altogether.

On the front page of the *New York Times* in the fall of 2007, there appeared three stories about privateering presented as if they had nothing to do with each other: the Blackwater killings of civilians in Iraq, the FDA's lack of inspectors for food and drug safety, and the bill to fund SCHIP (the State Children's Health Insurance Program). Let us look at what joins them together.

Blackwater

The military is a branch of the federal government. It exists to protect the country in case of invasion or imminent threat. It has many functions in addition to fighting, including the training of troops, the transporting of weapons and troops, the guarding of military installations and diplomatic personnel, running technical equipment, setting up bases, transporting equipment, feeding the troops, and so on. The military is a "service"—under civilian control and made up of U.S. citizens who volunteer to serve their country by protecting its citizens. There is a strict military code of conduct and international rules for what soldiers can and cannot do.

Blackwater is a private army of paid soldiers—mercenaries— referred to as "contractors" and "security guards." It has enormous facilities and trains 40,000 soldiers a year. The Iraq War would not have been possible without Blackwater: its private army guards installations, including the Green Zone, the huge city within a city in Baghdad; transports troops and diplomats; engages in training; and so on. Blackwater says that it can put 20,000 of its troops on the ground ready to function on short notice.

Blackwater has a huge fleet of military helicopters, and has received over a billion dollars in contracts in Iraq since the Bush administration came to power. It charges the U.S. government $445,000 a year per security guard. Its CEO, Erik Prince, is a billionaire, and a major financial supporter of the Republican Party. Ninety percent of its revenue has come from government contracts, two-thirds of which are no-bid contracts. That means that the American taxpayers have paid for most of Blackwater's capital—its bases, helicopters, weapons, and other equipment. And since its personnel are mostly former members of the U.S.

military, U.S. taxpayers have paid for their training. Yet the U.S. Congress has no control over Blackwater, and as of this writing, Blackwater operatives in other countries are neither under U.S. legal jurisdiction nor the legal jurisdiction of the country they are in. They are a law unto themselves. They also have a reputation for being trigger-happy, and in the incident that brought the company to national attention, killed seventeen Iraqi civilians, including a mother and her baby.

Blackwater turned up in the Hurricane Katrina tragedy, hired by Homeland Security. Blackwater was also hired by FEMA, which had its budget cut and could no longer function on its own to do hurricane relief. It had to hire Blackwater. At present Blackwater is looking to expand its operations in the domestic sphere. It is attempting to build a huge base in southern California near the Mexican border, in the hopes of getting business guarding the border and providing security and transportation in the case of earthquakes, fires, and floods, since it has equipment that FEMA does not.

The thought of a huge, well-funded, well-stocked private army run by right-wing ideologues and supporters of conservative politics is frightening enough. The idea that major parts of our country may become dependent on Blackwater and may have to pay exorbitantly for its services, while under its control, is even more frightening.

The threat to democracy that Blackwater represents was made clear in an interview with Representative Darrell Issa (R-CA), who was asked about Representative Henry Waxman's call for an investigation of Blackwater. Issa said, "If Henry Waxman today wants to go to Iraq and do an investigation, Blackwater will be his support team. His protection team. Do you think he really wants to investigate directly?"[1] And the New York *Daily News* reported:

When a team of FBI agents lands in Baghdad this week to probe Blackwater security contractors for murder, it will be protected by bodyguards from the very same firm, the Daily News has learned.

Half a dozen FBI criminal investigators based in Washington are scheduled to travel to Iraq to gather evidence and interview witnesses about a Sept. 16 shooting spree that left at least 11 Iraqi civilians dead.

The agents plan to interview witnesses within the relative safety of the fortified Green Zone, but they will be transported outside the compound by Blackwater armored convoys, a source briefed on the FBI mission said.

"What happens when the FBI team decides to go visit the crime scene? Blackwater is going to have to take them there," the senior U.S. official told The News.[2]

Blackwater is a privateer in every respect. The government's ability to fully perform its protective function has been gutted, and the country has been made dependent on companies like Blackwater, which are huge and have been capitalized at public expense. Its charges are exorbitant, its profits enormous. Wherever it functions, it governs—it takes on the power and duties of a government—but it is ruled by profit and is not accountable to those it governs. Nobody elected Blackwater and nobody can vote it out of office. But it has huge financial, legal, PR, and lobbying resources to influence our government to act in its favor.

The Food and Drug Administration

On September 28, 2007, the *New York Times* reported that the Food and Drug Administration audits less than 1 percent of clinical drug trials in the United States. It has only two hundred inspectors, some of whom are part-time, to audit 350,000 testing sites. And when serious problems are found, FDA administrators have downgraded the findings 68 percent of the time.

As the FDA had its funding for regulators cut and as industry-friendly officials were appointed, the responsibility for drug testing fell on the companies, which have billions of dollars invested in their drugs. We now know that private tests results were fudged for Propulsid (Johnson and Johnson), Bextra and Cele-brex (Pfizer), and Vioxx (Merck), resulting in many deaths.

In the area of food safety, the FDA has been underfunded for years and has a lack of inspectors and trained personnel because of budgeting shortfalls. The Waxman committee in 2006 esti-mated that year's shortfall at $135 million. The result is that food safety regulation falls to private corporations. The FDA had learned of a salmonella outbreak at ConAgra's Georgia peanut operation and told ConAgra that it was depending upon the com-pany to address it. The company did not.[3] The FDA received com-plaints of *E. coli* at spinach producers in the Salinas Valley before three deaths occurred, and had sent alerts to the producers, who did not address the problem. And when food imports increased from China and other countries, no inspectors for food safety were hired. In addition, the Bush administration and Republicans in Congress have resisted the call for even labeling country of ori-gin for foods sold in the United States.

Food and drug safety are excellent examples of privateering. Conservatives in government cut funding for FDA inspectors, making it impossible for the agency to engage in its moral mission of protecting the country's food and drug supply. That responsi-bility then fell to private corporations, whose primary mission is profit, not public protection. Inevitably, profit wins out. The drug companies fudge drug test data and make billions on drugs they know will harm the public. Food producers ignore warnings for the sake of profit. Food importers do not spend the needed money to monitor food imports. Not until people—or pets!—die does the problem come to light.

The FDA is only one such case of privateering. The Consumer Product Safety Division has similarly been underfunded for years by conservative policies. The result was a scandal: because of a lack of inspectors, millions of dangerous toys from China con-taining lead paint had been coming into the United States for many years, and millions of children had been directly exposed to them, presumably with harmful effects. Because of conservative privateering policy, the Chinese manufacturers and the American importers became responsible for product safety when inspectors were cut. For the sake of profits, those corporations did nothing to protect millions of children playing with the toys containing lead.

Privateering is central to the conservative plan for America. Conservatives nonetheless keep calling for "smaller government" and "spending cuts"—except for the military, the Energy Department, corporate subsidies, and any parts of government that fit the conservative worldview. What conservatives mean by a "strong defense" is bigger government where the military is concerned, with more spending on the military, and a considerable percentage of the money going to private corporations that are large military contractors and make high profits on those contracts. In both the call to cut spending on corporate regulators and the call to spend more on military contractors, conservatives are engaging in privateering.

Health Care

Privateering is at the center of the health care issue.

First, let us distinguish between health care and health insurance. Health insurance companies make their money by denying health care: either refusing to insure people with preconditions, turning down recommended procedures, or limiting the amount to be paid out for some condition—say, paying a maximum of $20,000 for cancer treatments, after which you have to sell your house to get them.

This is the opposite of the way most markets work. In a typical market, companies that provide more of their product tend to make more money. In health insurance, the product is health care. But the more care an insurance company provides, the less profit it makes. In a normal market, greater competition helps consumers. But with health insurance, competition is competition for profits, not for delivering care. Greater competition for profits thus means competition to deliver less care, which harms consumers. Health insurance is thus an anti-market phenomenon.

Second, health insurance greatly adds to the cost of care. While Medicare has administrative costs of 3 percent, HMOs have administrative costs of about 25 percent. Most of that money is spent on determining ways to deny care. On top of that, HMOs make a considerable profit, so that administrative costs plus profit amount to more than it would take to insure everyone under a Medicare-for-all or single-payer plan.

Third, health care falls under the moral mission of the government to protect its citizens from the ravages of disease, or injury, or the natural decay of the body as one ages. Sooner or later all our citizens will need health care.

Other forms of protection for the public do not require insurance. The police don't ask whether you have insurance and are up on your premiums when a burglar breaks into your house, nor does the fire department when your house catches fire. Basic protection is, or should be, a function of government, and that includes health security.

But conservatives favor privateering—eliminating the capacity of government to provide health security through Medicare and then placing health care in the hands of insurance companies whose main mission is making money and who make their money by denying care. Conservatives do not believe that everyone should have health care. For them it is a commodity. If you aren't making enough money to pay for the commodity, then you don't deserve to have it.

Neoliberal democrats, who might think that Medicare-for-all or single-payer would be the best plan, sense conservative opposition and surrender their moral position in advance. Neoliberals still see markets as a means to a progressive moral end, whereas conservatives see the market as being a moral end in itself. Neoliberals believe that they can achieve the effects of empathy by working for the interests of others—that is, other demographic groups (uninsured poor children, veterans, the elderly). They believe that with appropriate regulation and laws, markets can achieve most material or economic needs. That's why "pragmatic" Democrats are supporting insurance-based health plans with some federally funded insurance for the poor. The result of such plans would be that insurance companies will continue trying to deny as much care as they can get away with—only there will be 50 million more people to deny care to.

The conservative policy is a privateering policy. Keep the government from being able to, say, buy drugs at a huge discount and pass the savings on, so that drug companies can make huge profits. Keep the government from insuring all poor children, lest they grow up wanting government health care the rest of their lives.

Health care is different from the first two cases. Here government functioning is prevented from coming into being, not destroyed. But the phenomenon is the same: government is kept by privateering enablers from doing its job, and private companies make lots of profit as a result, often on government contracts.

Is privatization always bad? By no means. But to see if it's appropriate, I ask some simple questions. Will the moral mission of government, the protection and empowerment of citizens— otherwise called the common good—be served or undermined? Will democracy be served or undermined?

What does cognitive science have to do with the issue of privateering? Plenty. Neoliberals who stick to Old Enlightenment reason have not raised it as an issue because their mode of arguing doesn't permit it. Universal reason says that you only have to give the facts and figures and everyone will reason correctly using them and be convinced. But one can only have facts and figures about special cases of privateering—about Blackwater, or about the FDA, or about health care. You have to see the general case in order to fight against it. Cognitive science takes you beyond Old Enlightenment reasoning and forces you to notice the common structure in the privateering cases. Only when you grasp the idea of privateering can you even think of amassing facts and figures about it.

And cognitive science tells you something else. The only way the public can become conscious of privateering is if it is framed correctly and powerfully. Anything anyone learns is a matter of brain change. You can't learn anything without your synapses changing. And the brains of the public change only when a given frame is activated over and over. That's why progressives should be pointing out cases of privateering and discussing it in public every day. Influential newspapers like the *New York Times* and the *Washington Post* or the national televised news programs could introduce the idea into our culture if they noted the widespread causal influence of privateering in story after story, and identified it as conservative policy.

Conservative theorists are well aware of privateering, and have been writing about it in glowing terms, pointing to a celebrated history. The original privateers were state-licensed pirates who preyed upon the merchant ships of other nations, especially in war, but also in peacetime. They were as vicious as pirates, but they not only took all the valuables being transported, they also brought the victim ship back to port and sold it for profit. They could do so because they were state-licensed. And they were financed by investors, who often made a very hefty profit on their investments.

Larry J. Sechrest and Alexander Tabarrok of the Independent Institute have written tracts detailing a romantic history of the privateers. Starting with conservative assumptions about the free market, they suggest that private contractors be used in battle, not just as security guards, and that having mercenaries fight wars for profit is good thing.[4]

The old privateers were state-sanctioned to take for themselves, by force, the wealth of people in other nations. During wartime, their acts were justified as weakening the enemy's economy and strengthening one's own. The question is now being raised as to whether "free trade" pacts permit new forms of such privateering. In a postcolonial era, our government, which promotes "democracy," cannot simply take over another country, enslave its people, and take its resources. Have we created a modern equivalent of old-fashioned "privateering"?

Our banks invest in corporations that use the money to buy access to the resources—the wealth—of the citizens of other nations, resources like oil, natural gas, minerals, agricultural land, water rights, and cheap labor. To protect those investments, called our "vital interests," we send troops and private for-profit "security guards" like those from Blackwater. Is this modern international privateering? I think it is worth a public discussion.

In a New Enlightenment, the question must be asked and taken seriously.

CHAPTER 8

Fear of Framing

Progressives too often fall into conservative framing traps. Avoiding them takes a new consciousness. The way out takes insight and courage. Old Enlightenment reason was supposed to be universal, literal, and unemotional. It did not admit that alternative worldviews are normal, that we think in terms of frames and metaphors that fit our worldviews, and that language can be chosen to activate frames, metaphors, and worldviews.

Many Democrats in Congress are so accustomed to Old Enlightenment reason that they don't know how to effectively use framing to strengthen the hold of their worldview. The Republicans have become expert at it, and the Democrats often don't know what's hitting them and how to respond. The longer they wait to respond, the harder it gets—and they don't understand why. They fall into traps and have no idea how to get out. They fear that Republicans will frame them in an unsavory light. As a result, they unintentionally do it themselves. The Democrats need a New Enlightenment.

Here's a typical example. A headline on the *New York Times* front page on October 9, 2007, read, "Democrats Seem Ready to Extend Wiretap Powers... Fears of Appearing Soft on Terror." The Democrats, the story said, were "nervous that they would be called soft on terrorism if they insist on strict curbs on gathering intelligence."

In a New Enlightenment, the Democrats would disrupt the link between freedom and "softness." They would "Stand up to the President," "Remain Strong on Liberty," and "Say No to

More Wiretapping." Framing is not just a matter of slogans. It is a mode of thought, a mode of action, and a sign of character. It is not just words, though words do have to be said over and over. The question is not just what Democrats say, but how they act—over time.

Old Enlightenment reason says words are neutral. If you believe that, you will accept the other side's frame: We need to wiretap citizens and get around the FISA constraints to catch potential terrorists. As soon as the framing is accepted, you are trapped. You are weak if you do and weak if you don't. You are weak on terror if you don't support the president. But if you go along, you are weak for not standing up to him.

If Democrats can't stand up to a president with a 30 percent popularity rating, how can they stand up to the nation's enemies? The only way out is shifting the frame to what they really believe but are too afraid to say. And then say it and say it and say it. With power. With vigor. In unison. Everywhere. And get lots of progressives booked on radio and TV stations saying it.

In January 2007, the Democrats took control of both houses of Congress. Their mandate, from the voters in the 2006 election, was to end the U.S. military occupation of Iraq.

The Constitution in Article I, Section 8, gives Congress, and only Congress, the power "to declare war" and "to raise and support armies, but no appropriation of money to that use shall be for a longer term than two years." Two distinguished constitutional scholars clarified those powers in testimony before Congress on January 30, 2007. David J. Barron, of the Harvard Law School, said, "Congress possesses substantial constitutional authority to regulate ongoing military operations and even to bring them to an end." And Louis Fisher, a constitutional specialist at the Library of Congress, wrote:

> The legislative judgment to take the country to war carries
> with it a duty throughout the conflict to decide that military

force remains in the national interest.... Congress is responsible for monitoring what it has set in motion. In the midst of war, there are no grounds for believing that the President's authority is superior to the collective judgment of its elected representatives. Congress has both the constitutional authority and the responsibility to retain control and recalibrate national policy whenever necessary.[1]

In short, the framers of the Constitution framed Congress as the "Decider" on any overall military strategic mission, including troop levels, general deployments, and so on. The president is the executive who has the duty to execute that overall strategic mission.

These experts were brought in to testify because the president had claimed that he, as commander in chief, had such powers. The president framed Congress as merely a bursar of funds for his military actions. He was reframing the Constitution. And contrary to the mandate given by voters to the Democratic majority, the president wanted to escalate the military occupation in Iraq, not end it. He intended to double the number of combat troops there with what he called a "surge." Now, a "surge" is a short-term deployment of troops, usually for a few months, to do a short mission. But the president's deployment would be longer-term than that, more like an "escalation" than a "surge."

Democrats in Congress tried to force withdrawal from Iraq at first by sending the president military funding legislation tied to a timetable for withdrawal. The president countered in the court of public opinion with a framing campaign that went as follows:

The United States is at war with an enemy threatening our national security. The president is the "unitary executive," the commander in chief in charge of all use of the military; we can't have five hundred commanders. The Congress is merely a bursar of funds, trying to "micromanage the war," "tell the generals in the field what to do." Withdrawal would be "surrender," and timetables for withdrawal "told the enemy when we were surrendering."

Without more troops, there would be a "bloodbath." Withholding funding for the war would "endanger our troops in harm's way," "keep them from having the proper protection." It was "playing chicken with the safety of our troops." Congress, not the president, would be to blame for any deaths and injuries to the troops.

The political battle was a framing battle. The framers of the Constitution were being outframed by the president, and the Democrats in Congress felt helpless to stop it.

Here's how it played out in stages: The original justification for going to war in Iraq was to stop Saddam Hussein from using weapons of mass destruction against us. It was a Self-defense narrative. The administration deceived Congress on the evidence for the existence of WMDs. When no WMDs were found, the justification switched. It became a Rescue narrative: the United States was going to rescue the Iraqi people from Saddam Hussein and introduce them to democracy, which they would immediately embrace. The Democrats, who should have known better, allowed themselves to be deceived about the WMDs—or, worse, went along for political reasons—and gave the president authority to fight a war in Iraq. In May 2003, President Bush declared victory in Iraq. Literally, the war was over: our army had defeated Saddam Hussein's army, and an occupation began.

The Rescue narrative no longer applied. As civil war gradually broke out, our troops were caught in the middle, attacked by Iraqis from both sides. The Victims we were to rescue became indistinguishable from the Villains we were to defeat and kill. Our "enemies" became indistinguishable from those we were there to rescue and protect. The "war" was the civil war of Sunnis versus Shiites. The "insurgents" were also Iraqis—Sunnis and Shiites who were fighting each other and didn't want us there. Some al Qaeda members had even been recruited since we arrived. The old Iraqi army had been disbanded. The newly recruited Iraqi army was largely incompetent or corrupt, and couldn't be trusted. Seventy percent of Iraqis wanted us to leave. Sixty percent said it was moral to kill Americans. We came as liberators and stayed as occupiers. It was no longer the United States against a well-defined enemy army where military efforts could win the day and rescue well-defined victims. But the Bush administration had to keep the War frame in order for Bush to be a war president, not an occupation president, and thus keep war powers. He had to keep invoking "al Qaeda," though its influence was small, in order to give the appearance that the troops in Iraq were defending America. He never mentioned the fact of "occupation" and called the resistance to occupation "insurgency" as if it were a unified enemy, which it never was. He referred to it as the "enemy" in order to keep the War frame alive.

On July 2, 2006, I published an article pointing out the consequences of allowing the president to keep the War frame in the public mind, and suggesting that the truth be told: it was an occupation.[2] Those in charge of congressional messaging saw a danger: if you were a parent who had lost a child in the war, or had a child fighting in Iraq, would you want to be told that your son or daughter had died, been maimed, or was risking life and limb for an occupation? War suggested gallantry, worthwhile sacrifice. Occupation did not. The leadership did not want to risk it.

One Democrat did: Jim Webb of Virginia, who campaigned against the "occupation"—he used the word—and won. When he went toe-to-toe with the president after the 2007 State of the Union address, he threw away the script he was given by the party and did brilliantly. There was a chance for him to be a major spokesman. That chance never materialized. The Democrats went back to accepting the War frame, allowing George Bush to continue to be a "war president." The Democrats were content with that because, as the war went badly, his popularity ratings went down. They settled for framing him as incompetent, hoping his unpopularity would rub off on the Republicans in the next election.

The January 2007 hearings cited earlier, where the Congress's constitutional power was upheld by expert testimony, could have been a time when Congress began educating the public on its constitutional mission, that it was the Decider, not the president.

Moreover, the Congress could have ended the occupation just by doing nothing—by refusing to grant any more funds. But it didn't.

Republicans continuously ran nationwide framing campaigns, with spokespeople all over the country putting out their framing. If you accept the other side's framing, you lose. That's what the Democrats did, and they keep doing it. They accepted the president's frame, that their only authority lay in disbursing funds, not in setting the strategic mission. They did not say—and repeat again and again—that Congress sets the strategic mission and the president's job is to carry out that mission, and the president wasn't doing his job. They spoke of the "power of the purse," which just reinforced the president's framing of them as mere bursars. They kept arguing within the president's frames.

The president framed Congress, not himself, as responsible for the safety of the troops. And they went along with that. In part they feared that the public would hold them responsible for future casualties. In addition, progressives, whose moral principles start with empathy and responsibility, felt that since the president in the past had shown that he didn't really care about the welfare of the troops, they had to shoulder his responsibility. The more Congress tried to impose timetables on the president—with plenty of funding to protect the troops—the more the president acted in charge, telling Congress what he expected of them.

Trapped within the president's frame, on May 25, 2007, just before the Memorial Day holiday, a large group of Democrats caved. They took the withdrawal timetable out of their legislation and gave the president what he wanted—at least for three months. Having accepted the War frame, having not challenged the president seriously on the framers' frame, and having accepted the president's framing of them as responsible for the safety of the troops, they gave in. Here's what Representative Louise Slaughter said, defending her vote:

> As such, we had a choice. We could send Mr. Bush the same bill, or allow something to pass that wouldn't be vetoed. And

we elected to let something pass—to let Republicans, if they so choose, fund their own war.

Considering that 90% of the Out of Iraq Caucus was with us in this decision, there must have been at least some reason for it. In fact, there are two in my opinion. With this White House, and with this Republican minority, it is safe to say that a standoff with the Administration would have meant that our troops would be left in harm's way, only now with even less funding to back them up. I don't think that would have been right to do—to make them do even more with even less. The President doesn't seem to care how much our troops suffer. All evidence indicates that he will make them fight if they have needed funding or not.

Secondly, a standoff would have allowed the President to keep using our soldiers as pawns, accusing Democrats of abandoning them while it is really his war that has left them to fend for themselves.[3]

Many prominent Democrats voted against the bill—Nancy Pelosi, Hillary Clinton, Barack Obama. Senator Edward Kennedy did call it "an abdication of responsibility." But there was no recognition of the succession of framing failures that led 90 percent of the Out of Iraq Caucus to vote against their own position.

Democratic leaders like Harry Reid and Rahm Emanuel tried to put a happy face on the result, framing the vote as a step toward an ultimate rejection of the president's Iraq policy. But the larger issue—how to reclaim the framers' framing of the role of Congress—was not discussed. Nor was the question of how to avoid such framing traps in the future.

Why did this happen? There are many reasons. A main one is a continued embrace by progressives of the eighteenth-century view of the mind, and hence a failure to understand framing as deep, conceptual, largely unconscious, and operating by the mechanisms of the brain. What they needed to do instead, starting the day after the election, was to repeat over and over that

Congress is the Decider, to frame themselves as defenders of the Constitution and Bush as a traitor trying to overthrow the Constitution and as heartless in leaving our troops in harm's way in an impossible situation.

But they were afraid that if they took responsibility, the administration would pin the failures of Iraq on the Democrats for pulling out too early. Such an attack could have been headed off: they needed to repeat over and over the truth that we were running an occupation that there was no way of winning and that Iraqis had formed a resistance against us, and that we had gotten caught in the middle of their civil war. The blame for the situation fell on the president.

Again we see a fear of framing—a fear of how the other side will frame your vote and a fear of framing the truth on your own. On wiretapping, the issue is one of liberty. The president wanted to take ours away. The case can be made anywhere in America if you say it loud enough, articulately enough, and often enough. Congress is there to protect our liberty—period. The president is betraying the nation—usurping the power and responsibility of Congress and taking away your right to speak freely in private. Liberty must be defended.

Framing the truth so that it can be understood is not just central to honest, effective politics. It is central to every aspect of human life. It takes knowledge and honesty, skill and courage. It is part of being a full human being. It is not just the province of political leaders; it is the duty of a citizen.

Fear of framing is debilitating, not just to you, but to everyone who depends on you.

Getting Unframed

The June 2, 2007, Democratic presidential debate was on CNN. The host was Wolf Blitzer. Blitzer is a wolf in sheep's clothing—a conservative who poses as a neutral journalist. All through the debate, he asked questions using conservative frames. Some candidates managed to shift the frame to their ground, but all too often they tried to answer and were trapped in a conservative frame. This led up to one of the great moments of recent political television.

BLITZER: I want you to raise your hand if you believe English should be the official language of the United States.

Barack Obama refused to take it anymore. He got up, stepped forward, and said:

OBAMA: This is the kind of question that is designed precisely to divide us. You know, you're right. Everybody is going to learn to speak English if they live in this country. The issue is not whether or not future generations of immigrants are going to learn English. The question is: how can we come up with both a legal, sensible immigration policy? And when we get distracted by those kinds of questions, I think we do a disservice to the American people.

I jumped up and cheered. In my living room.

The first lesson about the use of framing in politics is not to accept the other side's framing. One part of that is politely shifting the frame, as Obama did. "You know, you're right..." But there are situations like presidential debates where the host should not be allowed to get away with conservative bias via framing. Obama did it just right, challenging the question itself. His response could be taken as a mantra: "This is the kind of question that is designed precisely to divide us."

Oil: The Forbidden Word

Fear of framing can keep you from asking the most important of questions. But every now and then forbidden words leak out.

Alan Greenspan, the former head of the Federal Reserve,

writes in his memoir, *The Age of Turbulence: Adventures in a New World*, "I am saddened that it is politically inconvenient to acknowledge what everyone knows: the Iraq war is largely about oil." Greenspan even advised Bush that "taking Saddam Hussein out was essential" to protect oil supplies.

Yes, we suspected it. But Greenspan put the mother of all facts in front of our noses: the United States invaded Iraq for the oil. It may seem obvious, but even after Greenspan came out with it, the very idea is too hot to handle. The Democrats did not seriously follow up, even the most antiwar of them. Yet the question must be asked. Iraq must be looked at through that frame. Frames change meaning.

Think about what it would mean for our troops and for the people of Iraq to seriously entertain the thought that the United States invaded Iraq primarily for oil. A democracy that went along with U.S. policy and guaranteed the oil would have been best. But the main objective was the oil. And we're going to keep troops there because of oil.

Our troops were told, and believed because they trusted their president, that they were in Iraq to protect America, to protect their families, their homes, their friends and neighbors, our democracy. They were there to find WMDs. When it came out that there were none, and it was known, there was no national outcry. The troops were supposedly there to fight al Qaeda. But when we went in, there was no al Qaeda in Iraq. It was known in advance.

Were the troops betrayed? Did those troops fight and die and get maimed and have their marriages break up for oil company profits? Would our troops say, "Okay, we're putting our lives on the line for Hunt Oil and ExxonMobil"? Or would they see it as an utter betrayal of our men and women in uniform and their families, a betrayal of their sacrifices, day after day, month after month, year and year—and for some, forever! Children growing up fatherless or motherless. Men and women without legs or arms or faces—for oil company profits.

And hundreds of thousands of Iraqis killed, more maimed, and millions made refugees. For oil profits.

And what profits they are! Take a look at a study of Iraqi oil contracts by the Global Policy Forum, a consultant to the United Nations Security Council.[4] Or read the editorial page of the *Daily Times* in Pakistan.[5]

The contracts that the Bush administration prepared for the Iraqi government to accept are not just about the distribution of oil among the Sunnis, Shiites, and Kurds. The contracts call for thirty-year exclusive rights for British and American oil companies, rights that cannot be revoked by future Iraqi governments. They are called "production sharing agreements," or PSAs, a legalistic code word. The Iraqi government would technically own the oil, but could not control it; only the companies could do that. ExxonMobil and others would invest in developing the infrastructure for the oil and would get 75 percent of the "cost oil" profits, until they got their investment back. After that, they would own the infrastructure (paid for by oil profits), and then get 20 percent of oil profits after that (twice the usual rate). The profits are estimated to be in the hundreds of billions of dollars. And the Iraqi people would have no democratic control over their own major resource. No other Middle Eastern country has such an arrangement.

Incidentally, polls show the Iraqi people overwhelmingly against "privatization," but "production sharing agreements" were devised so they are technically not "privatization," since the government would still "own" the oil; they just wouldn't control it. The ruse is there so that the government can claim it is not privatizing.

But none of this will work without military—or paramilitary—protection for the oil companies and their employees. That is what could keep the troops, or Blackwater, there indefinitely. The name for this is our "vital interests."

I have been struck by the use of the word "victory" by the right wing, especially by its propaganda arm, Freedom's Watch.

Usually, "victory" is used in reference to a war between countries over territory, where there is a definable enemy. That is not the case in Iraq, where we have for four years had an occupation, not a "war," and there has been no clear enemy, no one to sign a peace treaty with. We have mostly been fighting Iraqis we were supposed to be rescuing. "Victory" makes no sense for such an occupation. And even General Petraeus has said that only a political, not a military, settlement is possible. In what sense can keeping troops there for nine or ten years or longer, as Petraeus has suggested might be necessary, be a "victory"?

What is most frightening is that conservatives may mean what they say, that they may have a concept of "victory" that makes sense to them but not to the rest of the country. If the goal of the invasion and occupation of Iraq has been to guarantee access to Iraqi oil for the next thirty years, then any result guaranteeing oil and oil profits for American oil companies would count as "victory."

Suppose the present killing and chaos were to continue, and we keep our troops there indefinitely, while allowing the oil companies to prosper under our protection. Might that be a "victory"? Or if the Iraqi army and police force were to develop in a few years and keep order there protecting American investments and workers, perhaps that too would be "victory." If the country broke up into three distinct states or autonomous governments, that too might be "victory" as long as oil profits were guaranteed and Americans in the oil industry protected. If so, it wouldn't matter if a Republican president keeps the troops there or a Democratic president does. It is still an oil company "victory."

Indeed, Kurdistan's PSA contract in 2007 with Hunt Oil suggests the latter form of "victory." As Paul Krugman observed in the *New York Times* on September 14, 2007, "the chief executive and president of Hunt Oil is a close political ally of Mr. Bush. More than that, Mr. Hunt is a member of the President's Foreign Intelligence Advisory Board, a key oversight body." Hunt Oil seems to have had the first taste of "victory."

If that is "victory," what is "defeat" and who is being "defeated"? The troops who would have to stay to protect the oil investments would, person by person, suffer defeat—a defeat of the spirit and, for too many, of the body. And most of America would suffer a defeat, especially our taxpayers who have paid a trillion dollars that could have gone for health care for all, for excellent schools and college educations, for rebuilding Louisiana and Mississippi, for shoring up our infrastructure and bridges, and for protecting our environment. Victory for the oil companies, defeat for most of America.

Was Greenspan right? Is this what "victory" could possibly mean? I do not want to even think that the answer might be yes. The thought itself rankles. Is there a hidden frame, one too explosive to mention, even for Democrats? Were all those Democratic proposals for bringing home troops pointless, when tens of thousands of troops and mercenaries would be needed to protect our "vital interests."

Or are our "vital interests" not so vital?

While we are trying to use less oil to slow down global warming, are we sending troops into combat abroad to get more oil?

Fear of framing has been keeping us from the all-too-real discussions.

In a New Enlightenment, such framing discussions, especially in the media, would be normal.

CHAPTER 9

Confronting Stereotypes:
Sons of the Welfare Queen

Ronald Reagan made up a stereotype. He was lying, but it didn't matter. Campaigning in 1976, Reagan referred to a Chicago "Welfare Queen" who had ripped off $150,000 from the government and was driving a "Welfare Cadillac."

"She has eighty names, thirty addresses, twelve Social Security cards and is collecting veteran's benefits on four non-existing deceased husbands. And she is collecting Social Security on her cards. She's got Medicaid, getting food stamps, and she is collecting welfare under each of her names."[1]

The media dutifully tried to find her, but there never was such a person. It didn't matter whether she existed or not. Reagan made her into a symbol of everything that was supposedly wrong with welfare. How? What is it about the human mind and brain that makes this possible?

The answer lies in Prototype Theory, an account of the internal structure of categories, and how members of categories, real or imagined, can stand for categories themselves.[2] The imagined Welfare Queen came to stand for the whole category of welfare recipients.

Human minds create a number of types of prototypes. Any important category has at least three types of prototypes: a typical case, an ideal case, and a nightmare case. The typical case is used to draw conclusions about normal category members. The ideal case is used as a standard of quality, against which others are measured. The nightmare case is the case you want to avoid, or that best dramatizes the perils of a policy.

Then there is the salient exemplar: a well-known case that stands out, perhaps because it is highly publicized. The existence of a salient exemplar changes probability judgments—people judge a typical case as more likely to be like the salient exemplar.

Reagan made the invented Welfare Queen into a salient exemplar, and used the example in discourse as if it were the typical case. The Welfare Queen was a lazy, uppity, sexually immoral black woman who was a cheater living off of the taxpayers, driving a Cadillac paid for by taxpayers, having children just to get money for them. As a salient exemplar, the probability judgment that a welfare recipient would be like that went up, even though the majority of welfare recipients are white and few own vehicles of any kind. When Reagan used the exemplar in context as a typical case, he characterized most welfare recipients that way—just two short steps from one invented example to the whole category.

Of course, what made this possible were strict father framings. First, there was the conservative logic that morality requires discipline, discipline in the market leads to prosperity, and lack of honest prosperity means laziness, lack of discipline, and therefore immorality. The Welfare Queen myth fit the frame—and would not have worked if it had not. The Cadillac symbolized something valuable and upper-class that was not earned but uppity.

Then there is the conservative moral order, the racist and sexist version with whites above nonwhites and men above women. This places white men doubly above black women. Reagan used the Welfare Queen myth while campaigning in the South for racist white votes. What the myth did was to create a new frame in which welfare became an issue of race. To be against welfare was to be against good white taxpayers supporting lazy uppity blacks.

The brain mechanism for this was metonymy.[3] Here's how metonymy works: Within a single frame, there are certain fixed associations. In the frame for a restaurant, the customer is seated at a table and orders a dish. This creates an association between the customer and the table, and the customer and the dish. Neurally activating the idea of the dish or the table can activate the idea of the customer via the association. This allows one waitress to say to another, "Table six wants his check," or "The hamburger with fries left without paying."

In Reagan's created frame where the welfare recipient is a lazy uppity immoral black, and where that fits a social stereotype of blacks, eliminating welfare is giving those unworthy blacks what they deserve—nothing!

From an Old Enlightenment rational point of view, this makes no sense, starting with the self-interest of welfare recipients themselves. There were plenty of poor, white, worthy welfare recipients in the South. Eliminating welfare would obviously go against their interests. Nonetheless, they voted for Reagan and supported his stand against welfare. The reason? They accepted strict father morality and its reasoning: if you're not prosperous, you're not disciplined enough, so you're not moral enough, and you deserve your poverty. They accepted the Moral Order metaphor and the racism that went with it. And Reagan's Welfare Queen metonymy didn't fit them. They may have been on welfare, but they weren't Welfare Queens.

In the summer of 2007, there was a series of horrifying murders of teenagers in Newark, New Jersey. Two of the killers turned out to be "illegal immigrants." Congressman Tom Tancredo of Colorado, a conservative anti-immigrant crusader, flew to Newark. His task was to make the two "illegals" into the sons of the Welfare Queen. The mechanism was to take a salient exemplar—"illegals" who really were dangerous criminals—and treat them as typical case prototypes of immigrant workers. He did this by importuning the parents of the murdered teens to sue the City of Newark for not rounding up, arresting, and sending back its entire "illegal" immigrant population. In Tancredo's mind, the salient exemplars of the dangerous criminal immigrants became typical cases of immigrant workers, and the police should have been cracking down on all of them.

Tancredo called Newark a "sanctuary city"—a conservative phrase evoking a conservative frame, in which officials of moral cities root out and arrest "illegal immigrants" who have broken the law and deserve to be punished, while officials of immoral cities refuse to punish the lawbreakers and immorally offer them "sanctuary."

In the same week, Mitt Romney called New York a "sanctuary city." Here Romney was using metonymy to attack his principal rival, Rudy Giuliani, former mayor of New York, as immoral for not coming down hard on the "illegals" in New York. Giuliani was casting himself in his personal narrative as tough on lawbreakers, and Romney was using the metonymy to undermine Giuliani's image, while currying favor with the anti-immigrant conservative base.

Here we see clearly the difference between the politics of empathy—which supports sanctuary for immigrants, seeing them as honest, hardworking poor people who deserve city services and who should not be terrorized by local officials—and the politics of authority, which sees them mainly as lawbreakers who should be rounded up and punished.

The Welfare Queen is still very much alive.

CHAPTER 10

Aim Above the Bad Apples

To progressives, those in authority are accountable to the public. To conservatives, only underlings are accountable to those in authority. When things go wrong they find a bad apple. We have to aim above the bad apples.

Proverbs often tell us something very deep about a culture. "One bad apple spoils the barrel" evokes a folksy scene, back in the era of the family farm and general store, when apples were kept in a barrel. An apple can rot, and rot can spread from apple to apple. If nothing is done, that one apple can spoil the whole barrel, which would be big loss—lots of apples to eat or sell. The moral about apples is simple: get rid of the bad apple and the barrel will be saved. There was nothing wrong with the rest of the apples in the barrel, or with the idea of keeping apples in a barrel. It was just that one bad apple that was to blame.

The metaphors here are ones we've discussed. Morality is Purity; Immorality is Rottenness. And immorality is a contagion that can spread, infecting everyone in its wake.

We understand the proverb in terms of these metaphors. It is about people, not apples. The barrel is a container—metaphorically, an organization containing people. Like the good apples in the barrel, the people in the organization are good—all moral people. One or a few immoral people in an otherwise fine and upstanding organization can make others go bad—or look bad—and give the whole organization a bad name. All you have to do is find the bad apples in the organization and get rid of them. The organization is redeemed. There never was anything wrong with it. The problem was the bad apples.

We call this the Bad Apple frame. It is used all the time in politics. Its use goes like this: There is a systematic practice in an organization that is either illegal, immoral, or at least under-handed. If the practice were publicly recognized, it would greatly harm the reputation of the organization and threaten the careers of high-level members of the organization. There are two related uses of the Bad Apple frame:

1. To protect the organization and its mode of operation. The Bad Apple goes; the organization is redeemed and keeps oper-ating as before.
2. To find a target in the organization to blame so that everyone else in the organization escapes blame.

Conservative Republicans use the Bad Apple frame all the time. Take Abu Ghraib. Torture was Bush administration policy. The Justice Department knew about it and drew up supporting documents, the Defense Department gave orders, language was created—"extreme rendition"—to describe it, there was system-atic training for it, some of it was knowingly outsourced to pri-vate companies or other governments, and the commander in chief was responsible. It was part of the system of running the military operations in Afghanistan and Iraq.

But when Abu Ghraib came to light, the Bush administration used the Bad Apple defense, and found the lowest people on the totem pole to blame and prosecute.

Or take the death of Pat Tillman, who was shot by a mem-ber of his own unit three times in the front of the head. Tillman was a famous football star who had given up a lucrative foot-ball contract to join the Special Forces fighting in Afghanistan after 9/11. During his service, he served a tour of duty in Iraq, became disillusioned with the Iraq War and the Bush administration's war policy, and had begun to make his opinions known. He was sent back to Afghanistan. His death was first reported to be at the enemy's hands, and he was posthumously called a hero and awarded military honors as part of a cover-up. After five weeks, the army changed its story, saying that he was "accidentally" killed in a friendly-fire incident. In an unusual move, all his clothes and possible evidence in the case had been destroyed. An autopsy report later turned up that said he had been shot three times from close range in the front of the head. There is a suspicion that he was assassinated. Apparently he had contacted people in the antiwar movement, and it has been claimed that he would have become an antiwar figure had he returned home.

The Pentagon conducted its own investigation and declared that the death was accidental due to friendly fire, but that it should not have been covered up. The Bad Apple found was retired lieutenant general Philip R. Kensinger Jr., who said at the trial seventy times that he couldn't remember what had happened. His punishment was losing a star—from three to two, an $8,000-a-year pension loss. End of investigation.

Then there is Scooter Libby. He was the designated Bad Apple for the systematic lying and distortion of evidence by the Bush administration in justifying its invasion of Iraq. All the prosecutor could pin on him was lying under oath about revealing Valerie Plame's identity. President Bush commuted his sentence, so he would not have to spend time in jail. He had protected the administration.

Or take Enron. Enron bilked the State of California for billions of dollars in schemes with extraordinary names. In "Death Star," Enron would overschedule its expected power transmissions to create the illusion that the state's grid would be overloaded, then receive state payment for "relieving" the congestion. The beauty of this con, the company's memos noted, is that "Enron gets paid for moving energy to relieve congestion without actually moving any energy or relieving any congestion." It's the sort of protection deal that would make Tony Soprano proud.

The "Fat Boy" scam (a.k.a. "Inc-ing") also involved over-scheduling power transmission—for example, to a company subsidiary that didn't really need all of it. Then Enron would sell the "excess" power to the state at a premium.

"Ricochet," also called "megawatt laundering" (by analogy to money laundering), was the power equivalent of a real estate land flip: buy in-state power cheaply, flip it out of state to an intermediary, then resell it to California at a highly inflated "imported" price.

Similar schemes were apparently used throughout Enron and the energy transfer industry. The practice was ignored by FERC (the Federal Energy Regulatory Commission), which had former energy company employees appointed to do the "regulating." The Bush administration and the Republican Congress refused to investigate. Dick Cheney blamed the victim, California, of "using too much energy." The California losses were used in the Republican campaign to recall Democratic governor Gray Davis and elect Republican Arnold Schwarzenegger.

These practices came to light when Enron collapsed financially because of many illegal practices. The Bad Apples were Jeffrey Skilling and Ken Lay. Enron's collapse cost 20,000 people their jobs and many lost their life savings.

Public sympathy went to Enron employees who lost the money they had invested in the company. Enron's dirty business—carried on by many who lost their retirement funds—was forgotten. The energy transfer industry is intact. The Bad Apples are gone.

Why does the Bad Apple frame work? Because in the Hero-Villain narrative, the Villain is a person, not a system, an institution, or an ideology. You can convict a person of a crime, but not an ideology or a system of operation. It is easier to imagine a person than a system. The way our brains function favors the use of the Bad Apple frame.

Is it possible to change this? Is it possible to discuss systemic, ideological, or institutional villains overtly in ways people understand?

The first step is to recognize the use of the Bad Apple frame when we see it. The next step is to use a frame that reveals the truth. Enron's bilking of California with the help of Bush appointees on FERC who turned the other way was an instance of privateering.

Part of a New Enlightenment would be a public recognition of how such framing works. The use of the Bad Apple frame would not only be news, but the question would then arise: what people or what system is really to blame?

CHAPTER 11

Cognitive Policy

It is time to give a name to a practice that conservatives have engaged in for the past three decades but progressives have not. The practice is "cognitive policy." A cognitive policy is the policy of getting an idea into normal public discourse, which requires creating a change in the brains of millions of people.

Conservatives have spent huge sums to enact cognitive policies, to introduce as normal ideas like private medical and retirement accounts (to replace Medicare and social security), school vouchers (to replace public schools), the flat tax (to replace the progressive income tax), big government (to attack social programs), private contractors (to replace government responsibilities for protection and empowerment), faith-based solutions (to erase the separation of church and state), and on and on. Conservatives conduct such cognitive policy making every day of every year. It is explicit, well organized, and well funded. Its aim is to change brains in a conservative direction. And it has been working. Progressives rarely conduct cognitive policy making.

Policy for progressives is usually material, specific proposals to remedy market failures for some demographic group. The major recent exception has been Al Gore's movie and book, *An Inconvenient Truth*, which set out to bring into public discourse—and the public brain—the idea of the reality of global warming. But this was not a public policy brought up through legislation or through the usual policy think tanks. Instead, it came out of Hollywood. Progressive policy think tanks rarely construct and carry out explicit cognitive policies—with the major exception of Rockridge Institute, whose job is to do so explicitly.

Cognitive policy is a framing campaign that precedes specific material policies. It introduces the deep frames, the moral frames, that come first. It is a major mistake to think that framing is just there to sell preexisting policies. All material policies are based, explicitly or implicitly, on prior morally-based frames.

The first justification of any policy, often unconscious and implicit, is its moral correctness—from either a strict or nurturant moral perspective, depending on who is offering the policy. It operates in a circle: framing precedes policy. And because of this, a material policy can create a cognitive policy—a way of framing reality to reveal a deep truth and change brains to recognize that truth.

I want to demonstrate this by going through a complex example of a specific policy proposal for reducing carbon emissions. It has been called "Sky Trust." It is a proposal competing with various cap-and-trade and carbon tax proposals, and it is, at this writing, not well known. Its originator is Peter Barnes, the founder of Working Assets and author of *Capitalism 3.0*.

Sky Trust begins with the presupposed moral basis of the problem, and the consequences of taking it seriously: America has a moral obligation to reduce its carbon emissions 80 percent by 2050, that is, by 80 percent in forty years.

Given that moral obligation, here are some desirable features of any such plan:

- Any solution, to be workable, has to really accomplish the reductions. That is, it must work. It should result in air that is 80 percent cleaner in the United States at least.
- If it is to work, it must be administratively simple. No huge bureaucracy. No high administrative costs. No piles of paperwork. No imposition of administration on businesses all over the country. No army of inspectors.

- If it is to work, it must be transparent and easy to verify. That is, there should be little or no chance of cheating or lack of oversight.
- It should be gradual but steady, imposing as little as possible in the way of a dramatic shift for business, without changing too little.
- It should be predictable. Businesses should know what to expect over forty years so they can make long-term plans.
- For moral reasons, it should be economically progressive. Most of the costs should fall on those who can most easily bear them.
- It should be politically popular, something most people want—or at least prefer to the alternatives. It should be unifying, something the whole country can get behind.
- It should maximize the use of market principles. It should avoid central planning of the economy.
- It should encourage entrepreneurship. It should lead to the development of renewable energy that is as economical as possible, mostly through private investment. It should spur creativity and the use of American know-how.
- It should minimize or eliminate politics. Ideally, no money should flow through the federal government, so as to minimize or eliminate the effects of lobbying by special interests of any kind.
- It should create as many jobs as possible in the United States.

The moral basis of these desired features should be clear: Maximize protection for both ordinary people and business. Minimize harm. Minimize the need for obedience to authority. Stimulate creativity and opportunity. Minimize disruption of everyday life and business.

These are moral desiderata that precede policy. In addition, there is a truth that has finally been widely accepted. Because it contributes to global warming, carbon-based energy is harmful to the world, and dirties our air as well, harming people and wildlife.

This is where Sky Trust begins. It starts with two background frames. The first concerns firms that market and distribute carbon-based fuels (oil, coal, and gas). Through their lobbying, carbon-based energy companies (oil, coal, and gas companies) have kept clean and renewable energy sources from being developed. They have acted like drug pushers, inducing companies all over America to invest in plants that use their fuel and therefore dirty our air. Such companies are the point of entry of harmful pollutants into our economy. There are relatively few major distribution points for such harmful fuels—only about a thousand. They are easy to find and monitor.

The second frame is about the atmosphere as property. The air is valuable. The people of the United States own the air over the United States. Not the government, the people. A large number of companies have up till now been dumping their pollutants into our air, without any dumping fees being paid to those who own it. Those companies have been free riders. They have not been paying the full cost of doing business. Instead of cleaning up their pollutants, they have passed the costs on to others in the form of dirty air, asthma and other respiratory diseases, and global warming. The owners of the air have certain property rights: to have their air as clean as possible, and to be paid dumping fees for pollution dumped into it.

These two frames constitute the cognitive policy explicit in Sky Trust. Sky Trust is fundamentally about getting these ideas into public consciousness and public discourse. The material policy in Sky Trust is there to do two jobs: to reduce carbon dioxide emissions effectively in a way that wins public support, and to get into the public mind the idea that we all own the air, that the air is valuable—much more valuable when clean than when polluted.

The material aspect of Sky Trust has two parts: the cap and a dividend.

First, the cap is placed on carbon-based fuel distributors at

their distribution points, where the fuel enters the economy.
Here's how the cap works:

- Each year, fuel distribution companies engage in an auction
to buy pollution permits—permits to sell a certain amount
of polluting fuel. The auction is done by computer, with electronic transfers of permits and funds.
- The cap begins with permits for the amount of fuel sold in the
first year; the number of permits available in the country is
reduced 2 percent per year for forty years.
- Each distributor can sell only the amount of fuel that it has
permits for. The amount sold can be easily monitored.
- As the number of permits decreases, they become more valuable and cost more to buy.
- The more fuel a company wants to sell, the more permits it
will have to buy.
- Fuel companies will thus have an incentive to invest in renewable and clean sources of energy.
- The price of carbon-based fuels will rise, providing an incentive for other companies to invest in renewable, clean sources
of energy.
- Administrative costs are low: monitoring costs for about a
thousand sites, accounting and electronic transfer costs.

The cap proposal is independent of the dividend proposal and
can be carried out even if the dividend proposal is not. A Sky
Trust is set up with each U.S. citizen owning one equal and non-
negotiable share, as a birthright. Here's how it works:

- The money from the sale of carbon permits will go into the
Sky Trust—a trust like other trusts.
- The money will be collected in the form of electronic bank
transfers monitored via computers.
- Each U.S. citizen will get an equal share of this money—a
dividend for the use of his or her share of the air. The money

could be considerable, perhaps more than a thousand dollars per person per year at the start, and rising thereafter.

- The money will be electronically transferred into the bank or credit card accounts of each citizen, month by month, so that it helps pay their bills.
- The money can be used for anything at all. In particular, it will help offset rising energy costs.
- The money will be spent throughout the economy and provide an economic stimulus, creating jobs.
- The government will never touch the money directly, and it will be immune from political uses and the effects of lobbying by special interests.

That is the proposal. It includes a cognitive policy based on prior frames, and here you can see clearly just what the frames are. But that is not all. The policy, if carried out, will create a new frame in the minds of many Americans: the Common Wealth frame, which generalizes from the air to other sources of common wealth—things owned by all Americans, and in which they deserve a share. It can be extended widely, too. Take the airwaves, for example. They are extremely valuable, and right now the rights to their use have been just given away to media companies that make huge profits on them. That is our property, given away to private investors in media companies. Should there be an Airwave Trust, and an auction for the right to use the airwaves? And what about rivers and oceans? And if we own the air, the rivers, and the oceans, and share in their use value, shouldn't we preserve them and keep them clean for our heirs as well?

This is not an endorsement of the Sky Trust policy. I just want to make a point about the political mind: that policies are realizations of prior frames, many of them embodying moral principles, and that the establishment of a policy may result in a new way of seeing the world. And above all, I want to headline the importance of cognitive policy.

When Mitt Romney was asked about "the commons," he said that it sounded to him like communism. But Sky Trust, which makes the atmosphere a commons, is a form of capitalism, indeed, a form of capitalism so extreme that it makes capitalists out of everyone—even newborn children.

The most famous article on the concept of the commons is Garrett Hardin's "The Tragedy of the Commons."[1] Hardin argues that any commons—something owned by everyone and available for everyone's use—will eventually be destroyed through overuse, just as the British common lands, which were for grazing livestock, were eventually privatized and developed.

Barnes's Sky Trust proposal is a counterexample that proves Hardin wrong. The "use" is the dumping of pollution. Its value is first the cleanliness of the air, and then the monetary returns from the auction of pollution permits. The use is capped in the Sky Trust proposal, with the cap lowered every year for forty years. Both of the values increase every year.

There are two morals here. First: you can't separate policies from the frames that constitute the ideas the policies are based on. Because the policies presuppose the frames, even serious discussion of them can activate those frames in the brains of the public. Second: cognitive policy is every bit as important as material policy.

A final point: there are sensible variations on the Sky Trust. For example, some proportion of the income could be used for an investment trust, to invest in sustainable energy. Another variation would allow the public to invest for profit in the Sustainable Energy Trust, with pollution permit income functioning as a subsidy. Or the investment trust could turn any profits back to Sky Trust to be distributed to the owners of the air—everyone.

But the essence of Sky Trust is about changing brains: allowing the public to conceptualize their common wealth—the air, the airwaves, the rivers, the nature preserves—as real wealth, as something very valuable and worth upgrading and preserving. Sky Trust would do this by literally making it so. It is a material policy that would also carry out a far-reaching cognitive policy.

CHAPTER 12

Contested Concepts Everywhere

We have been discussing the two very different modes of moral and political thought dividing America. Strict and nurturant modes of thought are everywhere, and almost always unconscious. The result is a lack of communication about real problems and virtually no discussion of the real divide in American political life.

One of the most serious places where the divide occurs but is hidden is in our most important ideas: freedom, fairness, equality, opportunity, security, accountability. It turns out that they mean very different things—sometimes opposite things—to progressives and conservatives. Yet in public discourse, the difference is often difficult or impossible to see.

Why the difference in meaning? Why is it often hard to see? And why should this happen?

To make sense of it, we will have to go back over half a century and take a little detour through the history of cognitive science.

In London, on March, 12, 1956, there was meeting of the Aristotelian Society. A philosophical war was on in England. Followers of Bertrand Russell's formal logic approach to philosophy assumed that concepts were defined as in logic, by a list of necessary and sufficient conditions, and that meaning was based on truth in the world.

Ludwig Wittgenstein had challenged Russell's view, arguing that meaning is a matter of use, that concepts are based on "family resemblances" and are not fixed but can expand, just as the concept of number has expanded over the millennia from integers to fractions to real numbers to complex numbers to transfinite numbers.

J. L. Austin had argued that communication matters for meaning, and had studied the role of speech acts like questions and orders, which can be neither true nor false. Meanings, he argued, must be enlarged beyond truth and beyond Russellian logic.

Into this fray came Walter Bryce Gallie, then a young Cambridge political scientist, who delivered a fateful paper called "Essentially Contested Concepts."[1] He showed that concepts like "democracy" and "art" are meaningful, but will never have fixed meanings. They have agreed-upon central cases. But because the central cases have a complex structure and involve values, and because different people have different values, those values will necessarily extend the concepts in different directions. As a result, people will always be contesting the meanings of "democracy" and "art" because their values will always be different. The conclusion: the meanings of such concepts cannot be absolutely fixed.

It was, of course, inevitable that "essentially contested concept" would itself become contested. Scholars like H. L. A. Hart, John Rawls, Stephen Lukes, and Ronald Dworkin, all with agendas in philosophy and law requiring that concepts be fixed, contested Gallie's account.[2] They took the agreed-upon central case as the real concept and claimed the contestations as mere "instantiations" or "conceptualizations" of the concept—whatever that was to mean.

From a neural point of view, that makes no sense. Concepts don't exist in some abstract philosophical universe, where they can somehow be distinguished from "conceptions" or "instantiations." Each person has a concept that makes sense to him or her. That concept is instantiated in the synapses of the brain. No brains, no concepts.

For that person, her concept of freedom is *the* concept of freedom. She uses it to think with. When a hard-core conservative uses the word "liberty" and applies it to "economic liberty" and "religious liberty," he has in mind the conservative version of the word's meaning. And when a progressive uses the same word—that the freedom to marry is a matter of a gay person's "liberty"—he has in mind a progressive version of the concept's meaning.

There is, however, an interesting question to be asked from a cognitive science perspective: are instantiations in the brain of contested concepts structured so as to distinguish the agreed-upon core from the entire contested version? We will see that this is a real possibility, but it does not mean that the uncontested core is the concept. This cannot be discussed in the abstract without some details.

In 1992, Alan Schwartz, now a professor in medical decision-making at the University of Illinois at Chicago Circle, was Berkeley's first cognitive science major, double-majoring in women's studies. For his thesis, he looked at the concept of feminism from the perspective of cognitive science. Feminism is a hotly contested concept within the feminist community itself, with versions like liberal feminism, radical feminism, Marxist feminism, biocultural feminism, ecofeminism, woman of color feminism, and lesbian feminism.[3]

Schwartz, following Gallie, found that there was a common core: a collection of gender roles giving men advantage in society over women, a view that those gender roles are unfair, and a commitment to changing those roles. But this common core was so underspecified that, by itself, it didn't tell one much. There were different versions of what the gender roles should be changed to, different reasons for changing them, and different methods to be used. In each case, the different versions of feminism could be predicted from the central core and other value systems: liberalism, Marxism, and so on—as Gallie suggested. To each feminist activist, the word "feminism" was not, however, the underspecified core, but the rich version to which she subscribed.

Schwartz had substantiated Gallie's analysis, and contributed to a deep understanding of feminism in the process.

In January 2005, I watched George W. Bush's second inaugural address, where he used the words "freedom," "free," and "liberty" forty-nine times in twenty minutes. Half of the uses were common-core uses and the other half were radical conservative uses that made no sense to progressives. Freedom is an obvious candidate for an essentially contested concept, so I took up the challenge of doing a cognitive analysis in detail.

Here's what I found: There is an uncontested core of the concept of freedom, which everyone seems to accept. Conservatives tend to have strict moral values; progressives, nurturant moral values. If you take these two contested moral values and bind each to the uncontested core of freedom, you get exactly the two contested versions of freedom—one progressive and one conservative.

But it wasn't an easy analysis. The data to be accounted for were so massive that it took a book to go through it—*Whose Freedom?* I'll give you the flavor of it briefly, since it's an important component of what the cognitive and brain sciences can contribute to a New Enlightenment.

Freedom

The most basic idea of freedom is freedom of motion. Nothing bothers a child so much as being kept from moving his or her body. There are three fundamental types of movement: locomotion, movement from one place to another; movement of the arms to grasp objects; and movement of the body to perform actions. In all cases, preventing desired movement causes negative emotion, from infancy on.

The system of primary metaphor applies to movement. Achieving a Purpose is metaphorically conceptualized in two ways: reaching a desired destination (I reached my goal) and getting a desired object (the job just fell into my lap). Both are primary metaphors, apparently universal and learned early. Via these metaphors, Freedom of Action to Achieve a Purpose is Freedom of Motion to a Destination. Correspondingly, a restraint on freedom of action is metaphorically a restraint on freedom of motion. We see this in metaphorical expressions for restraints on freedom of action like being enslaved, in chains, in jail, tied up, handcuffed, tied down, tied to a ball and chain, held back, kept down, burdened, and so on.

Restraining freedom of motion and freedom of action both activate negative emotions. Thus, taking away someone's freedom is seen as immoral. You may be free to walk down the street, but not free to knock down somebody else and tie him up.

Similarly, Aids to Freedom of Action are understood metaphorically in terms of Aids to Freedom of Movement. This is positive freedom, "freedom to." Thus you can be given a helping hand, given a start, empowered, and so on. Metaphorically, Failing is Falling, and so among the aids to freedom of movement are things that help you if you fall, for example, safety nets, cushions, and so on. In short, we reason, imagine, and talk about freedom of action in terms of the logic and language of freedom of motion. Thus the general conception of freedom of action is grounded in the physical experience of freedom of movement via primary metaphor—that is, neural metaphor, circuitry that self-organizes on the basis of correlations in everyday experience.

Political freedom builds on this notion of freedom of action. Political freedom concerns the role of government in providing for both positive and negative freedom—both freedom from and freedom to.

On the negative freedom (freedom from) side, government has a central role in providing for Protection—civil order and civil liberties, so you can go about your business without fear and be protected from military invasion, and from epidemics, the harmful effects of natural disasters, economic catastrophe, harm from unscrupulous or irresponsible businesses, and so on.

On the positive freedom (freedom to) side, government provides Empowerment—basic infrastructure that empowers people to achieve their goals: elections, education, roads, communications, energy supply, water supply, public buildings, libraries, banking, markets and the stock market, the court system, and so on. Without these, American business and most of modern American life would be impossible.

Those are just the basics of political freedom. There are further progressive and conservative extensions of basic political freedom—in different and incompatible directions. But the heart of our understanding of freedom is freedom of movement, and the heart of political freedom is for a government to maximize freedom of movement and action, both freedom from and freedom to. What that means and how it is to be done is where the contestation comes in.

We can now see how strict and nurturant worldviews naturally extend the concept of freedom in different directions. Consider the "free" market. To a radical conservative, who functions with a general conservative worldview in all issue areas, the market functions according to strict father principles: it rewards discipline and playing by market rules, namely maximizing your profit; and it punishes lack of discipline or not playing by market rules, not trying, or being unable, to maximize profit. Government interferes with the free market, with "economic freedom," in the following ways: Regulation can interfere with profit and with the "free" use of property. Taxation takes away a significant portion of profit, hence taking away incentive and lessening discipline. Unions, benefits, and worker safety rules take away profit. And lawsuits for harm to the public threaten profit and profit-making practices. This worldview doesn't focus on the empowering aspect of government.

Progressives see regulation as working for freedom from harm—protecting the public from harm by irresponsible or immoral businesses. They see fair taxation as a form of empowerment by government (freedom to), where those who make more use of government empowerment should pay more back to maintain it for all. Worker safety rules protect working people from harmful work practices (freedom from), and unions create a fairer labor market (freedom to).

Fairness requires that people who work for a living should earn a living, and that workers who produce more should get a fair share of the profits from increased productivity (freedom to). Lawsuits are seen as the public's last line of defense against unscrupulous or irresponsible corporations (freedom from).

For progressives, their views follow directly from empathy with the public at large. For conservatives, their views follow directly from strict father morality applied to the market. It is sometimes said that conservatives are more concerned with freedom than are progressives. That is not true. Conservatives are just more vocal and articulate. As FDR said, freedom from want and freedom from fear are both freedom issues. It is the job of government to help maximize freedom for all its citizens. But conservatives want it to maximize conservative freedom and progressives want it to maximize progressive freedom.

Disagreement Everywhere

You can't get away from contested concepts. There will always be disagreement about the meanings of our most important moral and political ideas.

Take responsibility. Conservative thinking stresses individual responsibility—no matter what. Progressive thinking stresses interdependency and social responsibility, alongside individual responsibility.

Take equality. Conservative thinking requires competition for rewards and a hierarchy of "merit." For competition to be meaningful, rewards must be kept or the incentive to compete will be taken away and the motivation to be disciplined will be lost. Merit can be based on something either inherent (you were born with it), or acquired through discipline, or both. If you succeed through family wealth or social connections, that's okay because you were born with it. What you have, you should be able to keep, and things like being born with wealth, in the upper classes, and with social connections should not count in "equality of opportunity." If you succeed on the basis of inherited wealth or social capital, your success is still deserved. The stereotypical case, though, is to succeed through discipline and to earn success—even though the stereotype may not apply all that widely. Equality in general conservatism then can only mean equality of "opportunity," not outcome.

What about concentrations of great wealth—which are also concentrations of great political power? As long as the wealth is "merited"—say, not stolen or embezzled or obtained in a way that can be proven to be illegal—the concentration of wealth and the concentration of power that goes with it is fine, no matter how great.

Progressives begin with empathy for others. That means principles like equal pay for equal work. If you work for a living you should earn a living. Inherited wealth and social advantage do count in the concept of "equality of opportunity" and do not count as part of "merit." Political equality means equally shared power; there is no ability to force political "obedience." Great concentrations of wealth are not just fine, because great wealth controls access to limited resources (such as nice places to live, great private universities), and access to political leaders results in unequal political power, which violates political equality.

Take fairness. Fairness is fundamentally about equality of distribution, even in capuchin monkeys! The following experiment was performed at Yerkes National Laboratory in Atlanta.[4] Pairs of capuchins were trained side by side to do the same task for the same reward (a piece of cucumber). Then one, but not the other, got a better reward (a grape). The monkeys who got only the cucumber rebelled. They often refused to participate in the experiment any longer, refused to eat the cucumbers, and in some cases hurled the cucumbers back at human researchers.

We have already seen predicted differences in the notion of equality. Those differences will carry over to equality of distribution. Distribution is not always about food quality or quantity. It is complicated. Take the distribution of student places in a major public university. What should it be based on?

In the Proposition 209 debate in California, conservatives framed their argument as one of fairness in competition, where admission was a reward in the competition for high grades and test scores. Fairness, they argued, should be based on those indicators of "merit" alone.

What should not count as unfairness according to the conservative argument: social, cultural, and financial capital; being able to go to good schools previously; knowing how to take tests; having parents committed to your education; coming from a culture that values education; coming from a community that has all the trained professionals it needs.

Progressives had the opposite view of fairness: all of the above disparities created social unfairness. Grades and test scores are not in themselves a fair measure of a person's talent. In addition, progressives had a different way of understanding the mission of the university. It includes a moral mission: to provide trained professionals for all the state's communities, many of them racial and ethnic communities.

Progressives saw fairness in social as well as individual terms. Race and ethnicity were seen as statistical indicators of social, cultural, and financial capital—factors providing an unfair disadvantage, statistically not individually, on the basis of race and ethnicity. In addition, taking race and ethnicity into account were seen as central to a state university's moral mission of providing trained professionals to underserved communities. The lack of trained professionals was seen as unfair to those communities.

The progressives did a terrible job of framing their version of fairness. The conservatives did a superb job of framing theirs. The conservatives won.

Accountability

One of the most interesting examples is the concept of accountability. To progressives, it means accountability to the public on the part of those in charge. To conservatives, it is completely different. Those in charge are moral authorities. They hold their underlings accountable to them! In the Abu Ghraib scandal, the lowest-ranking people involved were punished. Conservatives did not see that those who gave the orders to torture, such as the secretary of defense, should be held accountable for the torture. Instead, it was the lowest underlings who were responsible. Progressives, naturally, took the opposite view.

In No Child Left Behind, the president cut off funding he had promised to improve schools. Progressives thought that he should be held accountable for school failure, because he cut off funding. But the president, as a conservative, held the lowest possible people under him accountable for their test scores—the schools, the teachers, and the students. Social, cultural, and class factors were not to count. You second-graders—you are accountable!

Authority is another interesting example. In conservative thinking, authority is a given and it is to be obeyed. Progressive thought has a very different view. Authority and respect have to be earned. A nurturant parent has to really be empathetic and responsible to be respected, trusted, and accepted as an authority. In progressive thought, an authority has to respect and be responsible to those he is responsible for. He or she has to be able to give good reasons for decisions that affect others, and is expected to take them into important deliberations. That doesn't mean a progressive authority doesn't make real decisions. It's just that the whole way of thinking about authority—and hierarchies of authority—is different.

By now, you should get the general idea. The entire Old Enlightenment set of ideas is essentially contested. Every such concept has a common core that is too abstract to be of use. In each case, the common core is extended (unconsciously) by an application of either the conservative or progressive moral worldview. But for activist conservatives and progressives, those "extensions" *are* the concepts—the only ones that make sense.

There is a neurobiological reason. Each "extension" from the common core is made in an individual brain by neural binding, which may be long- or short-term. Someone who identifies with either a strict or nurturant moral worldview will acquire long-term bindings to the core, and in the brain, the part that is core and the part that is worldview form an indistinguishable whole, just as my old red VW, despite its shape and color being computed in different parts of the brain, forms a single image to me. From the brain's perspective, progressive freedom is a different concept from conservative freedom.

Consider this example: Paul Starr, defending liberalism in *Freedom's Power*, writes, "At the heart of the liberal project is what it has always been: to create a free, fair, and prosperous society."[5] As we have seen, "free" and "fair" are contested as discussed above. "Prosperous" for conservatives refers to the country as a whole, not counting the grossly unequal distribution of wealth. Stock market prices, or GDP, are commonly taken as indicators of overall wealth, with most of it concentrated right at the top. Now let us consider this more closely from the perspective of the brain. First, the brain is structured so that many frames and metaphors have general content: they are underspecified and can apply to many kinds of special cases. We saw this in our discussion earlier of the Governing Institution as Family metaphor, which eliminates the family-level details about strict and nurturant families, leaving the conservative and progressive worldviews.

Second, neural binding permits such general-level worldviews to be "bound" to the uncontested cores of freedom, fairness, and prosperity, to yield two opposite and contested versions of each of these foundational ideas. The result of the neural binding is a neural circuit with its own integrity, functioning as a whole: when George W. Bush—or any extreme conservative—speaks of freedom, he means something like the conservative version, as if it were the only legitimate version. That is not the "prosperity" that progressives are talking about. It is not just a matter of words. What matters are the ideas and values behind the words—the conservative and progressive value systems—and all the other frames involved. They are different for conservative and progressive modes of thought.

Causation

One of the most profound differences between strict and nurturant modes of thought is in the area of causation. In the strict father model, there is individual responsibility and direct action operating: the father gives a directive, the child is expected to carry it out, and if not, the father punishes. Causation is direct and individual.

In the nurturant parent model, causation is sometimes direct and individual, but just as often it is systemic. Nurturance involves developing attachment, empathizing with and forming connections to others. The moral absolutes are Help, Don't Harm, and Do Unto Others. These are not specific direct actions. They involve understanding an overall social and interpersonal context, with lots of empathy. You have to function as part of a social and interpersonal system less governed by specific rules and more "felt out" in terms of how you relate to others and sense their needs and requirements. You learn systemic, as well as direct, causation.

When one mode of thought or the other is being used in reason, the systemic-versus-direct causation difference often appears—not as an absolute, but as a tendency. For example, what are the causes of crime? The conservative answer most typically given is: Bad people. Lock 'em up and throw away the key. This is direct causation. The progressive answer is usually something like: A culture of poverty, discrimination, and lack of education. This is systemic causation.

This difference shows up in many places. Take global warming, which is a star example of systemic causation. Many conservatives didn't believe the evidence and still don't. Part of the genius of Al Gore's movie, *An Inconvenient Truth*, was the graph linking the rise in the earth's temperature directly to the rise in carbon dioxide in the atmosphere. Now, you can't literally put a thermometer down on the earth and take its temperature. The earth's temperature is a metaphoric entity arrived at via statistical methods. The same with the carbon dioxide concentration. Statistics allow for the construction of a scientifically meaningful measure of each, which is reflected in the graph. The graph turns systemic causation into direct causation, making the argument accessible to conservative thinkers.

It happens that direct causation thinking is far more widespread than systemic causation thinking. Direct causation occurs normally in the languages of the world. Causation is based on the primary metaphor that Causes are Forces. The direct use of force is easily understood. Indirect, diffuse force is harder to understand. This puts progressives at a disadvantage.

A New Enlightenment cannot simply assume that there is one kind of causation for everyone. It will have to distinguish systemic and direct causation. There is no getting around it.

The brain has the capacity to turn any important concept into contested versions when there are deep value differences at stake. A New Enlightenment will have to recognize and cope with such realities of the brain and the mind. A deep rationality will require a metadiscourse—a mode of thinking and talking about the way minds really work. The old tradition in political theory and intellectual history will need to be augmented to go beyond the naïve use of the grand words—Freedom, Equality, Fairness, Democracy, Opportunity, and the rest—as if they were univocal, as if they had one clear and uncontested meaning. A New Enlightenment must go deeper than the debates based on normal conscious understanding. What is normally unconscious must be made conscious. And political debate needs to be informed by the sciences of the brain and the mind, as those sciences develop.

PART III

THE TECHNICAL IS
THE POLITICAL

The Politics of Academic Thought

The Old Enlightenment view of reason is alive and well in a great many technical disciplines, especially in the social sciences. The result is that social scientists make use of unconscious real reason—including frames, conceptual metaphors, and prototypes—but don't notice and think they are being literal and logical. Or they may think that Old Enlightenment reason is the way people really reason, and thus make mistakes.

If this were only an academic matter, I wouldn't write with such urgency. But it affects every aspect of our political life—from foreign policy to economic policy to educational policy. Experts, perhaps more than anyone else, assume that they and their policies are rational, that they are being logical and unemotional, that their theories directly fit reality, and that their ideas are universally applicable because they directly fit reality. And if they use mathematical models, they tend to assume that reality really is structured by their mathematics.

We begin this section with some additional research areas in the cognitive and brain sciences, to give a sense of the politically important research in those fields and how it is about to explode onto the national scene. Then we move on to the metaphorical structure of the rational actor model, a mathematical structure that supposedly characterizes rational action itself. It is widely used in economics and international relations, and is being extended to biology. As part of the critique of the rational actor model, we take up prospect theory, how it applies to economics and foreign policy, and how it reveals ways that real human reason fails to fit "rational action." After that, we discuss the inadequacy of the metaphor of competition in evolution and its application in evolutionary psychology. That metaphor for evolution, discounted by Darwin himself, has been used to shore up the idea that interest-based rationality is the natural human state.

Finally, we move to linguistics, where an Old Enlightenment–based theory hid from view the reality of frames, prototypes, metaphors, and contested concepts, and that is being replaced by a brain-based neural theory of language that explains the phenomena we have observed throughout this book. Neo-Enlightenment linguistics in the tradition of Noam Chomsky had hidden the vital role of language in contemporary politics.

In each case, the cognitive and brain sciences show shortcomings, significant ones, in social science expertise—shortcomings on which major political decisions may depend. The twenty-first-century mind requires rethinking a great deal of social science research. This is anything but a mere academic exercise, since the most influential of progressive policymakers have been trained in the social sciences at elite universities. To the extent that the social sciences need to be radically updated by the cognitive and brain sciences, so the most influential of progressive social and political thinkers need a corresponding updating. This section is dedicated to beginning that process.

CHAPTER 13

Exploring the Political Brain

The twenty-first century is only just beginning. There is a lot more to say, even now, about the brain, the mind, and their implications for politics. Other important research is going on now, especially in two areas: brain research on whether political preferences can be told from fMRI studies, and studies in political psychology on how conservatives and progressives might display different psychological profiles. It is time for those of us in diverse fields to put our brains—and brain studies—together.

Each field has its insights and its limits. Consider fMRI ("functional" MRI) experiments, which provide what are portrayed in the popular literature as pictures of the brain. They are not pictures of the brain. They are pictures of something else, which is informative and important, but not the brain itself.

Thinking requires the firing of neurons, and such firing takes energy. Brain cells need oxygen to fire. Blood carries the oxyhemoglobin protein to those neurons, which, via a chemical reaction, take the oxygen from those proteins, producing deoxyhemoglobin (hemoglobin with the oxygen removed). A brain region with a lot of neural activity will have a higher than normal ratio of oxyhemoglobin to deoxyhemoglobin. The magnetic field of the fMRI machine can measure this ratio. You are seeing "pictures" of this ratio.

The spatial resolution of the machine is a few millimeters, in which there can be hundreds of thousands, perhaps millions, of neurons, each doing different things, with hundreds of millions to billions of circuits. The time resolution is about one second, enough for each of those neurons to fire, say, a hundred times. The fine details of what the circuitry connecting the neurons is doing cannot be seen at all. The circuitry involves between a thousand and ten thousand inputs to and outputs from each neuron, none of them visible from the "pictures."

In short, the machine can only distinguish activity of some sort or other by perhaps millions of neurons with billions of connections firing a hundred times a second in complex circuits. It's like looking at an enormous office building from a satellite: you might see a lot of lights turned on, but you have no idea what is being said or thought. Frames are indeed neural circuits, but they are so fine-grained that no one could possibly "see" a frame in a brain.

In my field, cognitive linguistics, when combined with neural computational modeling, we can study—using very different methods—precise conceptual frames, conceptual metaphors, and cultural narratives that can account for the inferences actually used in unconscious reasoning about politics.

As you have seen, we can study the details of the Bad Apple frame, the War frame, types of moral metaphors, and details of prototypes and metonymies. And we can study best-fit conditions, complex frames and metaphors, systems of frames, mutual inhibition between systems of frames (leading to biconceptualism), and so on.

Indeed, it is in cognitive linguistics where the actual content and linguistic expression of frames is studied. Emotion research with fMRIs, however vital, cannot tell you conceptual content—what you are emotional about. Emotion research alone cannot distinguish one idea from another, much less progressive from conservative ideas. But it can tell you important things.

Drew Westen's excellent book *The Political Brain* is probably the best-known work on politics to date based on fMRI research.[1] Westen studies emotion, and as a result some readers may get the false impression that there are two different kinds of mental activity, emotional and rational. It's a false distinction, as Westen is well aware. Damasio has shown that rationality requires emotion. True, the dorsolateral prefrontal cortex is more active in certain kinds of reasoning, say, in mathematical computation or logic, but even there emotional work is being done.

Westen correctly—and brilliantly through remarkable experimentation—shows that emotion can be unconscious. This is extremely important, given the common assumption that emotions are things you can consciously feel. I am certain that unconscious emotion must play a huge role in the lives of virtually everyone—and that it is central to politics.

Westen has removed any doubt there may have been that, in electoral politics, it is vital to pay attention to the emotions, especially the unconscious ones, expressed by candidates and activated in voters. He talks of an "emotional constituency"—groups of voters with the same emotional reactions on a given issue or candidate.

One might conclude from Westen that the cognitive unconscious is all emotional. In fact, unconscious frames, narratives, prototypes, metaphors, and extensive neural bindings are all used in unconscious reasoning. And one might also get the impression from Westen that most reasoning is conscious. The opposite is true. The usual estimate is that about 98 percent of reasoning is unconscious and reflexive.

When Westen, a neuroscientist, speaks of the content of "networks," he is not speaking as a neuroscientist, since fMRI methods cannot "see" any such networks, much less tell what they mean. As he points out, he is mostly talking about networks that characterize frames.[2] As a neuroscientist, it is appropriate that he use the brain-based terminology of "networks" when referring to frames.

The moral here is that the cognitive and brain sciences have many methods and each has different things to contribute. Cognitive semantics, for example, has the most to contribute on the detailed study of frames, metaphors, metonymies, prototypes, inferences, language, and so on. Neuroscience does better at studying emotions in relatively large chunks of the brain. Only when the results are taken together and integrated does one get the kind of elaborate picture presented here.

There is still another subfield of cognitive science to consider—political psychology. Researchers in that field ask different questions than I have asked, and use very different methodologies. To give you a taste of the field, consider one of the most celebrated of recent studies, "Political Conservatism as Motivated Social Cognition," by John T. Jost and colleagues.[3]

The researchers studied three crucial areas of psychology: personality, epistemic and existential needs, and ideological justification, as they applied to politically conservative subjects. They found that the conservative personality was marked by a need for authoritarianism and dogmatism (or an intolerance of ambiguity); that the epistemic and existential needs of a conservative person included a need for closure (in order to avoid uncertainty), regulatory focus (in order to cultivate discipline), and terror management; that the typical ideological rationalization was one of social dominance and system justification. In short, their research indicates that conservatives show a higher personal need for order, structure, and closure.

Follow-up research looked at conflict monitoring: how well one can detect a mismatch between the way one is used to responding and an actual situation. This ability has been shown to correlate with activity in the anterior cingulated cortex (ACC). Conservatives showed less ability to respond to complex and potentially conflicting situations, as measured by ACC response.[4]

This field of research originated with the Margaret Mead/Gregory Bateson studies in the 1930s and '40s on childrearing and authoritarianism and later with the classic (though much maligned) study by Theodor Adorno and colleagues on the authoritarian personality, which looked for the roots of fascism,[5] recently updated by Bob Altemeyer.[6]

The methodology used in political psychology is, to a large extent, that employed extensively in social science research, and as usual, questions have been raised about the methods used by certain researchers. Adorno and his colleagues have come in for extensive criticism, though recent careful studies, like that by Jost and colleagues, have reached many similar conclusions.

A more fundamental problem has to do with the very ideas of personality and psychological needs. From the perspective of neuroscience, it is not clear what personality and psychological needs are. Is personality defined by a collection of narratives that you live out? Or by a worldview specified by frames and metaphors, determining how you interpret your experience? Or by a collection of traits, whatever "traits" are neurally? The very idea of personality, from the perspective of neural computation, needs a clarification. Neural circuitry does things. What exactly does the neural circuitry for personality do? Does it live out narratives? Does it impose worldviews and frames on experience and generate expectations and inferences? Can you tell "personality" from "worldview"?

But despite these questions, important results are forthcoming from such research. Robb Willer and colleagues looked at correlates of the support for war, specifically the Iraq War and support for attacking Iran.[7] Political conservatism, general distrust, fear of terrorism, racial prejudice, and social dominance were major predictive factors.

What I think we most need now is cooperation to knit together the various subfields of cognitive science as they bear on politics.

CHAPTER 14

The Problem of Self-interest

When I was a student, I had a neighbor who always greeted me with a glowing "How's the battle?" It was his way of cheering me up, while recognizing that life wasn't easy.

Now, as a metaphor analyst, I recognize that his greeting made use of the primary metaphor Difficulties are Opponents, with the metaphorical inference that Acting in a Difficult Situation is Struggling against an Opponent. That is why you can overcome difficulties, why you can be up against a deadline, or why successful completion can be seen as a triumph!

You never know where a primary metaphor will show up. The same one was used by Darwin in *The Origin of Species* (1859):

> I use this term [struggle for existence] in a large and metaphorical sense including dependence of one being upon another, and including (which is more important) not only the life of the individual, but success in leaving progeny. Two canine animals, in times of dearth, may be truly said to struggle with each other, which shall get food and live. But a plant on the edge of a desert is said to struggle for life against the drought, though more properly it should be said to be dependent on the moisture.

Brendan Larson, a young biologist, has been studying the metaphorical understanding of evolution.[1] He points out, as Darwin himself did, that notions like struggle and competition are metaphors. Darwin had grown up in Scotland, immersed in the ideas of competitiveness in economics and the Church of Scotland's strict father God. The ideas of struggle and competitiveness were everywhere in that environment, and he came by those metaphors as part of his upbringing and everyday life at home. But he knew they were metaphors. "Struggle" covered the minority of real cases where animals literally do fight to survive, but he also used "struggle" to refer to the opposite: "symbiosis" or "structural independence" or even cooperation and what has come to be known as "mutuality."

Consider a mountain on an island in the South Seas, where the rain falls on one side and it is dry on the other. Suppose the island has green and brown moths. In the rainforest, the green moths are less likely to be seen against the vegetation than the brown moths, and the birds will pick off the brown ones more easily. On the dry side, the brown moths will be hidden from the birds, but the green ones will tend to stand out and be eaten.

Does this mean that the green and brown moths are "competing" against each other—in a life-and-death struggle with each other—with the greens winning the literal struggle against the browns in the rainforest, while the browns overcome the greens on the dry side of the mountain? Come on! That's a ridiculous way to think of a species thriving when it fits an ecological niche, and another species surviving less well—or dying out—in that niche. "Struggle," as Darwin said, is a misleading metaphor.

Metaphors are common in science,[2] and the struggle and competition metaphors have stuck as ways to think about evolution. Douglas Erwin writes, "Natural selection, driven by competition for resources, allows the best-adapted individual to produce the most-survivable offspring."[3] It is the usual metaphorical story, and it won't work literally for the green and brown moths—no competition for resources. Indeed, it won't work literally in most cases.

But in evolutionary psychology, the metaphor is taken literally. Steven Pinker denies that "competition in evolutionary science is merely an obsolete metaphor, it is inherent to the very idea of natural selection, where advantageous variants are preserved at the expense of less advantageous ones."[4] When evolutionary psychologists apply this metaphor to human beings, an implicit claim is made about natural behavior, namely, that competition based on self-interest is natural—it is what enabled human beings to survive, and it is both natural and good now.

This has come into popular political culture as well. Think of how many times you have heard political candidates talk about the need to increase the "competitiveness"—of our country versus other countries, of our workers versus other workers, and of lower-class students versus students in the upper classes.

How does the twenty-first-century view of the brain and the mind change all that?

As we have seen, the discovery of mirror neuron circuitry and associated pathways shows that empathy and cooperation are natural. There are also "super-mirror neurons" that fire when you perform an action, but shut down when the same action is observed in others.[5] They appear in the anterior cingulate (hypothesized to detect conflicts), in the orbitofrontal cortex (active in planning that involves reward and punishment), and the pre-supplementary motor area (active in organizing simpler actions into more complex ones). In short, they appear to modulate or control the mirroring function of mirror neurons, and perhaps control empathy in situations of emotional conflict and in planning behavior with social consequences. This suggests that empathy is the natural state, but has to be monitored, modulated, enhanced, and sometimes shut off.

These discoveries challenge classical social, economic, and political theories based on self-interest. If empathy is natural, then self-interest is anything but the whole story. In many cases, self-interest itself may have to be justified in providing an explanation. Self-interest explanations can no longer be given with impunity.

Imagine if evolution were described using the metaphor "the survival of species best nurtured by their ecological niches."

Applied to human beings, it would say that societies should be structured to nurture their citizens, that is, help them and empower them as much as possible. The message of that evolutionary metaphor would be utterly different. It would mean cooperation and thinking of how society is structured overall and might be better structured for its citizens. It would stress interdependence and cooperativeness, not competitiveness. Metaphors matter.

It should be noted that altruism itself is a contested concept. The term was coined by Auguste Comte, who took it as a moral imperative that people should act for the benefit of others. But in a culture dominated by the idea of self-interest, altruism came to be defined within a self-interest frame as the willful sacrifice of one's own interests or well-being for the sake of something that is non-self. If self-interest is natural, then altruism must either be a sacrifice, or an indirect form of self-interest itself.

Although there is considerable literature documenting biological altruism,[6] the most popular evolutionary account of altruism as a form of self-interest is reciprocal altruism—the trading of favors: it is in my interest to serve your interests in a society where that is the norm. Reciprocal altruism evolved, as Pinker says, "because cooperators do better than hermits or misanthropes." This form of self-interest, he claims, explains why we have evolved social and moralistic emotions: "Sympathy and trust prompt people to extend the first favor. Gratitude and loyalty prompt them to repay favors. Guilt and shame deter them from hurting or failing to repay others. Anger and contempt prompt them to avoid or punish cheaters."[7] And because these emotions can be communicated via language, reputation is important. The motivator is always self-interest.

Notice how mirror neuron circuitry and empathy change this picture. First, start with a distinction between self-maintenance and self-interest. All organisms do tend to be self-maintaining. To go on living they have to breathe, move, eat, avoid being harmed or killed, and so on. Self-interest goes well beyond mere self-maintenance. It concerns motivation: are you motivated by having as many goodies as possible go to you, not to others? To say that self-interest is natural is to say that this motivation is not just natural, but motivates all social and moral life—and that we have to adapt to it in order to survive!

As soon as we introduce mirror neuron circuitry and empathy as natural, they become an alternative explanation for the evolution of social and moral emotions. Doing things for others is natural if you feel what they feel. Trust is natural when the self-other distinction is blurred. You can trust yourself; you can read someone else's emotions; so you can trust someone else whose emotions you can read and feel. Loyalty is natural to someone who is not distinct from you. Suppose you have expectations of someone and what they do exceeds them. If you identify with how they feel, gratitude is natural. When you expect others to have the empathy for you that you have for them and they fail you, anger and contempt are appropriate. Empathy also explains why attachment is so important in child development, as well as what attachment gives to parents, why parental love develops, and why family ties tend to be closer than normal social ties.

Explanations that rely on self-interest have a rival, and a more sensible one. Taking empathy as natural utterly changes explanations—and it changes our understanding of what social life should be and can be.

Finally, recent research by H. Kern Reeve and Bert Hölldobler on group selection argues that groups can function like "super organisms" and survive relative to other groups under conditions of scarce resources when members of the group do not compete with each other. Evolution, they claim, selects groups on the basis of in-group cooperation, not competition—whether ants, biological films, or human beings.[8]

The concept of self-interest has also been dominant in economic and political theorizing. Rationality, defined in terms of the eighteenth-century-view of mind, saw reason as primarily serving to achieve personal goals; hence it was seen as irrational to be against your self-interest. The rational actor model in economics is a tool to maximize self-interest, called "utility." The concept of utility is strange in two ways: First, it assumes that utility is always linear, that you can always form a linear preference hierarchy, which is far from true. Second, it assumes that utility, if it is not economic profit (the default case), is something that benefits you in some other way that can be meaningfully compared with profit and perhaps placed on the same scale.

Adam Smith's "invisible hand" metaphor made seeking profit into a moral act, since it supposedly maximized the profit of all. Utility replaces economic profit with well-being. The rational actor model then is seen as maximizing overall well-being for you—that is, utility: in other words, self-interest, whatever that self-interest might be. The failure of the old view of reason calls into question the old view of self-interest with it. It's not that self-interest disappears altogether. It still exists. But it does not simply define natural behavior. It is far from the whole story.

The idea of self-interest is foremost in politics if it is assumed that voters vote "rationally"—on the basis of their interests. We know that is far from true. In foreign policy, self-interest becomes the "national interest"—military strength, overall economic health (measured by GDP), and political influence.

As we have seen, the idea of reciprocal altruism is showing up in forms of foreign policy—that it is in our national interest to help other countries serve their national interests. Then they will be there when we need them. This is one of the themes of Robert Wright's book *Nonzero*, which promotes game theory models with non-zero-sum games in foreign policy.[9] It is still based on the old rationality and self-interest, it still assumes that self-interest is natural, it still assumes the old national interest; it just says that reciprocal altruism maximizes it. Bill Clinton loved the book. After all, it was the policy that he and Madeleine Albright promoted, and the idea was the basis of his free-trade policies. It was neoliberal thought in action.

Democrats put themselves in a precarious—and I think ultimately hopeless—position when they are really motivated by empathy, but wind up reasoning and arguing from interests—when they promote programs and tax policies to serve the "interests" of the middle class, or the uninsured, or victims of discrimination, or immigrants. They set themselves up for attacks as being unfair to ordinary Americans and promoting "special interests." They set themselves up as being a special interest themselves, for courting voting blocs. And worse, they never argue on the basis of empathy, the real motivator of the policies. They fail in two ways: they fail to activate empathy—their own moral foundation—in the brains of voters, while they succeed in activating self-interest, which conservatives specialize in.

CHAPTER 15

The Metaphors
Defining Rational Action

M y first application of metaphoric thought to politics occurred in the late 1980s. I decided to see what was taught in courses on international relations and sat in on such courses at Berkeley, which has one of the country's most prominent political science departments. Perhaps the most central idea was the rational actor model, an attempt to better understand and solve the world's problems by boiling them down to a mathematical model.[1]

The "rational" approach to foreign policy was governed by a set of conceptual metaphors, taken as simple common sense, as metaphors often are. As a special case of An Institution is a Person, there was A Nation is a Person. One of the consequences of taking this metaphor seriously is that what is internal to a country cannot matter in any strategy that uses the metaphor.

In addition, a common metaphor for rationality is used, namely, Rationality is the Maximization of Self-interest (or "utility"), which entails that it is "irrational" to act against one's self-interest. These two metaphors are then combined to yield: A Nation is a Rational Actor.

A further metaphor is needed to characterize what counts as "self-interest" for a nation. It too is commonplace. Just as it is in a person's self-interest to be strong, healthy, and socially influential, so we have the common metaphor that the National Interest is Military Strength, Economic Health (defined by the GDP and the stock market), and Political Influence. Putting these together, we get as an entailment the central thesis of the rational actor model in international relations: *Every nation acts rationally to maximize its military strength, economic health, and political influence.* Note that this use of the rational actor model excludes such matters as culture, religion, national identity, social and political structure, the nature and level of development, and so on. Rationality, on this conception, is taken as universal and occurring at the level of the state.

Foreign policy discourse is commonly conducted with another complex metaphor, based on an extension of the Nation as Person metaphor, namely, the Nation is a Person in the World Community, in which there are Neighboring States, Friendly States, Enemy States, Rogue States, Dysfunctional States, and so on. A noteworthy part of this metaphor is that it includes Adult and Children States, where Maturity is Industrialization. Thus the nonindustrialized nations are seen as "developing" or "underdeveloped" nations. The attitude toward them is commonly that they should take the advice of the adult/industrialized nations as to how to develop (accept neoliberal economics and "free markets"), or face "fiscal discipline" from the IMF and World Bank.

Since each nation-person is trying to maximize its self-interest, and since the world has limited resources, there is natural competition among nation-states. Additionally, the Nation as Person metaphor comes with a commonplace metaphor for competition: A Competition is a Game. This makes it seem like simple common sense to apply the mathematics of game theory to foreign policy.

Back in the 1950s, this is exactly what was done at the RAND Corporation. In those days, mathematical game theory was limited pretty much to zero-sum games, in which not all the participants could be winners. That form of game theory led to the foreign policy of Mutually Assured Destruction (MAD) in which the United States and the Soviet Union competed to build huge nuclear arsenals that threatened each other with nuclear war. If one nation attacked with nuclear weapons, the other would attack back with nuclear weapons, and both would lose; that is, much of the world would be destroyed. The nuclear arms race came about because, no matter how many weapons one country had, the other country would try to gain advantage by making more. "Being ahead" in the game was having more weapons.

At the time, a young game theorist named John Nash (who later became my freshman math teacher at MIT) decided that it was too dangerous for the world to have only such games at its disposal for foreign policy. He demonstrated that in every game with any number of players, in which every player can choose from a finite number of strategies, there is a solution (typically non-zero-sum) where further changes of strategies cannot gain anything for anyone. Though no one may get everything he wants, there is a state of the game (called a "Nash equilibrium") in which no one can do any better. Competition to get further ahead stops for everyone.

This defined a new form of "rational action" for game theory, in which it is rational to seek a Nash equilibrium. Many years later, Nash won the Nobel Prize in Economics for this discovery.

The application of some version of the rational actor model in some field is always an exercise in metaphor, in which something that is not inherently a rational actor in this technical sense is thought of as one. In economics, firms and consumers are commonly thought of as being rational actors. In foreign policy, nations are thought of as rational actors. Moreover, in order to apply the mathematics of the model, a mathematical model of the relevant parts of reality must be made, so that the model can be "fit" to it. This requires the creation of what are called "stylized facts"—clear, unambiguous assumptions about the situation that leave out what is considered "irrelevant." What counts as relevance is not in the mathematics but is a matter of judgment.

Why Metaphor?

Mathematical models are used throughout the social sciences. What is rarely recognized is that metaphor is used in modeling in three ways: first, to the situations to which the models are applied; second, within the construction of the models themselves; and third, within the "stylized facts"—the situation as "oversimplified" so that the mathematics can fit.

Why is it important to know this? Metaphors have entailments; they map source domain reasoning to target domains. If one is not careful, the metaphorical entailments may be hidden and go unnoticed, but they will have effects if the model is actually used as the basis for policy. The whole point of using mathematical models is *not* to have hidden effects of using the models.

According to Old Enlightenment reason, rationality is supposed to be logical and literal. It is supposed to have no metaphors. When metaphors are used, they may be hidden by the Old Enlightenment view of rationality. That is why a New Enlightenment must focus on the metaphors used in its technical apparatus—in the use of mathematical models, where metaphors, and hence their unconscious inferences, are most likely to be hidden.

The rational actor model does not define real rationality. It does not characterize the way people really think, though it is sometimes used as an ideal for how people *should* think. It is a mathematical model with very specific characteristics, characteristics that are not widely known or appreciated. It can be applied fairly directly, with validity, only in certain very circumscribed situations. The model can also help us think through certain kinds of complicated problems, and theorists are working to expand the range of legitimate applications. All this is to the good. But "rationality" defined in this way has severe limits.

What Is Rational Action About?

Imagine a competition. It could be a war, or a competition for power among countries, or a market competition between firms, or just a competition between people trying to outsmart one another. Suppose the competition involved a long sequence of decisions about what to do next. Suppose each competitor (called an "actor") wanted a rational strategy to do as well as possible. How could we model such a situation using game theory?

In the model, each actor is thought of as starting in an initial "position." Making a given decision is thought of metaphorically as moving in a certain direction to a new position. The possible decision points can be thought of as defining branches of a tree. Each sequence of decisions is seen as a path through the tree. At the end of each path, there is a "payoff"—a gain or a loss—together with the probability of getting that payoff with that sequence of moves in this game.

Each model is a "decision tree" of this kind, with payoffs determined by the strategies that the actors use in making their decisions. The idea is that this is a rational approach to making decisions in competitive situations.

Getting Technical

What is the pure mathematics used in the rational actor model? What kinds of axioms do you need in order to prove theorems about the model? The axioms needed to characterize the model come from formal language theory and probability theory. Once you get the formal axioms, you notice that they are just formal math and, in themselves, say nothing about rational action. The axioms, like all axioms, have to be *interpreted*—there needs to be a mapping from the symbols constituting the axioms to something else.

That something else is a tree structure—the decision tree— technically a collection of nodes connected by lines, with a single "root" at the top and branches at each node except for those at the bottom. Each non-bottom node is associated with a symbol, each bottom node with two numbers (one positive or negative, the other between zero and one), and each path from the top to the bottom with another symbol. This is called a *rooted directed graph with labels*. So far, it's still just abstract math.

Now a set of common metaphors is used to interpret this

graph as a network of locations and paths, with the root of the tree being the starting location. The metaphors map nodes into locations, that is, bounded regions in space; lines are mapped into paths of motion directed from top to bottom; bottom nodes are mapped into destinations. The labels on the locations and paths are mapped into names for those locations and paths; and the positive or negative numbers at the bottom nodes are mapped into values assigned to being at those final destinations, while the numbers between zero and one are mapped into probabilities of achieving those values. The symbols associated with top-to-bottom paths are mapped onto travelers, understood as moving from top to bottom. Technically, this is a rooted directed graph, and directed graphs are commonly understood metaphorically in terms of motions from one location to another. The resulting metaphorical picture is one of travelers starting at a beginning location, then moving to other locations, and winding up at a final location, which has some positive or negative value for each traveler and a probability of his having arrived there.

A collection of universal conceptual metaphors then interprets that network of paths and locations. Those conceptual metaphors are:

- States are Locations (bounded regions in space). An example is the state of being *in* a depression, that is, *inside* a bounded region. You can also be *heading for* a depression, *on the edge of* a depression, *deep in* a depression, and *out of* your depression.
- Actions are self-propelled motions in a given direction.
- Each Traveler is an Actor.
- The Choice of Direction is a Decision as to which action to take.
- Achieving a Purpose is Reaching a Destination (called a "goal"). Actions are purposeful if aimed toward achieving a goal.
- The Value of Achieving a Purpose is a Benefit (if positive) or a Cost (if negative). Note that the linear order imposed by hav-

ing positive and negative numbers as values imposes a set of linearly ordered *preferences*.

- The Probabilities (numbers between zero and one) are mapped onto Degrees of Risk, with high probabilities being low-risk, and low probabilities being high-risk.
- The product of the probability and the value associated with achieving each purpose is called the *utility* of deciding to take the action-path to that endpoint. The best decisions are those with the lowest risks combined with the highest values.

Rationality is defined here as the ability to calculate preferred outcomes on the basis of the values of the outcomes and the risk involved. When there is more than one actor, limited resources, competition for benefits, and strategies for acting given the actions and strategies of others, then we are in the realm of game theory.

Game theory imposes a further metaphorical interpretation on this structure. In game theory, each of the Actors is a "Player"; each Action is a "Move"; and each Value for a Player is a "Pay-off." In a zero-sum game, one actor (the "winner") gets value one at the end, and the others (the "losers") get value zero. In a non-zero-sum game, no players lose (get value zero) and no player wins everything (gets value one), but all players win something (get values above zero and less than one).

Game theory is about strategies given a player's knowledge of the game. In this mathematical model, an Information Set for a Player is the set of states (nodes in the tree) at which a given actor has the same information about his next possible action. A strategy is an algorithm that specifies an action at each available information set. A Nash equilibrium is a set of strategies for all actors, such that no actor can get a better payoff by changing strategies.

Game theory is an enormously rich field of mathematical modeling. Its understanding implicitly involves all of the given metaphors. To prove theorems, one uses axioms. Axioms are logical expressions with symbols. Trees are graphs with a given imagistic

structure. Axioms are not literally tree structures. It takes metaphorical thought to understand that axioms with a certain logical structure will map to trees with a certain imagistic structure.
Graphs are not literally paths of motions from location to location.
It takes metaphorical thought to map graphs to paths of motions
of certain kinds. Actions are not literally movements, states are
not literally locations, and purposes are not literally destinations;
positive and negative numbers are not literally values, and numbers between zero and one are not literally probabilities. It takes
metaphorical thought to create such understandings. And complex metaphorical structures combining all of these metaphors
are not literally games. It takes further metaphorical thought to
conceptualize games and strategies in terms of such metaphorical structures. All of this metaphorical complexity is necessary to
link the formal mathematical axioms and theorems to "rational
action" in a strategic "game."

And then it takes further metaphorical thought to link game
theory strategies by players to, say, pricing strategies by firms, or
foreign policy strategies by nations, or even "survival strategies"
by species. Some rational action theorists even extend the metaphors to make claims about morality and the nature of society. It
is in its applications that the rational actor model can get dangerous if one is not careful.

Here are the model's properties—and the ways those properties do not always reflect reality:

- *Differences of quality are reducible to differences of quantity.* In important matters, quality is often not reducible to
  quantity. Results of courses of action cannot always be ranked
  linearly, or "preferentially." They may simply be different in
  many respects, without clear preferences. Extended models
  allow for multidimensionality in preferences: preferable in one
  property, but not another, where the two properties are not
  rankable. But even then, there may be no rankable properties,
  again because quality may not be reducible to quantity.

- *Actors are unitary, distinct, and always in control of their choices.* When an institution—a nation or a firm, a society or a species—is taken as an "actor," its "actions" may be multiple and indistinct, while the system that one is in may determine what actions are taken as much as the actors.
- *History can be broken down into a discrete sequence of actions by particular actors.* History is usually much more complex than that.
- *A course of action must have a beginning and an end.* The model requires a beginning state and a final state, in order to measure the benefits and costs of a course of action. Any past history prior to the beginning state doesn't matter. Any future after the final state doesn't count.

But in most important courses of action, past history does matter and future effects should count. The Iraq War is the clearest case of this. Think of George W. Bush standing on the aircraft carrier in his flight suit in early May 2003 under a banner saying "Mission Accomplished." In the War frame, the mission of winning the war *is* accomplished when the enemy army (Saddam Hussein's in this case) is vanquished, as it was in May 2003. The "rational" course of action began with the beginning of the war. But the history of Iraq did not begin then. It is thousands of years old, with Sunni-Shiite hatreds going back hundreds of years and still smoldering. The causal effects of the war did not end in May 2003. Indeed, the greatest and most horrific effects have occurred since then. The stylized facts have an "enemy" being fought, innocent "victims" we are rescuing and protecting. But that may hide the reality that many of them may be the same people. When you use the rational actor model, you have to make sure that past history doesn't matter and that future events really don't count.

The model is literal. There are no alternative interpretations of the facts being modeled—no alternative framings. But this rarely happens in important cases. The framing of events by people taking part in those events affects their behavior. Framing includes what has happened, what purposes are to be achieved, and what values achievements have.

"Externalized" costs are outside the model. Frames, by necessity, oversimplify reality. A rational approach to business by a major corporation may use some version of the rational actor model, but that model has to act on some frame for the business.

The frame may include the business itself, its employees, its assets, its liabilities, its products, its costs, its consumers, its profits. Such a frame would typically structure what counts as the facts. Such a frame "stylizes" the facts. A lot can fall outside of the frame, and hence not be noticed by the application of rational action.

Take pollution, for example. It has been traditional in America not to consider pollution cleanup as a cost of production, since the pollution was rarely cleaned up. The result was a cost to others—those who have to pay to filter water or buy bottled water, asthma victims who suffer and sometimes die from pollution, or a health care system that has to pay considerably for those who become ill in any number of ways from pollution, such as leukemia and other cancer victims. To a limited extent this might be remedied through the use of pollution caps and credits, caps on the amount of pollution a firm can produce, and certificates, which can be bought and sold, granting the right to pollute to a certain extent. This creates a market in pollution credits, which become more valuable and hence more expensive as the caps become smaller. The system has the effect of introducing pollution into the frame for doing business. But ecosystem destruction still lies outside the frames that define the stylized facts, and hence outside the rational calculation by firms.

Another example is the "cost" of gasoline. In the Commercial Event frame, the amount paid directly by the buyer to the seller defines the cost to the buyer. The cost is generally understood as what you pay at the pump (which include gasoline taxes paid to the government). But gasoline has "hidden costs" that are outside the Commercial Event frame. For example, the government—that is, the taxpayers—pay tens of billions of dollars in subsidies to oil companies for exploration, an estimated $50 billion a year for the navy and Coast Guard to protect oil tankers, and hundreds of billions a year in military costs to protect the operations of American oil companies abroad. These externalized costs are usually outside normal rational calculations.

Infrastructure costs are outside the model, while taxes are inside. Taxpayers put together their common wealth to build an infrastructure for everyone to use, especially in doing business: highways, a communications satellite system, the Internet, the educational system for training employees, the banking system for making low-cost loans available, the judicial system for adjudicating contract disputes, the SEC for making a stock market possible. Forms include taxes under "costs," but the use of the infrastructure is not considered as a "benefit" in the frame, and hence in the stylized facts. The rational actor model can only be as accurate as the frames that define the stylized facts that it operates on.

The model contains no cost for using the model itself. The very use of the rational actor model can change the world radically. The Mutually Assured Destruction model of the 1950s led to the arms race—the spending of a huge amount of money, the endangering of the world, and the current abundance and spread of fissionable nuclear materials. It is dangerous to use a model when its very use has a cost not included in the model.

The model is taken as defining reality. The rational actor model is highly constrained and quite particular, with entailments like those just given that are extremely strange. *An enormous danger in using such a model is that the model can be taken for reality.* Whenever you are applying the model, you are not only using all the metaphors defining the model but also the metaphors fitting the model to the stylized facts; that is, to a model of reality that is also not literal.

Unfortunately not all practitioners of rational action are so careful. There are some that take the stylized facts for being the world and take the model not as a collection of metaphors for making sense of the stylized facts, but rather as stating truths inherent in the world itself.

The model is taken as defining what it means for a human being to be rational. When human beings are understood as rational animals (assuming incorrectly that no other animals have any rationality), the rational actor model is too often taken as part of human nature—as defining what it means to be rational. A consequence is that it is often seen as natural for people to act so as to maximize their self-interest (or profit) and unnatural for them not to. Those who profit most are therefore seen as doing what comes naturally, and those who profit much less are seen as irrational, unnatural, lesser beings who don't deserve much no matter how hard they work. Barack Obama has called this attitude a form of social Darwinism and accused conservatives of it.

How the Rational Actor Model Contradicts Real Reason

This is a book about real reason—what the cognitive sciences have discovered about how we really think. So far we have seen that we think in terms of frames, narratives, metaphors, metonymies, and prototypes. The rational actor model is itself defined by metaphors, and its stylized facts are defined by frames. But frame-based and metaphorical thought are largely unconscious and *reflexive*, while the calculative thought of the rational actor model is conscious and *reflective*. If you limit what you mean by "reason" to conscious reflective thought, you might very well be led to believe that the rational actor model, or something like it, might define rationality. That is, you might see such a model as defining the rational structure of reality as well as human rationality—allowing human beings to fit their reason to the rationality of the world and hence survive and thrive.

Yet versions of the rational actor model have contributed to the arms race (via game theory and Mutually Assured Destruction) and global warming (via the externalization of pollution costs). It is that form of "rationality" that has most threatened our ability to survive and thrive.

At the same time, it has had all sorts of beneficial effects through its application in economics. And the idea of the Nash equilibrium has had beneficial effects in going beyond zero-sum-game reasoning by introducing the idea that there are cases in which everybody on the whole can be better off if people don't try to maximize their self-interest, but rather include considerations of the interests of others.

Such ideas were applied to foreign policy in the Clinton administration by Madeleine Albright. As Bill Clinton said in a *Wired* magazine interview in 2000:

> The more complex societies get and the more complex the networks of interdependence within and beyond community and national borders get, the more people are forced in their own interests to find non-zero-sum solutions. That is, win-win solutions instead of win-lose solutions.... Because we find as our interdependence increases that, on the whole, we do better when other people do better as well—so we have to find ways that we can all win, we have to accommodate each other.[2]

The rational actor model is a product of real reason. But the model itself makes the inherent claim that reason does not involve either metaphors or frames. It therefore cannot be a model of real human reason. And moreover, when we study the metaphors, frames, and what follows from them, we can see the limitations and possible dangers, as well as the benefits, of applying such mathematical models.

CHAPTER 16

Why Hawks Win

Daniel Kahneman, a cognitive scientist not an economist, won the 2002 Nobel Prize in Economics.[1] What he (with his late colleague Amos Tversky) did was explain how discoveries in cognitive science show the inadequacies of the rational actor model and how economics could benefit from studying how people really reason. This work began the field of behavioral economics.

Kahneman distinguishes *reflexive* from *reflective* thought, calling them System 1 and System 2 respectively. Reflective thought is what I've called the Old Enlightenment reason. As he observes, it is: slow, serial, controlled, effortful, and commonly rule-governed. The real action is in reflexive thought, what I have called the cognitive unconscious: unconscious, fast, parallel, automatic, effortless, and associative. He describes it as the kind of thought used when you look at a person's face and immediately know that he or she is angry, or afraid, or happy.

Kahneman showed experimentally that reflexive thought uses frames. Here is an experiment: Suppose that you are told that you are seriously ill, and have to decide whether to undergo a certain operation. It is a life-or-death decision. In case A, you are told that you have a 10 percent chance of dying with the operation. In case B, you are told that you have a 90 percent chance of surviving. Case A frames the decision in terms of death. Case B frames the decision in terms of survival. Literally, they are the same: there is no real-world difference in probability. But experiments show that many more people decide in favor of the operation if they are given the choice in terms of the Survival frame than in terms of the Death frame. This isn't "rational" from the perspective of classical economic rationality, but it is what happens. Positive framing has a different effect than negative framing when the facts about the world are held constant.

This is an instance of what Kahneman and Tversky called "prospect theory," which has shown that people make decisions in ways that differ from classical economic "rationality"—that is, that are characteristic of New Enlightenment *reflexive* thinking, rather than Old Enlightenment *reflective* thinking.

Classical economics claims that people make decisions based on "marginal utility"—the gain-versus-loss difference in one's overall economic standing. It assumes the fungibility of money: preventing a loss is the same as guaranteeing a gain. It is order-independent: first winning, then losing should be the same as first losing, then winning, if you lose and win the same amount. Economic man is rational, thinks logically, follows the laws of probability, and reasons according to an objective understanding of the world.

Kahenman and Tversky found that, in everyday economic decision-making and problem-solving, all of these are commonly violated. They found that:

- People think in terms of gains and losses relative to a reference point.
- People tend to choose frames that highlight gains rather than losses.
- People tend to avoid losses more than they prefer gains.
- People tend to prefer certainty to uncertainty.
- People tend to think in terms of prototypical frames.
- People tend to adapt to a new state and take it as a new reference point.
- People tend to substitute more "accessible" frames for more accurate but less accessible frames.

These principles explain real human mental behavior that classical economics calls "irrational." For instance, the tendency to avoid losses explains why a gambler who is losing does not cut his losses, but keeps gambling in the hope that he can win back what he's lost. Or why someone who buys a stock that loses its value considerably will hold on to it hoping it will regain its value. Or why a president, obviously losing in war, will keep sending more and more troops hopelessly into battle in the hopes of eventually winning, rather than cut his losses, get fewer people killed, and save hundreds of billions of dollars. Many of Kahneman's examples are like this: cases where real human reasoning violates economic rationality and leads to disaster.

Framing is at the heart of prospect theory. Framing is about thought, about how you conceptualize a situation. In the first case given above, the framing was in terms of death (10 percent) or survival (90 percent), but not both at once. The activation of a given frame tends to inhibit alternative frames.

Prospect theory shows that decision-making itself comes with a frame. The Decision frame has the following structure: a Reference Point; an Outcome; an Outcome Type with values: a Gain or Loss; a Probability of the Outcome; a Preference function for Gain; and an Avoidance function for Loss. The value of the Avoidance function is approximately twice that of the Preference function. Losses are worse than gains are good.

In any specific situation, the Decision frame combines with a framing of the situation, say, the 10 percent Death frame versus the 90 percent Survival frame for the operation, where Death is a Loss and Survival is a Gain. The literature on behavioral economics is filled with such examples. The phenomenon is real.

- People may drive across town to save $5 on a $15 calculator but not drive across town to save $5 on a $125 coat.
- Suppose you are given a choice between getting $1,000 with certainty or having a 50 percent chance of getting $2,500. Even though the mathematical expectation of the 50 percent chance is $1,250, people tend to choose the certain $1,000. With positive framing, certainty trumps uncertainty; risk

aversion is preferable to risk. But the same people, when confronted with a certain $1,000 loss versus a fifty-fifty chance of either no loss or a $2,500 loss, often choose the uncertain alternative. That is, they choose the mathematical expectation of a $1,250 loss over a certain $1,000 loss. With negative framing, uncertainty of loss trumps certainty of loss. In both cases, real choice overrides the "rational" mathematical expectation.

• Peter Bernstein cites an experiment by Richard Thaler in which students were told to assume they had just won $30 and were offered a coin flip upon which they would win or lose $9. Seventy percent of the students opted for the coin flip. When other students were offered a certain $30 versus a coin flip in which they got either $21 or $39, a much smaller proportion, 43 percent, opted for the coin flip.[2] Objectively, the choices were the same. But the framing of the coin flip mattered. Framed as a possible $9 loss, the risk of losing with a $30 reference point seemed acceptable. Framed as $18 difference with a $30 reference point, the risk of losing seemed too high to many subjects.

What I've just given is an oversimplification. It sounds as if the brain has two different unconnected systems. It doesn't. *Reflective* thinking (Kahneman's "System 2") uses the mechanisms of unconscious *reflexive* thought—frames, metaphors, and so on. That is, conscious thought makes use of and is built on the cognitive unconscious; for example, when classical economic theory conceptualizes labor metaphorically as a resource (like coal or iron), or when firms are conceptualized by metaphor as human beings acting "rationally" (using the rational actor model).

Moreover, as we have seen, the rational actor model itself is metaphorical through and through, with the metaphors below the level of conscious. Frames, prototypes, and metaphors are as much a part of Old Enlightenment thinking as they are of New Enlightenment thinking, only their use is hidden from view.

Kahneman and Tversky's prospect theory raised an important question: Why should the mind work this way? The answer is coming from the study of the brain. Research by Craig Fox, Russell Poldrack, and their colleagues at UCLA indicates that the brain's emotional system explains why the mind works as Kahneman and Tversky have described. When people experience potential gains, there is increased activity in the midbrain dopaminergic system (positive emotion), and potential losses show decreases in activity in the same region. Degrees of loss aversion correspond to activation levels in the ventral striatum and prefrontal cortex.[3]

Why does all this matter for politics?

Kahneman and Jonathan Renshon recently explained why hawks have such an advantage over doves in matters of peace and war—why policymakers tend to go along with the hawks. They cite six well-documented results from cognitive science about the human mind, all of which give the hawks an advantage.

- Optimism bias: Just as all the children are above average in Lake Woebegon, 80 percent of drivers rate their driving skill as above average. Around 35 percent of Americans believe they will eventually be in the top 1 percent in wealth. And generals on both sides of a conflict tend to be overwhelmingly confident they will win, and win easily, especially in America, where optimism rules and a general who doesn't think we will win may not be a general for long. Policymakers too have an optimism bias. Who wants to vote for a pessimist?
- The fundamental attribution error: People tend to overemphasize personality-based explanations, rather than situation-based explanations, for the behavior of others, but not for their own behavior. In cognitive semantics, this follows from the metaphor of Essence: that everyone has an essence (or "character") that governs their natural behavior. Combine this with the Hero narrative in which the Hero (you) are Good, and the Villain (your adversary) is Bad. The result is that, in the lead-up to war, each side has a tendency to misjudge the other side's

motives. *He* is hostile and aggressive; *I* am pushed into a cor-
ner and have to react aggressively.

• The illusion of control: People exaggerate the amount of control they have over important outcomes, while in fact outside
and random factors are actually at work. For example, the
Iraq War was expected to be a "cakewalk," when evidence to
the contrary was long known but ignored.

• Reactive devaluation: A proposal is worth less because the
other side has offered it. In experiments, Israeli Jews evaluated
a peace plan less favorably when it was attributed to the Palestinians than when it was attributed to the Israeli government.
Pro-Israel Americans saw a given peace proposal as biased
toward the Palestinians when told it was a Palestinian plan,
but saw the same plan as "evenhanded" when told it was an
Israeli plan.

• Risk aversion: People tend to avoid an absolutely certain loss,
in favor of merely a potential, though perhaps larger, loss.
Here are two choices: (a) a sure loss of $890; (b) a 90 percent
chance of losing of $1,000 and a 10 percent chance of losing
nothing. People tend to choose option (b), though (a) is statistically better. This tendency shows up in Iraq policy, where
Bush and the Republicans refuse to cut their losses and get out
now, instead clinging to the unlikely hope that if they stay longer things will get better, though staying longer would involve
a greater loss. The framing is, *We can't lose* and *We shouldn't
cut and run*—attributing to liberals' cowardice rather than a
rational choice to cut our losses.

• The salient exemplar effect: Citing a well-known example of a
rare phenomenon tends to make people think the phenomenon
has a high probability. Citing Chamberlain's mistaken judgment that Hitler could be negotiated with rather than fought
evokes a high probability that any judgment favoring negotiations over war would be a similar mistake. The attacks of 9/11
made people in Iowa and Ohio think that there was a high
probability that they would be subject to a terrorist attack.

To answer this chapter's question: hawks win because cognitive biases are in their favor. People tend to think using these biases:

- Optimism bias: The people will be throwing flowers. We can achieve victory. If we fight them there, they won't come here.
- The fundamental attribution error: Those fighting us are Islamofascists. They hate our freedoms.
- The illusion of control: The Iraq War will be a cakewalk. The surge will end the carnage.
- Reactive devaluation: It's not an occupation because al Jazeera calls it an occupation. It's not a rebellion against an occupying army, if "the insurgents" say it is.
- Risk aversion: We can't risk losing in Iraq. We have to stay until we win.
- The salient exemplar effect: We can't appease Ahmadinejad. We have to bomb Iran before they get nuclear technology.

Kahneman and Renshon point out, correctly, that each of these existing cognitive biases favors hawks over doves in discussions of war and peace. They do not conclude that hawks are always wrong, but only that such biases need to be recognized and factored into an evaluation of their arguments.[4]

We all need to learn to recognize these cognitive biases. The press needs to learn them. We need public discussion of them wherever they occur.

The Enlightenment bias is that *we* are rational, that such cognitive biases don't exist in *us*—no matter who *we* are—and that *we*, as conscious rational beings, have direct access to our thought processes and know our own minds.

A New Enlightenment must transcend the Enlightenment bias.

CHAPTER 17

The Brain's Language

What we are learning about the brain gives us a new understanding of and appreciation for language, how it is exploited in politics, and what the limits are for its political use.

Language is far more than a means of expression and communication. It is the gateway to the mind. It organizes and provides access to the system of concepts used in thinking.

Language can be used to change minds, which means it can change brains—permanently, for good or ill. It does not merely express emotions, it can change them; not merely arouse or quell them, but change the role of emotion in one's life and the life of a nation.

Language does not merely express identity; it can change identity. Narratives and melodramas are not mere words and images; they can enter our brains and provide models that we not merely live by, but that define who we are.

Language is an instrument of creativity and power, a means of connecting with people or alienating them, and a force for social cohesion or separation.

Language is sensual and aesthetic, with the power to woo or to repulse, to be beautiful or ugly, to be meaningful or banal.

Language has moral force; it can bring out the best in people and the worst. Memories are never just "stored"; they are always created anew. Language does not just evoke memories; it can change them and shape them, and thereby change history—the story of the past.

For all these reasons, language has political force.

Understanding language is not just nice, it is necessary. And that requires understanding the brain. The properties of the brain are what give language its power.

Language is a matter of neural connections—connections between speech sounds, writing, or signs in signed languages on the one hand and meaningful brain structures: frames, metaphors, narratives, image schemas, prototypes, metonymies, and so on.

Meaning is embodied. All meaning.[1]

There is no abstract meaning floating in air. There is no meaning in empty symbols that are just manipulated. There is no meaning in some disembodied correspondence of symbols to things in the world.

The brain extends throughout the body via the nervous system. All meaningful perception and action is mediated by our brains, whether physical, social, emotional, or interpersonal. But brains alone without bodies and physical and social interactions do nothing. It is the brain connected to the body functioning in the physical and social world that gives meaning and grounds real reason.

What makes language powerful is its capacity to activate, communicate, regulate, and even change all aspects of our understanding! Language mostly works through the cognitive unconscious, so we are usually unaware of the effects it is having.

Language is a mediating system in the brain; it consists of circuits linking meaningful, embodied ideas to physical linguistic form—speech, writing, gesture, and signs in signed languages.

Does the way we think shape language? Yes. Does language shape the way we think? Yes.

Words and Politics

When I teach frame semantics, I give my class a task: Don't think of an elephant! The point is that you can't do it. The reason is that words are defined in terms of frames, and when used, the words activate those frames, whether negated or not. This is important for people in politics to know. If you use the opposition's frames, even to negate or argue against them, you are helping them because you are activating their frames in the minds of the public, and their frames in turn activate their worldview.

The trick on conservative talk shows is that the conservative host asks the questions and so sets the frames. Do you favor tax relief? Should we win the war on terror or cut and run? Do you favor free trade or protectionism? Should our schools and teachers be held accountable for teaching their students? If you accept the question, you're in their frame and working within a worldview that may not be yours. If it isn't, all you can do is shift the frame to one that fits your worldview, not theirs. But to do that, you have to understand what their worldview is, what yours is, and how to frame the response. You also have to know not to just answer with facts and figures, but to make the facts and figures meaningful through framing and narrative.

The question is, why does language work this way?

The word "elephant" activates an image of an elephant and knowledge about elephants. Since, in this culture, we have no conventional ways of interacting physically with elephants, the word "elephant" does not activate a motor program. Compare this with the word "cat." We do have a motor program for petting cats, which is part of the meaning of "cat."

As Antonio Damasio and his coworkers have observed, people with inferior temporal cortex lesions (near the motor area) may lose the ability to recognize cats, but not elephants.[2] And those with lesions in visual regions of the parietal cortex may lose the ability to recognize elephants, since visual imagery is part of the meaning. All this happens automatically and is beyond conscious control. If I tell you not to think of an elephant, you can't do it, because you cannot consciously control your own neural system.

It's not just the word "elephant"; it's all words. And it's not just one frame that's activated unconsciously and automatically by words—it's a whole system of frames and metaphors. The more that system is activated, the stronger its synapses become, and the more entrenched it is in your brain—all without your conscious awareness. That is why the conservative message machine, operating over thirty-five years, has been so effective.

Language has systemic effects. To see this, let's take an example that I've discussed superficially in the past and look at it in depth: tax relief. The word "relief" is defined relative to a complex frame made up of two parts and a neural binding linking them into a single whole. We can parse the meaning according to its function in several different narratives.

Rescue Narrative
Semantic Roles
Victim (helpless, innocent), Villain (evil), Villainous Act (harmful), Hero (good)
Scenario
(Start a) Villain harms Victim;

(Central a) Hero struggles against Villain;

(Finish a) Hero defeats Villain;

(Final State a) Victim is Rescued, Hero Rewarded, and Villain Punished.

Affliction Narrative
Semantic Roles
Affliction (Negative State), Afflicted Party, Affliction-Cause, Reliever, Relief (Positive State)
Scenario
(Start b) Affliction-Cause causes Affliction to Afflicted Party;

(Central b) Reliever works against Affliction-Cause;

(Finish b) Reliever relieves Affliction for Afflicted Party;

(Final State b) Afflicted-Party gets Relief, Reliever is Praised, Affliction-Cause is Thwarted.

The Bindings for Rescue-from-Affliction
>Victim = Afflicted Party, Villain = Affliction-Cause;
>Villainous Action = Causing Affliction; Hero = Reliever,
>   Rescue = Relief;
>Reward = Praise for Relieving Affliction; Punishment =
>   Affliction-Cause is Thwarted;
>Start a = Start b; Central a = Central b; Finish a = Finish b;
>   Final State a = Final State b.

The word "relief" activates the concept Relief in (3b). There is a form-meaning circuit linking the form "relief" and Relief the meaning in (3b). Simply hearing "relief" activates all of the above frames unconsciously and automatically.

How can a mere word, a sequence of sounds, accomplish this? A sign activates a frame element, which activates a whole, often complex frame, which activates the system the frame is embedded in.

From the point of view of the brain, the notation has specific, nonsymbolic meaning. "Rescue" and "Affliction" are names for the circuits controlling the activation of those frames. When activated, they in turn activate the semantic roles in those frames, roles like Victim and Afflicted Party. These roles are connected to other parts of the brain that are active during experiences—say, the negative experience of anxiety or pain that constitutes an affliction, and the positive experience of the "reward circuit activation" combined with the inhibition of the pain or anxiety.

"Narrative" is the name of a circuit that activates an Event Structure schema (X-schema) that both defines a structure and can operate in time. "Start" is the starting action of the executing schema, "Central" is the central action, and so on. Each of these is neurally bound to an action (like Causes or Relieves) or a state (like Relief).

"Rescue-from-Affliction Binding" is the name of a neural circuit that controls neural bindings linking the two frames, so that the thing Rescued From in one frame is the Affliction in the other. The "=" is the name given to a neural circuit binding the circuitry for two entities, so that they are experienced as the same entity. After you learn the concept of Relief, the entire network structure pictured above is there in your brain waiting to be activated.

Language links words and phrases to structures like these via neural circuitry. These circuits, when activated, create an experienced simulation—most likely below the level of consciousness. It is that imaginative simulation experienced inwardly that constitutes "meaning." And that's just one word!

Now what happens when "tax" is added to "relief"? A lot happens, if the conceptual system has the right content. Conservatives over the years have set up that content with a constant flow of political discourse.

For the term "tax relief" to be meaningful, taxes have to be defined in a frame in which they are a financial loss: money earned by taxpayers and rightly belonging to them, but taken from taxpayers by the government. In addition, there has to be a metaphor in place in which Financial Loss is Pain, and Pain has to be in a frame in which an Affliction Causes Pain. Then—and only then—does adding "tax" to "relief" give rise to the metaphor Taxation is Affliction, with the mapping:

Affliction	⟶ **Taxation**
Cause-of-Affliction	⟶ Proponents-of-Taxation
Reliever	⟶ Opponents of Taxation
Relief	⟶ Lessening of Taxation
Reward	⟶ Praise for Lowering Taxation
Punishment	⟶ Proponents of Taxation are Thwarted

The inference is that those taxed—the public—are victims, the proponents of taxation are villains and hence evil, and opponents of taxation are heroes and hence good. But the use of "tax relief" does not merely evoke all this context. When it is repeated over and over again, it keeps evoking this context, and each time all the synapses on all the neurons in those pathways get strengthened. If you don't have this understanding of taxes beforehand, it will come into your brain after a while. And remember, there is no erasure in the brain (short of brain damage). To change the meaning, you have to have the neural structure to bypass it. All this from two words: "tax relief"—again with no effort on your part, no conscious awareness, almost instantaneous each time it is said.

Notice that there are contexts in which "tax relief" doesn't make sense. Suppose you are thinking with a progressive worldview, in which the role of government is to protect and empower citizens—to make possible highways, communication systems, public schools, the banking system, the stock market, the courts, and in addition to protect us not just by the use of force, but in the areas of health, disasters, clean air and water, civil rights, consumer protection, and so on. From this perspective, taxes make possible our freedom—freedom from, in the case of protection, and freedom to, in the case of empowerment. Suppose everyone knew this thoroughly, that it was repeated over and over day after day on TV and radio, and that we were aware of it every day of our lives as we went about our daily business.

If all this were taken for granted, if it defined the conceptual system in which "taxes" made sense, then "tax relief" might make no more sense than "freedom relief" or "democracy relief"— or, thought about from the perspective of bodily health, "exercise relief." If you appreciate every day that taxes make possible the wonders of American life—especially our freedoms and our general well-being—then, as much as we might not want to pay them, they would be anything but an affliction we need relief from.

Support for this comes from a neuroscience experiment at the University of Oregon by a psychologist and two economists.[3] Their experiment was drawn up to remove some of the usual incentives for being charitable, such as the fear of looking stingy or the prestige of being named in the program of a charity dinner. Each student was given $100 and told that nobody would know how much of it she chose to keep or to give away, not even the researchers who enlisted her in the experiment and scanned her brain. Payoffs were recorded on a portable memory drive that the students took to a lab assistant, who then paid the students in cash and mailed donations to charity without knowing who had given what.

The brain responses were measured by a functional MRI machine as a series of transactions occurred. Sometimes the student had to choose whether to donate some of her cash to a local food bank. Sometimes a tax was levied that sent her money to the food bank without her approval. Sometimes she received extra money, and sometimes the food bank received money without any of it coming from her. When the typical student chose to donate to the food bank, she was rewarded with that warm glow: increased activity in the same ancient areas of the brain—the caudate, nucleus accumbens, and insula—that respond when you eat a sweet dessert or receive money. But these pleasure centers were also activated, albeit not as much, when she was forced to pay a tax to the food bank.

In short, it is possible to understand taxes as making the good things in America happen and to literally feel good about contributing to the good of the country.

But conservatives have been working hard to make sure it doesn't happen. For nearly forty years they have been using the term "tax-and-spend liberal" to stereotype those in favor of social programs, and Ronald Reagan introduced the term "entitlements" into conservative discourse to refer to such "spending programs." "Entitlements," to conservatives, are seen as money given to, or spent on, people who have not earned it and therefore don't deserve it—in other words, money not merely wasted, but spent badly.

But such an idea makes sense only given a conservative mode of reasoning focused on individual responsibility, individual discipline, and two basic ideas: First, what you are paid in the market is what you have earned on your own, with no government enabling, and it is yours and yours alone by right. Second, getting something you haven't earned makes you dependent and takes away your discipline, making it harder for you to earn a living and live as a moral person.

For "tax relief" to make sense to a public that has heard "tax and spend," "entitlements," and "spending programs" for over three decades, these deep and pervasive ideas must be active. "Tax relief" is a better fit to these conservative ideas than to progressive ideas.

The idea that taxation is an affliction is inconsistent with the progressive idea of the empowering role of government. Inconsistency is realized in the brain as mutual inhibition. Because "tax relief" fits with conservative ideas, and depends on them to make sense, it will automatically activate those deep conservative ideas.

At present, conservatives have gotten their ideas about taxes—and the deeper frames that support those ideas—out to the public. Progressives have not.

The moral: there is a reason why conservatives have an easier time constructing effective slogans and messages. In addition to having a better message machine and more radio and TV stations, they got to the public first, instilling their worldview and their deep framing over thirty-five years—changing a lot of brains, and by repetition, making those changes permanent.

Think of it this way: what conservatives had been doing over many years was preparing the seedbed of our brains with their high-level general principles so that when "tax relief" was planted, their framing could take root and sprout. As a result, progressive messages don't take root, because the soil was prepared for conservative messages, not progressive ones.

Progressives have a lot of tilling to do—and maybe some heavy-duty roto-tilling in conservative soil. It will take time and concerted effort. Here's how to begin:

Whatever the topic is, bring in the progressive moral vision and what the role of government is. America is about empathy and responsibility: people caring both for themselves and for one another, and acting responsibly on that sense of care. Government has two roles: protection and empowerment for all its citizens. Nobody makes it on his own.... And then frame whatever the issue is in these terms. Taxes pay for continued protection and empowerment, for freedom from and freedom to.

If progressives can stick to these basics, activate empathy in our fellow citizens, and frame issues so that they notice all the protection and empowerment that government affords in their everyday lives, then we have a fighting chance that the minds and the brains of our countrymen will align once more with the fundamental values and goals of American democracy. We need to say over and over that this is what true patriotism is.

Moreover, we need language to evoke the frames that tell why conservatism is destructive to democracy:

- America says we're all in the same boat. Conservatism says you're on your own, buddy.
- America makes the least of us secure. Conservatism tells us to save your own skin and not to care about your neighbor.
- America says you are safe from government oppression. Conservatism says the state—at least when run by conservatives—can spy on your phone calls, break down your door, imprison you without a charge or a lawyer or even notifying your family, and then torture you.
- America says your personal life is your own. Conservatism says the state can force medical decisions on you and your family, tell you who you can and can't marry, and what words you can and can't hear on the radio.
- America stands for liberty. Conservatism stands for state control over your personal life.

American values are progressive values. Saying it matters.

It matters because language works by mental simulation.[4] Words evoke whole frames—whole mental structures. Those mental structures activate an embodied mental simulation, giving the words meaning. Neuroscience tells us that the same region of the brain used for seeing is used for imagining seeing, remembering seeing, and dreaming about seeing; that the same parts of your brain used for moving are used for imagining moving, remembering moving, and dreaming about moving. Imagination is mental simulation. It is often unconscious. The meaning of language is also embodied mental simulation, mental simulation based on what your brain can tell your body to do or experience it doing.

Part of the power of a word is that it can activate vast stretches of the brain because of spreading activation—frames activate other frames, which activate still other frames, and so on. But brain structures provide words with even greater power. Consider metaphor circuitry.

The circuitry constituting the primary metaphors Moral is Up; Immoral is Down, and Moral is Pure; Immoral is Disgusting is sitting there in your brain waiting to be activated. It has allowed for the extension of meanings of words having to do with vertical orientation (e.g., low) to matters of morality, as in "That was a low thing to do." After 9/11 members of the Bush administration started referring to members of al Qaeda in the caves of Afghanistan as "vermin" and "rats in their holes," activating the metaphors of Immorality is Down and Disgusting. No one in America had to be told what those words meant. And when Republicans started running TV ads with "democRATS" flashing subliminally on the screen, it was those unconscious primary metaphors sitting in our brains that they were trying to activate.

The political power of words lies not primarily in their form—that is, in speech—or even in the meanings they are directly linked to, but in the totality of brain circuitry that activation can spread to: the frames, metaphors, prototypes, metonymies, and the entire systems of concepts. Words matter. They shape our politics—and our lives.

CHAPTER 18

Language in
the New Enlightenment

Many academic disciplines, especially in the social sciences, have developed using the Old Enlightenment view of reason. Changing to a New Enlightenment version of those disciplines will not be quick or easy. Daniel Kahneman's achievement in bringing the New Enlightenment mind to economics is exemplary; he and his coworkers have shown, empirically, in detail, many of the ways in which the rational actor model departs from real reason and what to do about it. Research on freeing evolutionary thought from the competition and struggle for survival metaphors, as we have seen, is proceeding. But the academic world moves slowly. Change will take a while, but it will come.

My own discipline, linguistics, is still partly enmeshed in an Old Enlightenment paradigm, though it has come very far in freeing itself, starting as early as the mid-1970s. We are now in the stage described by Thomas Kuhn in which the new and old paradigms coexist with little interaction.

I have already discussed the political ramifications of New Enlightenment ideas like frames and conceptual metaphors. Since other disciplines will eventually have to go through such a process as the cognitive and brain sciences advance, I think it might be useful to put aside politics for a chapter to discuss how these ideas developed and what they were up against historically.

The Old Enlightenment Paradigm in the 1950s

In the late 1950s, when I was an undergraduate at MIT, a version of the Enlightenment reason paradigm was everywhere. Great excitement was generated by the Church-Turing thesis of the equivalence between Turing machines, formal logic, recursive functions, and Emil Post's formal languages. The question naturally arose: could thought be characterized by symbol manipulation systems?

The idea of artificial intelligence developed out of an attempt to answer this question. Marvin Minsky and John McCarthy, the founders, were at MIT. I met them there through friends who were their students. The Mind-as-Digital-Computer-Program metaphor—in which the mind is seen as carrying out computer programs by manipulating abstract symbols—was dominating both artificial intelligence and the information-processing approach to the cognitive psychology of the 1960s. The mind was seen as computer software, with the brain as hardware. The software was what mattered. Any hardware would do—or "wetware," as the brain was called. The corresponding philosophy of mind was called "functionalism": it was assumed that you could study the mind independently of the brain in terms of its functions, as carried out by the manipulation of abstract symbols. The brain, in this view, could safely be ignored.

American philosophy was largely ruled by philosophical logicians, many of whom believed that formal logic defined rational thought, and centered their philosophy on it: Willard Van Orman Quine, Saul Kripke, Richard Montague, Donald Davidson, David Lewis. I was privileged to know them all and communicated with them during the period when I was one of the linguists bringing formal logic into linguistics. Ordinary language philosophy in the traditions of Wittgenstein and Austin were creeping in, however, as was Continental philosophy.

Mathematics was in the grip of the formalist rigor of the Bourbaki—the French mathematicians who believed that all mathematics should be placed in the framework of formal logic (pure symbol manipulation) and set theory, and that mathematics *is* what results. The key to the mind was taken to be the manipulation of meaningless symbols—in artificial intelligence, in the new post-behaviorist cognitive psychology, and in the philosophy of mind, philosophical logic, and mathematics.

At that historical moment, Noam Chomsky re-created linguistics to fit the symbol manipulation paradigm. He used ideas from his mentor, Zellig Harris, who had thought up linguistic transformations and combined them with the mathematical theory of formal systems (called "formal languages") from the mathematician Emil Post.

Chomsky claimed that language too was a matter of the manipulation of meaningless symbols—formal syntax. His central metaphor was simple: A sentence is a sequence of symbols. A language is a set of such sequences. A grammar is a mathematically describable device for generating—that is, spitting out—all and only the sentences of English, or any other natural language.[1]

The mathematics existed: the formal language theory of Emil Post had been argued by Alonzo Church to be mathematically equivalent to the theory of recursive functions, to symbolic logic, and to Turing machines—the foundation of modern "programming languages."

Language, on Chomsky's account, had nothing to do with meaning or communication—and certainly not with anything bodily. Language was the study of form alone—pure form, symbols manipulated by formal rules. Chomsky was a functionalist; he saw the brain as irrelevant. Artificial intelligence, information-processing psychology, the functionalist theory of mind, formal logic, philosophy in the tradition from Bertrand Russell to W. V. O. Quine, and Bourbaki mathematics made an excellent fit with generative linguistics in the technical intellectual culture of the times.

Chomsky is the ultimate figure of the Old Enlightenment, a follower of René Descartes, trying to revive seventeenth-century rationalism, the Enlightenment theory of mind, seeing "Cartesian linguistics" as a predecessor to his own work.[2]

In Chomsky's linguistics, phrase structure trees—hierarchical symbol structures—were all-important. One of his central arguments involved "recursion," a process in symbolic computation with loops, in which the output of a process was input to it again. Thus relative clauses can have relative clauses in them, and those can have relative clauses in them, ad infinitum. Here is the Mother Goose version:

> This is the farmer sowing his corn,
> That kept the cock that crowed in the morn,
> That waked the priest all shaven and shorn,
> That married the man all tattered and torn,
> That kissed the maiden all forlorn,
> That milked the cow with the crumpled horn,
> That tossed the dog,
> That worried the cat,
> That killed the rat,
> That ate the malt
> That lay in the house that Jack built.

The phrase structure tree would have an *S* (for sentence—the main clause) at the top, and another *S* inside it (indicating a relative clause), and another *S* inside it, and so on for each line.

Chomsky's claim is that recursion is a matter of pure form—the manipulation of abstract symbols like *S*—and that language works that way. Language, he observed correctly, allows limitless variety from finite means. In his theory, this was supposed to be accomplished by formal (symbol-manipulating) "rules" that "generated" such trees. Here the functionalist assumption of the irrelevance of the brain is crucial, since brains don't have symbols and trees.

Chomsky made further Cartesian claims. Descartes had claimed that it was disembodied reason that was the essence of being human—that distinguished us from all other animals—and that reason in general, like proofs in mathematics, involved manipulating abstract symbols. Chomsky took this a step further, claiming language was pure form—abstract symbol manipulation—and that it was language that was the essence of our humanity and separated us from other animals.

This required, in the age of genetics, the idea that language was due to a genetic innovation shared by all and only human beings, and that what we acquired could be called a "language organ." Chomsky's followers, in the age of the brain, tried to locate that organ in the brain, suggesting that it might be Broca's area. But brain studies have shown that language always activates many brain areas. Broca's area actually appears to be a mirror neuron area linking speaking and hearing. No such "language organ" exists. It appears that language arises from circuitry linking many distinct brain areas, which are also used for nonlinguistic functions.

One important innovation of Chomsky's was that his theory required the existence of unconscious thought. His "rules of language" were anything but conscious. It cannot be underestimated how important this innovation was. It focused a generation of cognitive scientists on the study of unconscious mental processes.

It should be recalled that Chomsky's central metaphor was not based on prior empirical results. Instead, it fit the most popular paradigm of the times and defined a program of research, one that has had mixed results. As a discovery procedure—a way into the precise study of linguistic form—it has been extremely useful.

Chomsky had excluded meaning from the study of linguistic structure. In 1963, having been one of Chomsky's first students as an undergraduate, I found evidence to the contrary, cases where syntactic structure depended on meaning. "Meaning" in the 1963 context of symbol manipulation systems meant formal logic. I proposed extending Chomsky's theory by bringing formal logic into generative linguistics, in a theory I called "generative semantics."

By the late 1960s, generative semantics had become popular with many former followers of Chomsky's. Its early form fell within the symbol manipulation paradigm. Treating thought as formal logic worked as an important discovery procedure for linguistic semantics for a while. But by 1968, problems arose accounting for meaning within symbolic logic, and I and several colleagues—Jim McCawley, Ed Keenan, and Barbara Partee—turned to model-theoretic logic, which went beyond symbol manipulation to mathematical models using set theory.

Inklings of the New Enlightenment Mind

By the mid-1970s, linguists like Ron Langacker, Gilles Fauconnier, Len Talmy, Charles Fillmore, and I had turned up data that in principle could not be accounted for by any symbol manipulation paradigm or by model-theoretic logic. At the same time, results in the cognitive and brain sciences had started to come in that suggested that such data could be handled by a theory that integrated linguistics into the cognitive and brain sciences. Cognitive linguistics was born in 1975, and it has been developing in communities around the world ever since, studying a huge range of linguistic phenomena that cannot fit the symbol manipulation paradigm, but that makes sense in terms of the cognitive and brain sciences. Those that have the most immediate import for politics are frames, conceptual metaphors, and prototypes, as I have discussed in previous chapters. Here is how those ideas developed:

The idea that we think in terms of "frames" arose in the late 1960s and early 1970s. The sociologist Erving Goffman studied social institutions and practices in minute detail.[3] To make sense of what he observed, he used the metaphor of Life as a Play: each form of institution or practice is like a drama, with players, dialogue, and relatively well-defined actions. In a hospital, the patients, nurses, doctors, visitors, and orderlies all have different roles. The doctors perform diagnoses, prescribe drugs, and operate, but the patients and visitors do not. Operations occur in operating rooms, not in the lobby. Elevators are in the lobby, not in the operating rooms.

Life, Goffman says, is made up of successive and overlapping frames—narratives that people playing those roles carry out. We are acutely aware of them when, for example, we get a job in a new profession and have to learn what someone in our new role has to, can, and cannot do. The frame—and the roles—are visible, in practices.

But mostly the frames we live are unconscious and reflexive, as when you are ordering a coffee or asking directions or driving home. As Goffman says, the "user" of a frame is "likely to be unaware of such organized features as the framework has."

The idea of the frame had a different utility as academics began to observe computers as well as human culture. Marvin Minsky, one of the founders of artificial intelligence, observed in 1974 that information comes in structures he called "frames."[4] A frame for Minsky was a data structure for representing a stereotyped situation, like being in a certain kind of living room, or going to a child's birthday party or a hospital.

We can think of a frame as a network of nodes and relations. The "top levels" of a frame are fixed, and represent things that are always true about the supposed situation. The lower levels have many terminals—"slots" that must be filled by specific instances or data. Each terminal can specify conditions its assignments must meet. Collections of related frames are linked together into frame systems.

Around the same time, Roger Shank and Robert Abelson developed a similar account of what they called "scripts."[5] Their classic example was the Restaurant script, with slots: customer, maître d', waiter/waitress, cook, table, seats, menu, dish, dish prices, check, tip. The customer, maître d', waiter, and chef are constrained to being people, the dish is food, and so on. There is a sequence: first the customers are seated at a table by the maître d' and given menus, then the waiter takes their order, and so on. The stories we tell, say what happened at the restaurant, are structured in this way.

One can see in scripts the link between frames and narratives. Narratives are frames that tell a story. They have semantic roles, properties of the role, relations among roles, and scenarios. What makes it a narrative—a story—and not just a mere frame? A narrative has a point to it, a moral. It is about how you should live your life—or how you shouldn't. It has emotional content: events that make you sad or angry or in awe.

Charles Fillmore, founder of the field of frame semantics, has studied frames in more detail than anyone else. His evidence comes from a number of linguistic sources. The first is "semantic fields," clusters of related words or phrases. Examples of semantic fields are {knife, fork, spoon}, {Sunday, Monday, Tuesday,...}, {buy, sell, cost, price,... }, {table, chair, couch,...}, {accelerator, carburetor, brake, clutch,...}, {restaurant, waiter, customer, menu, dish, check,...}, and so on. In the simple cases (of which there are thousands), it is easy to tell what is in or out of a semantic field—so easy that no scientific funding agency would bother funding the experiment, though one could set one up as follows: Each of the following has three elements that belong together and one that does not belong with the others. Pick out the one that does not belong: {knife, couch, fork, spoon}, {buy, sell, Sunday, price}, {banana, carburetor, brake, accelerator}. The ones that don't belong, obviously, are "couch," "Sunday," and "banana."

Fillmore then asked what characterized the relationships among the elements in a semantic field. His answer was a "frame."[6] A Fillmore frame consists of frame elements called "semantic roles," like Minsky's "slots" and Goffman's "roles." Each semantic role has a set of constraints on what can "fill" that role. Then there are relationships among the roles. There are presuppositions: presupposed "truths of the frame" about the roles. There are possible scenarios: processes or sequences of actions that define what can happen in a frame. And possible contrasts between elements that fill a role.

Take, for example, the Commercial Event frame. The semantic

roles are Buyer, Seller, Goods, and Money. The Buyer and Seller are People.

The scenario has three parts:

First part: The Buyer Wants the Goods and Has the Money, and the Seller Wants the Money and Has the Goods.
Second part: The Buyer Transfers the Money to the Seller, and the Seller Transfers the Goods to the Buyer.
Third part: The Buyer Has the Goods, and the Seller Has the Money.

The scenario presupposes other frames: a Desire frame, a Possession frame, and a Transfer frame. The Commercial Event frame is part of a system, and is presupposed by, for instance, the Shopping frame, the Marketing frame, and so on. The Restaurant frame is complex and includes both a Commercial Event frame and a Serving-of-Food frame, where the Goods in the Commercial Event frame is the Food in the Serving-of-Food frame.

Fillmore has hypothesized that the meanings of all words are characterized in terms of frames, a hypothesis that has held up for over thirty years.

In recent years, neural computational models of frames have been constructed in the Neural Theory of Language (NTL) group at the International Computer Science Institute (ICSI) at Berkeley. The grammar and the lexicon are characterized in NTL theory in terms of what are called "constructions"—neural circuitry linking speech (and writing and signs) to meanings, that is, frames, metaphors, and so on, which activate mental simulations. The mental simulations carry out inferences. The result is a collection of neural computational models of words, grammar, language understanding, and language acquisition.[7]

Vittorio Gallese is one of the original discoverers of mirror neurons. He and I, working together in 2002, discovered something startling in going through primary mirror neuron data: all the information needed for the frame structure characterizing the concept of grasping can be found in the mirror neurons governing the action and perception of grasping.[8] In other words, a conceptual structure for physical actions exists in the neural system governing bodily movements and the visual perception of those movements. It was evidence that the most basic concepts characterized in frames could be physically embodied at the level of mirror neurons. It is hard to underestimate how far the idea that concepts are physically embodied, using the sensory motor system of the brain, is from disembodied Enlightenment reason—from the usual view of concepts as disembodied abstractions, entirely separate from the sensory motor system.

Embodiment and Conceptual Metaphor

Most of us are taught a twenty-five-hundred-year-old theory of metaphor, one that goes back to Aristotle. This age-old theory assumed that ordinary language was literal—that is, it expressed ideas that could fit the world directly. Metaphor, the theory claimed, was not a matter of thought, but rather an abnormal use of language, based on similarity. It was, the claim went, used primarily for poetic or deceptive purposes, especially in political rhetoric. A few philosophers (such as Vico, Nietzsche, and Cassirer) and literary critics (such as I. A. Richards) had noticed the existence of metaphorical thought, but none had figured out the scientific details of how it works. The old theory held sway until 1977.[9]

Michael Reddy, in a classic paper written in 1977 and published in 1979 called "The Conduit Metaphor," showed that metaphor is really conceptual—a matter of thought—with language secondary.[10] Reddy was looking at expressions that indicated issues of communication, and took them from his Columbia colleagues' comments on freshman themes. He found comments like: "try to pack more thoughts into fewer words," "the sentence was filled with emotion," "that remark is completely impenetrable," "your words are hollow—you don't mean them," "your concepts come across beautifully," and over a hundred more. Looking for the generalization over them, he concluded that the major metaphor for communication is: *Words are containers for ideas, and communication is putting ideas into words and sending them along a "conduit"—a means of communication—to a listener or reader who then extracts the meanings from the words.*

In early 1978, with Reddy's paper lying unread on my desk, I reached the same conclusion by looking at expressions for thinking and talking about love in terms of travel: *The relationship has hit a dead end. We can't keep going the way we've been going. We may have to turn back. The marriage is on the rocks. It's off the track. We're spinning our wheels in this relationship. We're stuck; our relationship isn't going anywhere. It's been a long, bumpy road. We've come a long way. We're going in different directions. We're at a crossroads. We may have to go our separate ways. I may have to bail out of this marriage.*

The generalization governing all these different expressions is conceptual in nature, a way to conceptualize love in terms of travel. The general idea can be expressed as a mapping from the frame for travel to the frame for love, with roles mapped to roles.

Travel	Love
Travelers	→ Lovers
Vehicle	→ Relationship
Destinations	→ Common life goals
Travel difficulties	→ Love difficulties

The mapping constitutes the metaphor. What is important is not the mere words, but the fact that you can think in terms of this metaphor. The metaphor maps knowledge about travel, as characterized by the Travel frame, onto knowledge about love in a Love as Travel frame, allowing you to reason metaphorically. For example, if you've hit a dead end in your relationship, you can't keep going the way you've been going. You may have to turn back. If you are going in different directions, that means you are unlikely to get to the same place—unlikely to reach common life goals, and you may have to split up.

Mark Johnson and I wondered about cases like Love is a Journey, where there is no apparent reason for Journeys to correspond to Love. We noticed something interesting about the Love is a Journey metaphor: it seemed to make use of metaphors of a more general sort. For example, take the submappings Common Life Goals are Destinations and Difficulties are Impediments to Motion. There are general metaphors that Achieving a Purpose is Reaching a Destination, that Purposeful Action is Motion to a Destination, and that Difficulties (in achieving purposes) are Impediments to Motion (to such a destination). These separate, and more general, metaphors seemed to playing a role in the Love is a Journey system of mappings.

But why, we asked, in Love is a Journey, is the Love Relationship taken to be a Vehicle? A vehicle is an enclosure, and there is another general metaphor that Relationships are Enclosures. Thus we speak of being in a relationship, of leaving the relationship, and sometimes even of being trapped in a relationship. Moreover, when two people are in a vehicle, they are typically close together. In addition, there is a separate and general metaphor that Intimacy is Closeness, with expressions like: *We're very close. We've drifted apart. We've split up. We've been together for ten years now.* A vehicle happens to be an enclosure in which the occupants are close and that is used to travel.

But what, we asked, does love have to do with destinations? In Western culture, people are supposed to have purposes in life—life goals, things you plan to achieve over a lifetime. We have a major cultural metaphor for life, namely, Life is a Goal-Oriented Activity. That is, life is supposed to be purposeful. Given the metaphor that Achieving a Purpose is reaching a Destination, long-term life goals are metaphorically seen as destinations to be reached over the course of a lifetime. We even have documents showing how far we have gotten by what age. They are called CVs, from *curriculum vitae,* Latin for "the course of life" (from *curro,* "to run"). People who are in love are, in this culture, supposed to not only have life goals, but compatible life goals, that is, destinations they can reach together. The Love is a Journey metaphor is about the difficulties in doing so: long, bumpy roads, dead-end streets, getting stuck, going in different directions, being at a crossroads, and so on.

In short, we can analyze the Love is a Journey metaphor into metaphorical parts, the general metaphors: Intimacy is Closeness; Relationships are Enclosures—special case: the Love Relationship; Life is a Goal-Oriented Activity; Achieving a Purpose is Reaching a Destination; Difficulties are Impediments to Reaching Destinations.

Most of these general metaphors, like More is Up, are based on correlations in common everyday experience, especially experiences we've had as children. Intimacy correlates with physical closeness; we are physically close to the people we become intimate with. What we have called "enclosures" are bounded regions in space. Our basic relationships develop within our family, with whom we share a bounded region of space, a home. Achieving a purpose regularly requires moving to a destination: if you want a cold beer, you've got to go to the fridge. And difficulties regularly correlate with things keeping you from reaching destinations: if the kitchen is blocked off, you won't be able to get to the fridge for that beer. Such correlations in experience occur over and over, in culture after culture.

In short, Johnson and I found that conceptual metaphors like Love is a Journey is a mapping that is comprised of submappings—simpler metaphors that occur independently and that are based on correlations in everyday experience. These are embodied metaphors, based on everyday embodied experiences—for example, experiences correlating achieving purposes (e.g., getting a beer) with reaching a destination (e.g., going to the fridge); experiences like living or working with someone in closely bounded area (an apartment, a house, or an office) and having a relationship with that person. As the years of research around the world continued, more cases of embodied metaphors turned up.[11]

It took until 1997 for this to be explained, when Srini Narayanan came up with the neural theory of metaphor: regular co-occurrence in experience means repeated simultaneous activation in different brain regions.[12] Spreading activation forms neural circuits connecting the regions. Those connections physically constitute a "primary metaphor." Examples are exactly the "smaller" metaphors we had noticed, such as Intimacy is Closeness; Relationships are Enclosures—special case: the Love Relationship; Life is a Goal-Oriented Activity; Achieving a Purpose is Reaching a Destination; Difficulties are Impediments to Moving to Destinations. Love is a Journey is a complex metaphor formed when primary metaphors are neurally bound together.

Our brains acquire such primary metaphors by the hundreds. By the time we are in mid- to late childhood, we have hundreds of primary metaphors structuring our brains, available to bind to frames and to other metaphors to form new metaphorical concepts.

Language connects to our conceptual structure of frames and metaphors in complex ways. In some cases, the words for source domain concepts are used for the corresponding target domain concepts, as when we speak of being at a "crossroads" in a relationship. But there are more complex cases. Take "spinning our wheels" in a relationship. There a conventional cultural image (typically unconscious) is activated, in which the lovers are in a car that is stuck in sand, mud, snow, or on ice, its wheels are spinning, and what we know about the image is that the occupants are putting a lot of effort into trying to make it go and are frustrated. The Love is a Journey metaphor maps that knowledge about the image to knowledge about the relationship: it's not going anywhere, and the lovers are putting a lot of effort into it and are frustrated.

Mark Turner and I noticed an even more complex relationship between primary metaphors and language.[13] In Shakespeare's Sonnet 73, the first quatrain is based on the metaphor that A Lifetime is a Year, with Old Age as Autumn and Winter as Death.

That time of year thou mayst in me behold
When yellow leaves, or none, or few, do hang
Upon those boughs that shake against the cold,
Bare ruined choirs, where late the sweet birds sang.

The second quatrain is based on the metaphor that A Lifetime is a Day, Old Age is Sunset, and Death is Night.

In me thou seest the twilight of such day
As after sunset fadeth in the west;
Which by and by black night doth take away
Death's second self that seals up all in rest.

In the last six lines, we find the conceptual metaphor A Lifetime is a Fire, Old Age is Glowing Coals, and Death is Cold Ashes.

In me thou seest the glowing of such fire
That on the ashes of his youth doth lie
As the deathbed on which it must expire
Consumed with that which it was nourished by.
This thou perceivest, which makes thy love more strong,
To love that well which thou must leave ere long.

The metaphors of A Lifetime as a Year, Day, and Fire make sense together. But why do they make sense together? Poets often conceptualize a lifetime in those ways. And why does Shakespeare, the greatest poetic mind of all time, put them all in one of his greatest sonnets?

On the surface these metaphors do not seem to be embodied. Lifetimes don't correlate in our experience with years, days, and fires. But on a deeper analysis, they are embodied. A year, a day, and a fire all share an image schema: a waxing-and-waning cycle of intensity—starting from nothing, slowly growing, reaching a peak, slowly declining in intensity, finally dwindling again to nothing. A lifetime too, lived out to full extent, has that overall shape, as does each breath we take. In all three, the cycle begins at darkness, then gets lighter and lighter, then slowly gets darker till dark returns. And in all three, the cycle begins with cold, gets warmer, reaches a peak of heat, and slowly gets colder till cold returns.

All three sections can thus be seen as special cases of these three conceptual metaphors combined by neural binding: Life is Light and Death is Darkness. Life is Heat and Death is Cold. Life is a Waxing-and-Waning Cycle.

Each is based on a correlation in experience: only when one is alive can one see light. At death, one loses sight. Only when one is alive is the body warm. At death it becomes cold. And a lifetime starts with a low level of strength and vitality, grows to a peak, and then declines.

Each section in the poem is a special case of these three deeper, simpler, and embodied metaphors—metaphors we all know and sense whether or not they are overtly present in the actual language of the poem. Shakespeare, being Shakespeare, knew that intuitively.

These three primary metaphors are structuring our under-standing of the poem without any overt language. They do so when they are bound together, giving rise to special cases of a year, a day, and a fire, which do show up in the language of the poem.

The point is not that Shakespeare was a genius. It's that brains normally work this way. This is just what we see in the case of strict father and nurturant parent worldviews. They are meta-phors that structure whole systems of thought, though they rarely show up in the language of the discourse they are structuring. Where they show up is in the forms of reason used and in the coherence of apparently disparate ideas.

Essential Metaphor

On the old theory, metaphor is extraneous to the meaning of a concept. But conceptual metaphor changes all that. The Conduit metaphor is the principal way we think about communication, but it is nonetheless a metaphor, a way of understanding communication in terms of the sending of physical objects.

The Conduit metaphor, by the way, is one of several metaphors for communication. Metaphors for ideas and thought tend to give rise to metaphors for communication. For example, in the Thinking is Moving metaphor,[14] ideas are locations in a terrain, and in thinking, the thinker moves from idea-location to idea-location. In logical reasoning, a thinker goes step by step, his mind not wandering. Communication is providing a guided tour along a path of thought, as in sentences like "Let me take you through the argument," "Are you following me?" and so on.

In the Knowing is Seeing metaphor, Thinking is Looking at objects, and Communicating is Showing, as in "Now I'm going to show you that you are wrong," "He pointed out that global warming is real," and so on.

And in the metaphor in which Ideas are Food and Understanding is Digesting, and Communicating is Feeding, as in "I've been feeding him stock market tips for weeks—so many he can barely digest them all."

Overall, the concept of communication is mostly metaphorical. What would communicating be without sending messages and getting ideas across? Without showing or pointing out? Without taking someone through an argument step by step? Without feeding people information? If you strip away all the metaphor, it's not clear how you could think about communication or communicate what communication is.

The same is true of love, which is an emotion that has little nonmetaphorical conceptual content that one can reason in terms of.[15] There are many metaphors for love beside the Journey metaphor—as a physical force (She knocked me off my feet, There's a magnetism between us); as a gift (I gave her my love); as madness (I'm crazy about her); as heat (A hot romance, His passion has cooled); as becoming a single entity or linked, and so on. Love just is not love without the heat of passion, without the physical force and magnetism, the madness, the gift, the journey, the fusing, and so on.

Conceptual metaphor is not just an add-on. It is an inherent and extremely rich aspect of thought.

Frames and Metaphors in Grammar

Vittorio Gallese and I, in noticing that frame information occurred in the mirror neuron data, also found that the mirror neurons and nearby neuronal groups provide information to characterize semantic roles for a general Action frame: Agent, Action, Patient, Location, and Purpose. We pointed it out for grasping, and observed that the same kind of information is available at the single-neuron level for all such actions that is for a general frame, with no specific action.

Such generalized frames have been studied in linguistics for more than four decades. Beginning in 1965, Charles Fillmore[16] and Jeff Gruber[17] independently started investigating how such general semantic roles worked in grammar, showing that such roles enter into general grammatical principles.

A huge amount of research linking such general frames and grammar has been done since then across languages. Other semantic roles that have been studied include the Instrument of an action, the Experiencer of an event, and the Stimulus of the experience, the Protagonist of the event (from whose viewpoint the event is simulated), the Source, Path, and Goal of movement, and so on.

What this research shows is that in the grammar of a language, neural circuitry can link such semantic roles to various positions in a linear ordering, or may mark them with case endings.[18]

What we grammarians call nouns, verbs, prepositions, clauses, and other grammatical categories appear to be grammarians' names for the circuitry linking physical form (speech, writing, sign) to conceptual categories. Traditional grammarians characterized a noun as the name of a person, place, or thing. The name part is the phonological form. The person, place, or thing is some sort of conceptual entity. "Noun" is the relation linking them. As such, "Noun" defines a category of names for persons, places, things, and their metaphorical projections, such as states, actions, and so on.

The noun "desk" consists of a phoneme sequence /desk/—a form—linked to a meaning consisting of a mental image of a desk shape, a motor program for interacting with desks, knowledge about desks, and so on. There are other kinds of nouns of course—states (metaphorical locations), actions (metaphorical objects), institutions (metaphorical persons).

Grammar is an interesting site for understanding how primary metaphors operate in our conceptual systems. Take the metaphor that States are Locations (bounded regions in space). It arises because of correlations between being in a state and being in a location. For example, if you want to get cool on a hot day, you might go under a tree. If a child wants to feel warm and secure, she might get under the covers in her bed. We constantly experience certain states in certain locations, which give rise to the primary metaphor. The metaphor is not about any particular state or location. It is about states in general and locations in general. Once the mapping is learned, it is fixed in our brains, ready to be activated, as it is almost anytime we think about a state. All particular states make use of the concept of a state in general, which is understood as a bounded region in space. That is why we can apply that metaphor to reason about states. If you are in a depression, you're not out of it. If you're on the edge of a depression, you're not yet in it and you're not far from being in it. The language and the logic of bounded regions in space is applied to states. And so states, as metaphorical places, are nouns, and hence happiness and depression are nouns.

Let's turn to simple sentences. Take the sentence "Sam bought the car from Harry." "Buy" is both defined relative to the Commercial Event frame, with semantic roles Buyer, Seller, Goods, and Money, and a scenario where the Buyer starts out with the money and the Seller the Goods; then they exchange; finally the Seller has the Money, and the Buyer the Goods. But the concepts of buying and selling in addition bind other frames to the Commercial Event frame. The concept of buying takes the buyer's point of view in simulation. The Buyer is the protagonist throughout the scenario. In addition, the general Action frame is bound to the Commercial Event frame, with the Buyer bound to the Agent role and the Goods bound to the Patient role. The Action is bound to the Exchange, with the Buyer-Agent seen as the causal agent in the exchange. In the mental simulation, the Buyer's concerns are the important ones—Will the car work? Can he afford it?

The verb "buy" has the meaning just given and is pronounced as "buy" in the present tense, and "bought" in the past tense. "Buy" is an action verb. An action verb in general—as a concept in grammar—is a circuit linking an Action in the Action frame to some unspecified phoneme sequence.

Now for word order. In a simple Action clause in English, the Agent comes first, then the Action comes after the Agent, and the Patient comes after the Action. From the neural perspective, an action clause looks like this: In the Action clause construction, the meaning is the Action frame; the form part of the construction consists of a linear ordering of forms—words and morphemes. The grammatical construction consists of a neural mapping that connects slots in that ordering to the Action frame roles: the first slot to Agent, the second to Action, and the third to Patient. This view of grammar is now being worked out in detail.

"Recursion" in the Brain's Grammar

Chomsky still claims that the structure of language is given by symbol manipulation and phrase structure trees. His principal argument in recent years has been recursion, where clauses can be embedded within other clauses apparently ad infinitum, as in the example given earlier from "The House That Jack Built." But there are no symbols or phrase structure trees in the brain. How does recursion work in a brain-based theory of grammar?

What are called "embeddings" are a consequence of frames and neural binding. Frame structure with binding supplies the hierarchical structure of the sentence. Take a sentence like "Bill believed Sam bought the book from Harry." The Belief frame has the semantic roles Believer and Content-of-Belief. The Believer role is neurally bound to Bill. The Content-of-Belief Role—a functional cluster of neurons—is neurally bound to the meaning of the clause "Sam bought the book from Harry." That meaning is given by the Buy frame, where Sam is neurally bound to the Buyer role, Harry to the Seller role, and the book to the Goods role.

The entire Buy frame forms an integrated neural circuit. In the neural theory of language, it is hypothesized that every frame contains a subcircuit called a control node, with the following properties:

- When the control node is activated, the entire frame circuit is activated.
- When any role in the frame is activated, the control node is activated, which then activates the rest of the frame.
- When the control node is inhibited, the entire frame is inhibited.

Now consider the control node of the Buy frame. When this node is neurally bound to the Content-of-Belief role of the Believe frame, we get the meaning of "Bill believed Sam bought the book from Harry."

This is called a sentential complement by grammarians, and the clause is called "embedded." Embedding is achieved by the neural binding of frame control nodes (for entire frames) to frame role nodes. We can keep this process of binding up to get further embedding: May believed that Max believed that Bill believed... that Sam bought the book from Harry—as many times as we like. This is how a neural grammar creates infinite possibilities from finite means.

But what about the Belief frame? Don't you need multiple instances of it in "May believed that Max believed that Bill believed..."? That's true. What is an instance? Recall that a node is a circuit that contains between tens and hundreds of neurons. In the theory of neural computation, instances of nodes are sub-circuits with the same computational properties as the whole circuit. As you go through the sentence, only a small number of Belief frame subcircuits are needed, with the control node of one subcircuit bound to a role node of another.

In addition to complements, there other kinds of embedded clauses. Here things get a bit complicated. A noun is the name of an entity. An entity is a category member and has properties and a referent—something it refers to. Thus the roles in the Entity frame include Referent, Category, and Property.

Semantically, a restrictive relative clause neurally binds the control node of a whole frame F to the Property role of an Entity frame, and it binds some role in the frame F to the Referent of the Entity.

For example, consider "the book Bill bought from Harry." The book is an Entity. In other words, "the book" is a form linked by a construction to an Entity frame, which has in it roles such as Referent, Category, and Property. The Book frame is bound to the Category role, making the entity a book. "Bill bought __ from Harry" is the form of a Buy frame with the Goods role having no phonological form. The relative clause construction is general, but in this case has the effect that it:

- Neurally binds the control node of the Buy frame to the Property role of the book.
- Binds the Goods role of the Buy frame to the Referent of the book.
- Orders the phonological form of the Buy frame following the book.

• Constrains the Goods role to be expressed in form by a relative pronoun or nothing—in this case, nothing.

The "embedding" of the surface form is a consequence of neural binding in the semantics.

Adverbial clauses involve bindings of frame control nodes to Roles in Proposition frames. Each Proposition frame comes with such roles as Time, Place, and Reason. For example, in "John was sad because Sarah left," the proposition expressed by "John was sad" has a Reason role, and the frame control node for "Sarah left" is bound to that Reason node. "Because" precedes a clause bound to a Reason role. Again the appearance of an "embedded" clause is the result of a binding in the semantics of a role node of one frame to the control node of another frame.

Neural grammar in fine detail has begun to be developed. It is important, because it helps to explain how language works in the brain and why it is so powerful.

It is inevitable that the theory of language will accommodate to brain science. The symbol manipulation paradigm for the mind and language, which is still popular in the few (four or five dozen) departments of linguistics in the United States, will fade entirely over the coming decades and be replaced by a brain-based linguistics.

But the brain-based theory of thought and language that is emerging has consequences in the academic world far beyond linguistics per se. It utterly changes philosophy, as Mark Johnson and I surveyed in *Philosophy in the Flesh*. Philosophy had been viewed as a priori theorizing independent of evidence.[19] The philosophy of language, for example, mostly proceeded without taking into account the massive knowledge about real languages. A brain-based account of language and mind challenges that view. Philosophy proceeded without recognition that many of its central concepts were metaphorical in nature, and that philosophical theories themselves each adopt certain metaphors as central truths. Anglo-American philosophical approaches tend to adopt the correspondence theory of truth and a view of meaning as truth conditions.

Both have turned out to be empirically false. But changing the very idea of philosophy itself is a no small matter. Philosophers are human. Their brains won't change overnight, any more than anyone else's will. But philosophy is important. Most contemporary theories of politics and morality have arisen from philosophy as a discipline. In a New Enlightenment, political philosophy, like other philosophy, will eventually be based on the twenty-first-century mind.

What If It Works?

Suppose the twenty-first-century understanding of the brain and the mind were widely known and fully appreciated. What might change? Here's where the changes in consciousness would begin:

We would understand that our brains evolved for empathy, for cooperation, for connection to each other and to the earth. We cannot exist alone.

We would embrace the fact that empathy is at the heart of American democracy. It is a positive force for human society at large. It is why we care about fundamental human rights. It is why we care about protecting our people in all ways, from criminals, fire, disease, disasters, impure food, dangerous working conditions, consumer fraud, and poverty in old age. It is why we care about empowerment of both individuals and businesses: roads and bridges for transportation, the Internet and satellites for communication, public schools for education, a banking system for capital, a court system for contracts. It is why we care about checks and balances against authoritarian power. It is why we place that care in a government we choose. Without such care, there would be no America.

We would see how empathy is also at the heart of ecological consciousness. It transcends political parties and national boundaries. Our connection to the natural world and to other beings, human or not, is central to our humanity. With the cultivation of empathy, ecological consciousness would permeate every aspect of life.

With the twenty-first-century mind comes a new sophistication about systems of frames. It should be harder to use framing for lying, cheating, and political blackmail now that the act of lying with frames can be named and pinpointed. That alone will help. But there is much more.

We would recognize that the two major American modes of political thought—strict and nurturant—exist, but in nonintersecting realms. Many Americans have versions of both, though active in different and distinct areas of life.

Progressive thought would be understood as having as its moral base the politics of empathy, with the responsibility and strength necessary to act on that empathy. The role of government would be seen as protection and empowerment. This would be understood as the moral basis of democracy. The moral authority of government would come from earned respect in carrying out those moral missions of government. Taxes would been seen as payment for both continuing protection and empowerment.

Conservative politics would be recognized as being the politics of authority, discipline, and obedience: the role of government might be large, but it would be skewed toward maximizing national military and economic power, maintaining public order with shows of force, creating and defending laissez-faire markets, encouraging privateers, protecting private property, and promoting individual responsibility and conservative forms of religion.

American democratic principles (such as the balance of powers, habeas corpus, fundamental rights) would be recognized as deriving from the progressive understanding of freedom, fairness, equality, opportunity, responsibility, accountability, and so on. It would also be recognized that all those concepts are contested and have conservative versions, and that a very different conservative view of democracy as tied to laissez-faire free markets would be publicly recognized.

A New Enlightenment would not be a utopia. It would be understood that conservatives are not going to go away, nor are biconceptual "partial conservatives." The question of whether

American politics should be based on empathy or authority will not disappear. Democracy would continue to be problematic since antidemocratic elements are always going to be present. But our new knowledge would bring the question out into the open.

It would be understood that there is no left-to-right line between progressive and conservative views, and no unified "moderate" worldview. "Moderate progressives" use conservative values and modes of thought in some issue areas, and "moderate conservatives" use progressive values and modes of thought on some issues.

The vital importance of childrearing would be recognized. The public would understand that a child's brain is largely shaped during the first three to five years by the large-scale death of neurons. The ones that go unused die off. Early childhood education would be recognized as vital. Studies showing that nurturant upbringing is far better for children—and for society—would be well known. Nurturant forms of childrearing and teaching would be instituted nationwide. Child-beating and other child abuse would be outlawed. Advocates of strict father upbringing—like James Dobson and Dr. Laura—would be recognized as harmful to children.[1]

The framing of issues in public debate would be a matter of open public discussion. Political leaders would be aware of the values behind the conceptual frames they are using. They would avoid using frames that best fit the other side's values, values they don't share.

Policymakers would become aware of the moral basis of their policies and would be expected to specify that moral basis explicitly.

Journalists would be aware when they are using politically motivated frames, and would discuss the alternative framings of the issues.

Pollsters and those who pay for polls would become more sensitive to the framing of questions. Political campaigns would not follow polls but use them to see how they can change public opinion to their moral worldview.

The need for a foreign policy focused on people, not just states, would be recognized, with foreign policy coming to embrace issues like hunger, poverty, women's and children's rights, public health, basic education, global ecology, water rights, the effects of global warming, the rights of indigenous peoples, and so on.

Kinds of common wealth—the air, the airwaves, the rivers, streams, and aquifers, the oceans, the national forests—would be recognized as more valuable preserved than used and as property owned by all and kept in trust, with permits for use sold at auction and caps placed on pollution and reasonable use.

Privateering would be a recognizable conservative strategy, with cases discussed in public. The principle of conservation of government would be recognized. Corporations would be recognized as forms of government—they govern people's lives in many ways. Deregulation and privatization would be understood not as the elimination of government, but as a shift from a government with accountability to the public to a government without accountability to the public, from public government with a moral mission (protection and empowerment) to private government with only the mission of maximizing profits.

Health would be seen as a matter of protection, not insurance. Making a profit by selling health insurance policies and then denying care would be recognized overtly and discussed accordingly.

Education would be seen as a matter of empowerment—of enhancing the full range of natural talents and opening up wondrous worlds to students. Teaching to the test would be abandoned, replaced by teaching to think on one's own. Advances in our understanding of the brain and the mind would be taught.

Accountability would flow upward—toward those in charge, not downward to those who are powerless or subordinate.

The immorality of the vast divide between the ultra-wealthy and the middle and lower classes would be manifest. Vast wealth translates into vast power, which in itself threatens democracy. It also drains limited resources (such as accessibility to land) that should be much more widely distributed.

I could go on, but I'll stop here.

Our minds work very differently than Descartes and Kant thought they did. We are far more fascinating creatures than our great political theorists—from Plato and Aristotle to Rousseau, Hobbes, Locke, Marx, J. S. Mill, and John Rawls, for instance— thought we were. A new understanding is emerging about what it means to be human. Our political institutions and practices reflect our collective self-understanding. When that changes dramatically, so should our politics.

But we'd better hurry up. The ice caps are melting.

Acknowledgments

A book like this cannot be written without a lot of help. A hearty Thank you! for very useful discussion to:

My wife, Kathleen Frumkin, who supplied daily insights and enormous support.

My son, Andrew Lakoff, and Daniela Bleichmar.

My brother, Sandy Lakoff.

My colleagues at the Rockridge Institute: Bruce Budner, Glenn W. Smith, Evan Frisch, Eric Haas, Sherry Reson, Joe Brewer, Scott Parkinson, Christina Smith, Will Bunnett, and Dashielle Vawter.

Politically involved friends: Robert Reich, Michael Pollan, Manuel Castells, Wes Boyd, Joan Blades, Peter Barnes, Don Arbitblit, Jeff Mankoff, Guy and Jeanine Saperstein, Steve Silberstein, Kathy Barry, Bob Burnett, Bob Epstein, Harley and Beatrice Shaiken, Chris Edley, Maria Echaveste, Quinn Delaney, Wayne Jordan, Catherine Trimbur, Mal Burnstein, Idelisse Maleve, Steve and Mary Swig, Carl Pope, Hannah Beth Jackson.

Friends among the Netroots: too many to list, but special thanks to Eli Pariser, Markos Moulitsos, Don Hazen, and Arianna Huffington.

The Neural Theory of Language and Cognitive Linguistics groups at UC Berkeley: Jerome Feldman, Eve Sweetser, Charles Fillmore, Srini Narayanan, Ellen Dodge, John Bryant, Nancy Chang, Eva Mok, Karen Sullivan, Russell Lee-Goldman, Michael Ellsworth, Marc Ettlinger, Sarah Berson, Russell Rhodes, Jenny Lederer, Zhenya Antic, Jisup Hong, Elisabeth Wehling, and Joshua Marker.

Neuroscienstists and cognitive scientists: Antonio and Hanna

Damasio, Vittorio Gallese, Marco Iacoboni, Drew Westen, Lisa Aziz-Zadeh, Robb Willer, John Jost, Ray Gibbs.

And frequent collaborators Mark Johnson and Rafael Núñez.

I also want to express my gratitude to the worldwide community of cognitive linguists and other cognitive scientists, whose work over the past three decades has so vastly changed our understanding of the brain, the mind, and language.

Notes

Introduction: Brain Change and Social Change

1. Andrea Rock, *The Mind at Night* (New York: Basic Books, 2005). "According to Dartmouth neuroscientist Michael Gazzaniga, 98 percent of what the brain does is outside of conscious awareness." Numbers like 98 percent, strictly speaking, make little sense since you can't really count thoughts. Yet the percentage seems about right. For example, in text analysis, if we write down everything needed to understand a text that is neither in conscious awareness nor written in the text, an estimate of 95–98 percent seems to be in the right ballpark.

1. Anna Nicole on the Brain

1. George Lakoff, "Structural Complexity in Fairy Tales," paper presented at the 1964 summer meeting of the Linguistic Society of America, Bloomington, IN (unpublished). This was an updating of Vladimir Propp's classic *Morphology of the Folktale*, showing how complex whole plots can be understood as simple plots woven together and systematically structured.

2. Roger Shank and Robert Abelson, *Scripts, Plans, Goals and Understanding* (Hillsdale, NJ: Erlbaum, 1977).

3. Jerome Feldman, *From Molecule to Metaphor* (Cambridge, MA: MIT Press, 2006). Feldman argues that combinations of simple "triangle nodes" are sufficient to characterize the neural computational properties of frames. Each "node" is a relatively small collection of neurons forming a circuit. In a triangle node, there are three such circuits, and the firing of any two activates the third. In addition there is a control node, a simple circuit that accomplishes this.

4. Erving Goffman, *Frame Analysis: An Essay on the Organization of Experience* (New York: Harper and Row, 1974).

5. Charles Fillmore, "An Alternative to Checklist Theories of Meaning," in *Proceedings of the First Annual Meeting of the Berkeley Linguistics Society* (Berkeley, CA: Berkeley Lingustics Society, 1975), 123–31. Charles

Fillmore, "Frame Semantics," in Linguistic Society of Korea, ed., *Linguistics in the Morning Calm* (Seoul: Hanshin), 111–38. Charles Fillmore, "Frames and the Semantics of Understanding," *Quaderni di Semantica* 6 (1985): 222–53.

6. Vittorio Gallese and George Lakoff, "The Brain's Concepts: The Role of the Sensory-Motor System in Conceptual Structure," *Cognitive Neuropsychology*, 22(2005): 455–79.

7. Antonio Damasio, *Descartes' Error* (New York: Grosset/Putnam) 1974), 174. Antonio Damasio, *Looking for Spinoza* (New York: Harcourt, 2003), 147–50.

8. Srini Narayanan, "Moving Right Along: A Computational Model of Metaphorical Reasoning About Events," *Proceedings of the National Conference on Artificial Intelligence*, 1999 (AAAI '99): 121–28. Feldman, *From Molecule to Metaphor*.

9. Dan P. McAdams, *The Redemptive Self: Stories Americans Live By* (New York: Oxford University Press, 2006). Dan P. McAdams, *The Person: A New Introduction to Personality Psychology*, 4th ed. (New York: Wiley, 2006). McAdams and his colleagues at the Northwestern University Psychology Department have shown that it is common for people to live out the Redemption narrative. He suggests that personality involves living out narratives.

10. http://www.gwu.edu/~nsarchiv/NSAEBB/NSAEBB122/index.htm# kubark.

11. Feldman, *From Molecule to Metaphor*, 213–15.

12. Antonio and Hanna Damasio, personal communication.

13. Marco Iacoboni, *Mirroring People: The New Science of How We Connect with Others* (New York: Farrar, Straus and Giroux, 2008). I highly recommend this excellent popular book on mirror neurons.

14. Naomi Klein, *The Shock Doctrine* (New York: Metropolitan Books, 2007).

15. For a full discussion, see chapter 7.

2. The Political Unconscious

1. Charles Fillmore, "An Alternative to Checklist Theories of Meaning," in *Proceedings of the First Annual Meeting of the Berkeley Linguistics Society* (Berkeley, CA: Berkeley Lingustics Society, 1975), 123–31. Charles Fillmore, "Frame Semantics," in Linguistic Society of Korea, ed., *Linguistics in the Morning Calm* (Seoul: Hanshin), 111–38. Charles Fillmore, "Frames and the Semantics of Understanding," *Quaderni di Semantica* 6 (1985): 222–53.

2. http://www.rockridgeinstitute.org/research/lakoff/tortreform.

3. Al Gore, *The Assault on Reason* (New York: The Penguin Press, 2007), 72.

4. Lynn Hunt, *Inventing Human Rights: A History* (New York: Norton, 2007).

5. J. E. Faust, "Obedience: The Path to Freedom," *Ensign*, May 1999, 45.

6. *New York Times*, March 29, 1994.

7. An excellent discussion of this history is Emma Rothschild's *Economic Sentiments: Adam Smith, Condorcet, and the Enlightenment* (Cambridge, MA, and London: Harvard University Press, 2001), especially chapter 2.

8. Adam Smith, *An Inquiry into the Nature and Causes of the Wealth of Nations*, R. H. Campbell and A. S. Skinner, eds. (Oxford: Clarendon Press, 1976), 157–58.

9. Ibid., 96.

10. Rothschild, *Economic Sentiments*, 64.

11. From the Nixon tapes. Quoted in Michael Moore's movie *Sicko*.

12. Drew Westen, *The Political Brain* (New York: Public Affairs, 2007).

4. The Brain's Role in Political Ideologies

1. Chen-Bo Zhong and Kate Liljenquist, "Washing Away Your Sins: Threatened Morality and Physical Cleansing," *Science* 313, no. 5792 (September 8, 2006): 1451–52.

2. Dan Jones, "Moral Psychology: The Depths of Disgust," *Nature* 447 (June 14, 2007): 768–71.

3. J. Moll et al., "Human Fronto-Mesolimbic Networks Guide Decisions About Charitable Donation," *Proceedings of the National Academy of Sciences USA* 103, no. 42 (October 17, 2006): 15623–28.

4. Marco Iacoboni, *Mirroring People: The New Science of How We Connect with Others* (New York: Farrar, Straus and Giroux, 2008).

5. J. Greene et al., "The Neural Basis of Cognitive Conflict and Control in Moral Judgment," *Neuron* 44 (October 14, 2004): 389–400.

5. A New Consciousness

1. Lynn Hunt, *Inventing Human Rights: A History* (New York: Norton, 2007).

2. George Lakoff, *Don't Think of an Elephant!* (White River Junction, VT: Chelsea Green, 2004). George Lakoff and the Rockridge Institute, *Thinking Points* (New York: Farrar, Straus and Giroux, 2006).

6. Traumatic Ideas: The War on Terror

1. http://www.cfr.org/publication/13432/.

7. Framing Reality: Privateering

1. http://www.youtube.com/watch?v=Zu90tBlkKXw.

2. http://www.nydailynews.com/news/wn_report/2007/10/03/2007-10-03_blackwater_to_guard_fbi_team_probing_it.html.

3. http://www.foodnavigator-usa.com/news/ng.asp?id=76029.

4. http://www.independent.org/publications/tir/article.asp?issueID=49&articleID=631; http://www.independent.org/publications/tir/article.asp?issueID=50&articleID=646; http://www.independent.org/newsroom/article.asp?id=119.

8. Fear of Framing

1. http://judiciary.senate.gov/testimony.cfm?id=2504&wit_id=432.

2. http://www.rockridgeinstitute.org/research/lakoff/occupation.

3. http://www.dailykos.com/story/2007/5/24/143738/794.

4. http://www.globalpolicy.org/security/oil/2005/crudedesigns.htm.

5. http://www.dailytimes.com.pk/default.asp?page=2007%5C09%5C19%5Cstory_19-9-2007_pg3_1.

9. Confronting Stereotypes: Sons of the Welfare Queen

1. *New York Times*, 1976-02-15, p. 51; www.washingtonmonthly.com/features/2003/0309.mendacity-index.html; www.huppi.com/kangaroo/L-welfarequeen.htm; http://en.wikipedia.org/wiki/Welfare_queen.

2. George Lakoff, *Women, Fire, and Dangerous Things* (Chicago University of Chicago Press, 1987). C. Mervis and E. Rosch, "Categorization of Natural Objects," *Annual Review of Psychology* 32 (1981): 89–115. E. Rosch (E. Heider), "Natural Categories," *Cognitive Psychology* 4: 328–50. E. Rosch, "Cognitive Reference Points," *Cognitive Psychology* 7: 532–47. E. Rosch, "Cognitive Representations of Semantic Categories," *Journal of Experimental Psychology* (General) 104: 192–233. E. Rosch, "Human Categorization," in N. Warren, ed., *Studies in Cross-Cultural Psychology* (London: Academic, 1977). E. Rosch, "Principles of Categorization," in E. Rosch and B. B. Lloyd, *Cognition and Categorization* (Hillsdale, NJ: Erlbaum, 1978), 27–48. E. Rosch, "Prototype Classification and Logical Classification: The Two Systems," in E. Scholnick, ed., *New Trends in Cognitive Representation: Challenges to Piaget's Theory* (Hillsdale, NJ: Erlbaum, 1981), 73–86. E. Rosch and B. B. Lloyd, *Cognition and Categorization* (Hillsdale, NJ: Erlbaum, 1978). E. Rosch et al., "Basic Objects in Natural Categories," *Cognitive Psychology* 8 (1976): 382–439.

3. George Lakoff and Mark Johnson, *Metaphors We Live By* (Chicago: University of Chicago Press, 1980); 2nd ed., 2003.

11. Cognitive Policy

1. Garrett Hardin, "The Tragedy of the Commons," *Science* 162 (1968): 1243–48.

12. Contested Concepts Everywhere

1. W. B. Gallie, "Essentially Contested Concepts," *Proceedings of the Aristotelian Society* 56 (1956): 167–98.

2. http://en.wikipedia.org/wiki/Essentially_contested_concept.

3. For a description, see George Lakoff, *Moral Politics: How Liberals and Conservatives Think* (Chicago: University of Chicago Press, 1996; 2002), 299–303.

4. www.americanscientist.org/template/Newsletter?memberid=null& issueid=1661.

5. Paul Starr, *Freedom's Power* (New York: Basic Books, 2007), 2.

13. Exploring the Political Brain

1. Drew Westen, *The Political Brain* (New York: Public Affairs, 2007).

2. Ibid., 264.

3. J. T. Jost et al., "Political Conservatism as Motivated Social Cognition," *Psychological Bulletin* 129, no. 3 (May 2003): 339–75.

4. D. M. Amodio et al., "Neurocognitive Correlates of Liberalism and Conservatism," *Nature Neuroscience*, September 9, 2007.

5. Theodor W. Adorno, *The Authoritarian Personality* (New York: Harper, 1950).

6. Bob Altemeyer, *Enemies of Freedom: Understanding Right-Wing Authoritarianism* (San Francisco: Jossey-Bass, 1998). Bob Altemeyer, *The Authoritarian Specter* (Cambridge, MA: Harvard University Press, 1997).

7. R. Willer, M. Feinberg, and D. Laurison, " 'Fear and Loathing' in Support for War: The Effects of Predjudice, Distrust, and Fear of Terrorism," Department of Sociology, University of California, Berkeley.

14. The Problem of Self-interest

1. B. M. H. Larson, "The Social Resonance of Competitive and Progressive Evolutionary Metaphors," *Bioscience* 56, no. 12 (December 2006). B. M. H. Larson, "Darwin's Metaphors Revisited: Conceptual Metaphors, Conceptual Blends, and Cognitive Models in a Scientific Theory," unpublished manuscript.

2. Theodore L. Brown, *Making Truth: Metaphor in Science* (Urbana and Chicago: University of Illinois Press, 2003).

3. www.nytimes.com/2007/06/26/science/26essay.html.

4. *New Republic*, October 19, 2006.

5. Marco Iacoboni, *Mirroring People: The New Science of How We Connect with Others* (New York: Farrar, Straus and Giroux, 2008), chapter 7.

6. An excellent introduction to the literature is found at http://plato.stanford.edu/entries/altruism-biological.

7. Steven Pinker, *The Blank Slate* (New York: Viking, 2002), 243.

8. H. Kern Reeve and Bert Hölldobler, "The emergence of a super organism through intergroup competition," *Proceedings of the National Academy of Sciences USA* 104, no. 23 (June 5, 2007): 9736–40.

9. Robert Wright, *Nonzero: The Logic of Human Destiny* (New York: Pantheon, 2000).

15. The Metaphors Defining Rational Action

1. A fully detailed, technical discussion of the metaphorical character of the rational actor model can be found in Lakoff and Johnson, *Philosophy in the Flesh*, chapter 23. That analysis was done by me and Robert Powell, a noted mathematician who teaches game theory in the Political Science Department at Berkeley.

2. Karen Breslau and Katrina Heron, "The Debriefing," *Wired* 8.12 (December 2000).

16. Why Hawks Win

1. I strongly recommend Kahneman's Nobel Prize lecture: nobelprize.org/nobel_prizes/economics/laureates/2002/kahneman-lecture.html.

2. Peter Bernstein, *Against the Gods: The Remarkable Story of Risk* (New York: John Wiley & Sons, 1996). Examples are taken from Thayer Watkins, http://www.sjsu.edu/faculty/watkins/prospect.htm.

3. C. Trepel, C. Fox, and R. Poldrack, "Prospect Theory on the Brain?: Toward a Cognitive Neuroscience of Decision under Risk," *Cognitive Brain Research* 23 (2005): 34–50. S. M. Tom, C. Trepel, C. Fox, and R. Poldrack, "The Neural Basis of Loss Aversion in Decision Making Under Risk," *Science* 315 (January 26, 2007): 515–18.

4. D. Kahneman and J. Renshon, "Why Hawks Win," *Foreign Policy*, Jan./Feb. 2007.

17. The Brain's Language

1. The first full discussion of the evidence for the embodiment of mind occurs in George Lakoff's *Women, Fire, and Dangerous Things* (Chicago: University of Chicago Press, 1987). The first modern philosophical treatment occurs in Mark Johnson's *The Body in the Mind* (Chicago: University of

Chicago Press, 1987). An updated account, including neuroscience, occurs in George Lakoff and Mark Johnson's *Philosophy in the Flesh* (New York: Basic Books, 1999). Raymond J. Gibbs Jr.'s *Embodiment in Cognitive Science* (New York: Cambridge University Press, 2005) is an excellent and thorough survey of the evidence for the embodiment of meaning. The neural computational foundation for the embodiment of meaning is given in Jerome Feldman's *From Molecule to Metaphor* (Cambridge, MA: MIT Press, 2006).

2. A. R. Damasio and D. Tranel, "Nouns and verbs are retrieved with differently distributed neural systems," *Proceedings of the National Academy of Sciences USA* 90 (1993): 4957–60.

3. W. T. Harbaugh, U. Mayr, and D. R. Burghart, "Neural Responses to Taxation and Voluntary Giving Reveal Motives for Charitable Donations," *Science* 316, no. 5831 (June 15, 2007): 1622–25.

4. The theory of mental simulation is laid out in Jerome Feldman's *From Molecule to Metaphor* (Cambridge, MA: MIT Press, 2006).

18. Language in the New Enlightenment

1. Noam Chomsky, *Syntactic Structures* (The Hague: Mouton, 1957), 13.

2. Noam Chomsky, *Cartesian Linguistics: A Chapter in the History of Rationalist Thought* (Cambridge, MA: MIT Press, 1966).

3. Erving Goffman, *Frame Analysis: An Essay on the Organization of Experience* (New York: Harper and Row, 1974).

4. M. Minsky, "A Framework for Representing Knowledge," MIT-AI Laboratory Memo 306, June 1974, condensed version, in P. Winston, ed., *The Psychology of Computer Vision* (New York: McGraw-Hill, 1975).

5. Roger Shank and Robert Abelson, *Scripts, Plans, Goals and Understanding* (Hillsdale, NJ: Erlbaum, 1977).

6. Charles Fillmore, "An Alternative to Checklist Theories of Meaning," in *Proceedings of the First Annual Meeting of the Berkeley Linguistics Society* (Berkeley, CA: Berkeley Lingustics Society, 1975), 123–31.

7. http://www.framenet.icsi.berkeley.edu.

8. Vittorio Gallese and George Lakoff, "The Brain's Concepts: The Role of the Sensory-Motor System in Conceptual Structure," *Cognitive Neuropsychology* 22 (2005): 455–79.

9. For an excellent survey of the earlier accounts of metaphor, see M. Johnson, ed., *Philosophical Perspectives on Metaphor* (Minneapolis: University of Minnesota Press, 1981). For an excellent introductory text, see Z. Kövecses, *Metaphor* (New York: Oxford University Press, 2002).

10. Michael Reddy, "The conduit metaphor," in A. Ortony, ed., *Metaphor and Thought* (Cambridge, UK: Cambridge University Press, 1979), 284–324.

11. George Lakoff and Mark Johnson, *Metaphors We Live By* (Chicago: University of Chicago Press, 1980); 2nd ed., 2003.

12. The explanation came from putting together the results of three dissertations done between 1997 and 1999: S. Narayanan, "KARMA: Knowledge-based Action Representation for Metaphor and Aspect," Ph.D. dissertation, Department of Computer Science, University of California, Berkeley, 1997. Joseph Grady, "Foundation of Meaning: Primary Metaphors and Primary Scenes," Ph.D. dissertation, University of California, Berkeley, 1997. Christopher Johnson, "Constructional Grounding: The Role of Interpretational Overlap in Lexical and Constructional Acquisition," Ph.D. dissertation, University of California, Berkeley, 1999.

13. G. Lakoff and M. Turner, *More Than Cool Reason: A Field Guide to Poetic Metaphor* (Chicago and London: University of Chicago Press, 1989).

14. George Lakoff and Mark Johnson's *Philosophy in the Flesh* (New York: Basic Books, 1999), 236.

15. Ibid., 70.

16. Charles J. Fillmore, *Entailment Rules in a Semantic Theory* (Columbus: Ohio State University, 1965).

17. Jeffrey Gruber, "Studies in Lexical Relations," Ph.D. dissertation, MIT, 1965.

18. See chapter 23 on embodied construction grammar in Jerome Feldman's *From Molecule to Metaphor* (Cambridge, MA: MIT Press, 2006).

19. Kwame Anthony Appiah, "The New Philosophy," *New York Times Magazine*, Decmeber 9, 2007; http://www.nytimes.com/2007/12/09/magazine/09ww1n-idealab-t.htm. Appiah defends the traditional view of philosophy as an armchair discipline against the idea that empirical scientific study has a place in philosophy.

Afterword: What If It Works?

1. For details, see chapter 21 in my *Moral Politics: How Liberals and Conservatives Think* (Chicago: University of Chicago Press, 1996; 2002).

Index